THE COST OF INEQUALITY

THREE DECADES OF
THE SUPER-RICH AND THE ECONOMY

Stewart Lansley

London

GIBSON SQUARE

Also by Stewart Lansley:

Poverty and Progress in Britain (with GC Fiegehen and AD Smith)
Poor Britain (with Joanna Mack)
Beyond Our Ken (with Andy Forrester and Robin Pauley)
After the Gold Rush
Top Man: How Philip Green Built His High Street Empire
  (with Andy Forrester)
Rich Britain: The Rise and Rise of the New Super-Wealthy
Londongrad: From Russia With Cash (with Mark Hollingsworth)

First published in 2011 by

Gibson Square

Tel: +44 (0)20 7096 1100

info@gibsonsquare.com
www.gibsonsquare.com

ISBN 9781908096067 HB

Printed by CPI.

CONTENTS

Introduction   5

1   An Economic Megashift   13
2   'Zapping Labour'   33
3   The Vanishing Middle   60
4   A Faustian Pact   86
5   The Incessant Pressure to Transact   111
6   The Age of Turbulence   136
7   Living on Borrowed Time   164
8   A Consumer Society without the Capacity
        to Consume   184
9   The Cuckoo in the Nest   203
10 Walking away with Giant Jackpots   225
11 The Bigger Picture   251
12 The Scale of the Task Ahead   275

Acknowledgements   303
Notes   305
Index   317

'The most essential long-term economic problem of this century is the risk that income inequality will get substantially worse... economic growth will be a positive development only if we do not see at the same time a huge increase in inequality, which could mean that the economic gains are concentrated in a rich class. The mere prospect of a winner-takes-all world ought to strike fear into our hearts.'

Robert J Shiller[1]

INTRODUCTION

While personal fortunes at the top have soared to levels not seen since before the Second World War, living standards for most Britons have fallen well behind general rises in prosperity. In the United States, nine-tenths of the population has faced stagnant incomes over the last three decades. As a result, the big divide in British and American society is now less between the top, the middle and the bottom, than between a tiny group at the very top and nearly everyone else.

Although recent years have seen several hard-hitting, and hotly debated, critiques of this deepening gulf, these have concentrated on issues of social injustice and fairness. Rewards at the top of finance and business, their authors argue, have become increasingly disproportionate and undeserving, the product of an increase in the con-centration of political and market power rather than a greater economic contribution.[2] One of the most influential of these critiques, *The Spirit Level*, has shown that highly unequal societies are much more likely to impose widespread social damage.[3]

These are important arguments but they deal mainly with the moral and social consequences of the surge in polarisation. An equally important issue, but one that has been largely ignored, is the impact of soaring inequality on the way economies function. This is the issue addressed in this book. Allowing the gains from growing prosperity to be colonised by such a tiny group has been very bad news for the domestic and the global economy. This is because there is a limit to the inequality that is consistent with economic stability and dynamism. That limit has been severely breached in recent times.

Over the last three decades, Britain, the United States and a rising number of other nations have divided into a two-track economy. It is the first track, one which makes money out of money, that has provided a super-fast route to personal wealth. The 'money economy' has and is still being used to deliver big returns to those who control it— a small, powerful group of a few thousand top bankers, financiers and corporate executives running the world's largest companies.

Nearly everyone else, in contrast, has ended up in the second track—the slow lane of the economy. This track—the 'productive economy' where new businesses are built, new products devised and wealth and jobs created—is the one on which economic success depends. It produces the goods and services that make up economic output, provides jobs for the bulk of the workforce and creates the wealth that enables rising living standards. But while the first track is thriving, this one is floundering.

Although the productive side of the economy has always depended on the financial side, the interests of these two tracks have become increasingly at odds. Actively promoted by successive governments over three decades, for misguided reasons as we shall see, the money economy has captured the dominant position, greatly out of proportion to the needs of the wider economy. In the process, finance has come to play a new role—that of a cash cow for a domestic and global super-rich elite.

Able to control the destiny of mass global flows of capital, that elite has used its growing political and economic muscle to extract an increasing share of existing wealth, sucking lifeblood out of the wider economy. Apart from making nations more vulnerable to external and internal shocks, it impedes the recovery of the global economy.

The country that sits at the top of the international league table for the growth of finance-generated inequality is the United States. According to the American business magazine, *Forbes*, the number of American billionaires jumped forty-fold in the 25 years to 2007. While most US citizens faced little better than stagnant real incomes over this period, the aggregate wealth of America's top 400 (adjusted for inflation) soared from $169 to $1500 billion. Across continental Europe, even once relatively equal countries have succumbed, albeit more latterly and more slowly, to this global shift to greater inequality.

Traditionally capitalism has thrived through the development of new products and new industries, by taking long-term risks with investment, by finding ways of becoming smarter, more inventive and beating the competition with better or cheaper products. That model of capitalism has not disappeared—witness the rise of Google, Facebook and Yahoo—but it has become a sideshow in the non-tech world (where in Britain is the new James Dyson?). Instead, the new era of deregulation has created the opportunity to make money, big money, not by being smarter, or by taking a long view, or by investing in new systems, but by a number of new business practices that manipulate the financial structures of existing firms.

'Business' activity today means mergers, hostile takeovers and rearranging balance sheets. On paper, these changes can make companies look more profitable and productive. But it is mostly an illusion, one that only brings short-term, one-off gains that have little to do with the core product or service of the business.

In a City-led strategy, the high-street retail banks in Britain more than halved the number of local braches from the late 1990s. Profit margins were greatly increased while retail banking did not become any cheaper, or, indeed, better. Boardrooms, led by the hand of a newly rejuvenated finance sector, one awash with access to great pools of global cash, have turned to buying, merging, breaking up, repackaging and selling on existing companies.

Scores of high-street names—from the AA to Debenhams—have been bought up by consortiums of corporate financiers. Far from bringing a more productive economy, healthier companies and more jobs, the financial engineering of these companies in a diversity of ways has often been detrimental to the firms, while fuelling the construction of a separate economy of the super rich.

The categorical division between the money and the productive economy is well illustrated by the 2007 crisis and its aftermath. After hopeful signs of recovery in 2010, productive activity in the world's richest economies has stalled and growth forecasts are being adjusted sharply downward. In an historic move, the American economy, the largest in the world, had its credit rating downgraded by the powerful ratings agency, Standard and Poor's, in August, 2011.

While the productive sector is fragile, the initial slump in the fortunes of the world's super-rich turned out to be very short-lived. By the beginning of 2011, most had bounced back from the nadir of 2008. Many bankers, financiers and corporate executives, on both sides of the Atlantic, remain unaffected by the continuing turmoil. The average Wall Street bonus in 2009—at the very height of the crisis—was close to its highest in history. *Forbes* counted a record number of 1210 billionaires in 2011, up by 28 per cent over 2007. Their combined wealth has risen from $3,500 billion in 2007 to $4,500 billion in 2010. Little more than a thousand individuals commanded a sum equivalent to a third of the output of the American economy.

In the UK, the City bonus pool in 2010 came close to pre-credit crunch levels. The average pay of the chief executives of Britain's largest 100 companies rose by 55 per cent in the first six months of 2010 to stand at almost £5 million. Big business is enjoying surging profit levels, with many of the nation's largest conglomerates sitting on near-record levels of cash, most of it standing idle.

In contrast to the rising fortunes at the top, living standards for most Britons, Americans and Europeans are on a downward slide. Across the UK, real incomes for most have been, at best, stagnant since 2005. In August 2011, Mervyn King, the Governor of the Bank of England, predicted 'a long and deep squeeze on real UK living standards.' Although the economic orthodoxy of the last thirty years—that escalating rewards at the top and high levels of inequality are the key to success—remains largely intact, leading commentators are now beginning to question the impact of this growing divide. As Sir Max Hastings wrote in the *Financial Times* on 10 June 2011, 'It seems mistaken to take for granted the tranquility of a large struggling majority, while a minority wins fabulous rewards... capitalism works only when rewards are seen to be shared.'

Building wealth- and job-creating companies on which robust economies depend means tackling the root causes of failure—a combination of the mass personal fortunes accumulated across the globe and a steady erosion of relative living standards. One of the fundamental faultlines in the British, American and a growing number of other rich economies, remains the imbalance between wages and profits, the result of three decades of a sustained squeeze on wages. Until this imbalance—the key source of surging inequality as argued below—is corrected, economies will continue to falter. The shrinking wage share of the last thirty years needs to be halted and reversed, taking it back to the norm of the immediate post-war decades, a period which brought sustained growth and stability.

There are important, if small, micro-initiatives being launched within the business world itself. Shareholder groups are rebelling against escalating executive pay packages. The International Monetary Fund has argued that economic success depends on reversing the long run slide in the wage shares of the world's major economies. Yet these initiatives on their own are not enough. The great concentrations of national and global wealth in the hands of a few need to be broken up if Western economies are to return to sustained economic success.

Economists have yet to call on political leaders for the scale of measures needed to dismantle the two-track economy. But this task is now urgent. The world has just been through the second deepest economic crisis of the last century. It is struggling to recover. The restoration of long term economic health depends on the two-sides of the economy being brought back into balance. Not everyone will agree with the details of the strategy laid at the end of the book. But the cost of inaction will be grave indeed. A failure to act risks a new phase of permanent or near-permanent recession, one that will condemn much of the population—in the UK, the US and elsewhere—to a prolonged period of depressed wages, stagnant living standards and blighted opportunities.

1

AN ECONOMIC MEGASHIFT

Thirty years ago, the United Kingdom was one of the most equal countries in the developed world. Today it is one of the most unequal.[4] This shift started at the beginning of the 1980s and put into reverse a half century of political and social change that had reduced the gap between the top and the bottom to its lowest level in history. This egalitarian drive began in the aftermath of the great stock market crash of 1929, a time of global economic upheaval. The crash was to prove a decisive turning point in the history of the fortunes of both the poor and the rich. From that point, the extremes of wealth that characterised the period to the end of the 1920s were gradually eroded.

Not only did many of the wealthy classes suffer sustained losses, the political climate towards the super-rich turned much colder. The crash, the subsequent recession and then the Second World War transformed public and political attitudes towards the rich for a generation and more. Rewards at the top became more modest, expectations were checked and there was much less flaunting of personal wealth. Successive governments moved to build a higher protective floor below which living standards would not fall. Incomes at the very top were capped by new social mores unsympathetic to excessive rewards and by the introduction of progressive taxes that clawed back a rising proportion of top incomes.

It was a story repeated across much of the globe. Most of the world's developed nations embarked on a long march towards greater equality. The steady reduction in the wealth and income divide was driven by the development of democratic institutions, a growing intolerance of the extremes of wealth and poverty and a new philosophy of state intervention. Monopolies were broken up. Tax rates on the rich increased.

Though they progressed at different speeds, and from different starting points, most rich nations by the early 1970s were characterised by unprecedented levels of equality. In the United States the sharpest falls in the wealth and income gaps came between the beginning of the 1930s and the early- to mid-1950s, a process of equal-isation that became known as the 'great compression'.[5] In 1958 *Business Week* summed up the American mood: 'The rich have been in hiding for twenty years.'[6]

In the UK—where a similar process was dubbed the 'great levelling'—the size of the biggest fortunes slumped and the numbers of super-rich fell sharply.[7] Again the sharpest fall in the concentration of income at the top came between the 1930s and the early 1950s. In 1953 one Inland Revenue officer claimed that there were only 36 millionaires in Britain compared with more than one thousand in 1939.[8] Large fortunes were also harder to come by in the City. The era of the commercial barons when huge fortunes could be made in banking had gone and were yet to be replaced by the voracious financial deal-making that was to come a few decades later.

Yet the 'great levelling' was not to prove a permanent revolution. The drive towards greater domestic and global

equality slowed from the early 1950s and then came to a
halt in the United Kingdom and the United States during
the 1970s. It then went into reverse. The story of these
two nations since that time has been one of a rapid return
to past levels of inequality, as measured by the degree of
concentration at the top. By the turn of the millennium,
the income gap in both countries had returned to levels
close to those last seen in the pre-war era. In an unparal-
leled historic reversal, the great levelling had given way to
the great widening. Almost half a century of economic
and social progress had unravelled in little more than two
decades.[9]

The scale of the reversal in the case of the UK is
shown in figure 1.1. The share of net income received by
the top one per cent shrank from 12.6 per cent in 1937 to

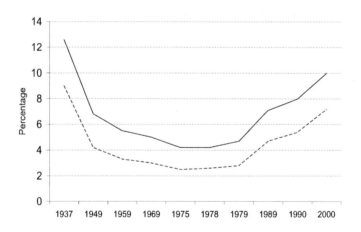

The fall and rise of income inequality, UK, 1937 to 2000 (Figure 1.1)
The share of net income (after income tax) received by the top 0.5% (dotted
line) and top 1% (straight line) of taxpayers.[10]

4.2 per cent in 1978. It then started rising, and was back to 10 per cent by 2000, much closer to the level last seen in the 1930s. The share of an even smaller group—the top 0.5 per cent—followed a very similar pattern.

Wealth—which is much more unequally distributed than income—has followed a parallel path. The wealth gap fell sharply for most of the twentieth century and continued to do so until the mid-to-late 1980s. It then started to rise again, following, with a lag, the pattern of incomes. In 2002, according to the latest reliable official figures, the top one per cent owned 23 per cent of 'marketable wealth', up from 17 per cent in 1988. While the share of the nation's wealth at the top has been rising, that of the bottom 50 per cent has been shrinking from 10 per cent in the mid-1980s to 6 per cent in 2002.[11] The distribution of 'liquid wealth' (cash, savings and shares) is even more concentrated at the top.[12] The Office for National Statistics has stopped publishing official figures on wealth shares, in part because of their unreliability compared with incomes. Moreover, these figures almost certainly understate the full extent of the wealth gap and the scale of its increase since the mid-1980s.[13]

These trends towards greater inequality have been driven by a remarkable revolution—a sharp rise in both the numbers of the rich and in the size of their fortunes. Since the mid-1980s the UK has witnessed a great surge in the rate of personal enrichment, one not seen since— and probably outstripping—the private fortune building that took place during the nation's last great wealth boom in the final quarter of the nineteenth century.

The number of UK citizens with incomes of over £1 million rose eightfold in the ten years up to 2006.[14] In the seven years to 2005, the number of Britons with more than £5 million in 'liquid assets'—held in equities, bonds, deposits and cash—rose at the rate of 15 per cent a year, despite the impact of the 2000 stock market crash.[15] In 1990, you needed a fortune of £50 million to make it into the list of the 200 richest residents in Britain compiled annually by the *Sunday Times*. By 2008, that figure had soared to £430 million, a near-ninefold increase.

The trend towards greater inequality has been even more extreme in the United States. Here the level of income concentration fell sharply from the late 1920s, flattened out in the 1960s, fell slightly during the first half of the 1970s and then, from the end of that decade, started rising again. By the mid-2000s it was back to levels last seen at the end of the 1920s.[16] Awareness of the reversal of the earlier process of equalisation first emerged from the late 1980s with the publication of several articles by American scholars. At first, debate about these findings was confined to a small group of academic economists arguing amongst themselves about the causes of this new trend. Then in early 1992, the debate became public when the findings were published in an article in the *New York Times* by the American academic, Paul Krugman, later to receive the Nobel Prize in Economics for his work on trade theory.

The article caused something of a storm. The question of inequality was and remains a sensitive one in the United States, a nation that likes to see itself as having created the most opportunistic society in the world. 'Even mentioning income distribution leads to angry accusations of "class warfare"' is how Krugman put it.[17]

In 1989, George H W Bush had succeeded Ronald

17

Reagan as President and continued the broad economic policies of his predecessor—a mix of freer markets, smaller government and lower taxes. Republican administrations from the 1980s had long claimed that 'Reaganomics'—as President Reagan's free-market experiment was known—had been highly successful, helping to boost growth and prosperity for all.

These new findings challenged a key aspect of this claim—that all Americans had benefited from the new economic direction. Indeed, they suggested that not only had those at the top hoovered up most of the gains from growth after 1979, real incomes at the bottom had stagnated or even declined. Although the response of some conservative economists was to accept the finding that inequality had increased and claim that it was a necessary price to pay for a more productive and faster growing economy, Krugman's article generated a good deal of hostility from the US Treasury and a number of conservative politicians and newspapers.

The Bush administration might have been able to live with a mild increase in inequality resulting from a few business leaders getting richer. But the evidence that significant numbers had enjoyed little rise in real incomes while some were worse off was much more politically sensitive. In response, the President's advisers launched a sustained counter-attack. Over the next few months, the findings were ridiculed in a number of articles first published in the *Wall Street Journal*. While this was a conservative daily read mainly by financial traders and Republican supporters, and the paper most wedded to free-market thinking, the mud-slinging soon spread to the more popular press.

These attacks took a number of forms. First they attempted to challenge the evidence, presenting new data which appeared to show the rise in inequality was a myth. When this new data was revealed to have no substance, the antagonists took another tack, claiming that improved social mobility—with poorer families increasingly able to rise to higher income levels—made comparisons of inequality at single points in time irrelevant.

In response, Krugman described the authorities' responses as full of 'mendacity and sheer incompetence'.[18] Although the row continued to blaze for years, the weight of evidence on the course of inequality became increasingly irrefutable. It all pointed in one direction—that the income gulf continued to widen throughout the 1990s and into the next century. Indeed, the argument about whether America had become more unequal was effectively closed in June 2005 with comments by Alan Greenspan, the longstanding and widely admired Chairman of the Federal Reserve. Greenspan, an outspoken champion of free markets, admitted before a hearing of the Congressional Joint Economic Committee that the divergence in the fortunes of different groups in its labour market had gone too far. 'As I've often said, this is not the type of thing which a democratic society—a capitalist democratic society—can really accept without addressing.'[19]

Two years later, in 2007, Greenspan's successor, the respected academic, Ben Bernanke, told the Omaha Chamber of Commerce that, after reviewing the evidence, he accepted the fact of growing inequality: 'No-one should be allowed to slip too far down the economic ladder.'[20]

One of the most important pieces of research that finally clinched the argument was carried out by two leading economic experts on the distribution of income. One of them, Thomas Piketty, was based at the École Normale Superieure in Paris, the other, Emmanuel Saez, at Harvard. What distinguished their work was the extended time period observed—from 1913 to 2006—and the use of individual tax return data which offered much greater accuracy at the top of the distribution than had previously been available.[21]

What their long span of data showed was that the course of income concentration in the United States had gone full circle over the 93 year period of their study. As shown in figure 1.2, the top one per cent took between a fifth and a quarter of incomes between 1925 and 1929—the five year period that preceded the Great Crash of 1929. Following the crash, the income share enjoyed by this group dived sharply through the depression of the 1930s, kept falling through the 1950s until eventually reaching a low of 8.9 per cent in 1976.

This long downward trend then went into reverse from the mid-1970s. By 2007, the share had risen almost threefold to 23.5 per cent—back to the level of the late 1920s. The share taken by an even smaller group of the rich—the top 0.5 per cent—followed a near identical path. As the *New York Times* noted in an editorial on the data on 4th April 2007: 'Not since the Roaring Twenties have the rich been so much richer than everyone else.' In an ominous sounding note, the editorial was entitled: 'It didn't end well last time.'

One of the most significant of Piketty and Saez's findings is that there have been only two periods over the

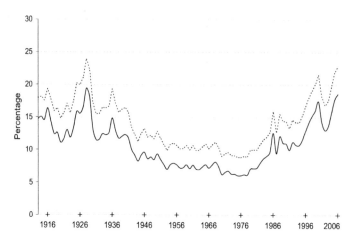

Income inequality in the United States comes full circle (Figure 1.2)
The share of national income (including capital gains) held by the top
one per cent (dotted line) and top 0.5 per cent (straight line) of
American households, 1913 to 2006, percentages. (The shares relate to
gross income and include capital gains.)[22]

course of the last century when the richest one per cent
of American households have held more than a fifth of
the country's income pool. The first embraced the whole
of the second half of the 1920s. The second began eight
decades later at the turn of the twentieth century, a period
that also preceded a time of economic turmoil. Moreover,
what was common about these two periods was not just a
sudden rise in the level of income concentration, but a
sharp increase in the level of debt, a similar set of
mainstream economic beliefs especially in the self-
correcting nature of markets and finally, a very similar set
of economic outcomes.

Although there is limited official information on
recent trends in the concentration of wealth in the US,

independent analysts have shown that the share of wealth enjoyed by the top one per cent has followed a similar path, rising from a low of 19.9 per cent in 1976 to 34.6 per cent in 2007. This is close to the levels of concentration last seen in the era before the great crash—the top one per cent took 36.7 per cent in 1922 and 44.2 per cent in 1929. The same study found that financial or 'liquid' wealth (all assets less housing) was even more concentrated, with the richest one percent owning 42.7 percent of total household financial wealth in 2007.[23] This is a higher degree of concentration than in the UK. As in the UK, the evidence is that the survey data on which these estimates are based are likely to understate the full extent of the wealth holdings of the super-rich.[24]

In the twenty years from the mid-1970s, America—the richest nation in the world—experienced a rapid upward 'wealth rush'. In the late 1970s, the cutoff to qualify for the highest-earning one ten-thousandth of households was roughly $2 million, in inflation-adjusted, pretax terms. By 2007, it had jumped to $11.5 million.[25] By 1999, the 30 top US family and individual fortunes were, collectively, roughly ten times the size of the 30 largest in 1982—a mere 17 years earlier. This was an increase greater than any comparable period during the 19th century.[26]

This dramatic surge in the levels of personal wealth held by the country's super-rich has been described by one of America's leading commentators on the history of wealth, Kevin Phillips, as an 'economic megashift'.[27] Such is the scale of the wealth boom, the United States is now living through a second 'gilded age'. This was the phrase originally coined in 1873 by the American satirist and author, Mark Twain, to describe the excess and opulence that accompanied the stark levels of wealth and income inequality in America at the end of the nineteenth century. It was a time that produced the world's first dollar billionaire, the oil magnate, John D Rockefeller and gave rise to the term 'robber barons' to describe the business practices of the leading American industrialists and financiers of the time.

Today's wealthiest citizens in the United States and the United Kingdom have acquired shares of the national income of their countries that are close to those enjoyed by their richest citizens eighty years ago, despite much more mature democracies and regulated economies. In the period from the end of the nineteenth century to the end of the 1920s, the constraints on fortune-making in both countries were much weaker, tax rates much lower and business regulations minimal. As Sir Max Hastings, a former editor of the *Daily Telegraph*, commented on the UK in 2005: 'Today's filthy rich are wealthier, healthier and more secure than ever... It seems remarkable that any high roller these days resorts to fraud to enrich himself. It is possible to bank such huge sums legally that criminality seems redundant.'[28]

In the UK and the US, the story of rising inequality has been largely one of greater income growth at the very top. The gap has also widened across the rest of the distribution in both countries, with, for example, the top doing better than the middle and the middle doing better than the bottom, but this is much less pronounced than the new inequality divide, a sharply rising gap between the top and the rest. It is this that represents the most significant gulf in both the US and the UK.

In both countries the greater concentration has been

driven by two key factors—a pay explosion at the very top along with a sustained squeeze on pay amongst middle and low income workers. In the UK the incomes of roughly the bottom three-fifths of the population have failed to keep pace with rising prosperity. As a result their share of national income fell from 40 to 33 per cent between 1977 and 2008.[29]

In contrast, those at the very top—especially top corporate executives, financiers and bankers—have been enjoying pay rises that greatly outstrip those of the rest of the workforce. The average pay of the chief executives of Britain's largest 100 companies, for example, grew by more than 11 per cent per annum in real terms between 1999 and 2006, compared with 1.4 per cent for all full-time employees. In 2006, the average earnings of a top 100 chief executive was nearly 100 times that of the average for all full-time employees. Twenty-five years earlier, it had been less than twenty-five times as high.[30]

According to a study by researchers at the London School of Economics, the biggest cause of the rise of income inequality in the UK in recent times has been the pay explosion in the City. In the decade to 2008, three-quarters of the increase in income concentration amongst the top one per cent went to finance workers, virtually all of it in bonuses.[31]

This is also true of the United States where it was the finance sector that drove the trend toward income concentration at the top. 'In 2004, for instance, non-financial executives of publicly traded companies accounted for less than 6 percent of the top 0.01 percent income bracket. In that same year, the top 25 hedge fund managers combined appear to have earned more than all of the CEOs from the entire S&P 500. The number of Wall Street investors earning more than $100 million a year was nine times higher than the public company executives earning that amount.'[32]

In the United States, the gains from economic growth have also become increasingly unevenly shared with an even greater rise in the gap between the top and the rest. In 1960, the ratio of the average annual pay of chief executives of large and medium sized American companies to that of all workers stood at 42 to one. By 2007 it had risen to 344 to one. This ratio is even higher in the case of America's largest companies: the chief executive of Walmart earns 900 times the pay of his average employee.[33] 'From 1990 to 2005, CEOs' pay increased almost 300 per cent (adjusted for inflation), while production workers gained a scant 4.3 per cent' according to one study. 'The purchasing power of the federal minimum wage actually *declined* by 9.3 per cent, when inflation is taken into account.'[34] At the beginning of the new century, the 13,000 richest families in America had almost as much income combined as the 20 million poorest households.[35]

Moreover, although the rise in inequality has been especially marked in the US and the UK, the growing gap has been a global phenomenon. Some countries have bucked the trend, remaining relatively equal by international and historical standards, but most have become more unequal since the 1980s, though at different speeds and starting points, and mostly not on the scale of the US and the UK.[36]

A study of 30 nations by the Paris-based club of rich countries, the Organisation for Economic Co-operation and Development (OECD) found that during the 20 year period from the mid-1980s, the concentration of income gathered pace across most of the developed world. 'The gap between rich and poor and the number of people below the poverty line have both grown over the past two decades. The increase is widespread, affecting three-quarters of OECD countries.' Countries that experienced an increase in income inequality between the mid-1980s and mid-2000s include New Zealand, Canada, Finland, Germany, Italy and Portugal. As the OECD concluded, 'there is widespread concern that economic growth is not being shared fairly.'[37] Another study has found a similar trend amongst non-OECD nations.[38]

Not so long ago the world's rich list was an almost exclusively western club. No longer. In 2007, the American business magazine, *Forbes,* counted 946 billionaires across the globe with a combined net worth of $3.500 billion, a figure larger than the Gross Domestic Product (GDP—the market value of all goods and services) of Germany, the third largest economy in the world. Close to a fifth of the top 100 billionaires came from developing nations, among them three self-made Indian industrialists, including Mukesh Ambani, the petrochemical tycoon, and Lakshmi Mittal, the British-based global steel magnate. It also included one Mexican—Carlos Slim Helu who soared up the world rankings through the privatisation of Mexico's telecommunications industry in the early 1990s—and one Russian oligarch, the owner of Chelsea football club, Roman Abramovich.[39]

Most East European nations experienced a sharp rise in inequality after the collapse of communism, a trend driven by the introduction of markets and the sell-off of state industries. A similar process of privatisation over the last twenty years has enriched a small group of political and business insiders across the globe from Mexico to Tunisia. In much of Latin America and Asia, rapid economic progress has also been accompanied by much larger wealth divides, with the benefits of growth also very unevenly spread. While the top fifth of Chileans earn almost 67 per cent of the nation's income, for example, the bottom fifth earn just over three per cent.[40] While strong growth in countries like India and China has increased living standards on average, and led to an expanded middle class, the rich in these countries have seen their incomes grow much more quickly than those of the rest of the population. In 2011, according to *Forbes*, China had 115 billionaires living on the mainland, second only to the United States (with 413) and ahead of Russia with 101.

Today the combined wealth of the world's richest 1000 people is almost twice as much as the poorest 2.5 billion.[41] Although average income gaps between some rich and poor countries have narrowed because of strong growth in parts of Asia and Latin America, the gap between the richest countries (the United States, Japan and some member states of the European Union) and the poorest (such as Ethiopia, Haiti and Nepal) has been widening.[42] 'The richest two per cent of adults in the world own more than half of global household wealth' according to a study by the Helsinki-based World Institute for Development Economics. The study—which said that its estimates of the top wealth shares were conservative— also found that: 'Members of the top percentile [the richest one per cent] are almost 2000 times richer (than the bottom 50 per cent).'[43]

While the evidence about the course of inequality is now indisputable, the arguments about its merits have yet to be laid to rest. Those wedded to free markets mostly continue to back the rise in inequality. A common claim is that more uneven rewards are the product of more effective markets, rewarding talent and effort more closely. Rising inequality merely reflects the greater contribution of the most productive. The rich themselves have their own language in defence of their wealth—that their activities 'create or save jobs', 'add value', that their rewards are 'in line with the risks they take'.

For some defenders of inequality, even modest egalitarianism is seen as economically dangerous. Martin Feldstein, Professor of Economics at Harvard, and a former advisor to President Reagan and George HW Bush, described those who are against increases in incomes at the top as 'spiteful egalitarians'.[44] Before she was disgraced and jailed in 2005 for lying about an illicit share deal, the high-profile American businesswoman and television celebrity Martha Stewart was fond of arguing that inequality not only did not matter, it was, to use her catch phrase, 'a good thing'. Her consolation on leaving federal jail five months later, aged 63, was that she was still estimated to be worth $1 billion.

These views are widely echoed in the UK. 'Egalitarianism has been the most corrosive, illiberal and murderous of modern beliefs,' is how the liberal philosopher, Anthony O'Hear, once put it in a provocative guest column in the left-of-centre weekly, the *New Statesman*.[45] One polemic celebrating wealth, the rich and modern capitalism, published by the free market think tank, the Social Affairs Unit in 2005, was titled *Rich Is Beautiful.*[46]

When the *Daily Telegraph* launched its new separate business section to an audience of Britain's leading business figures in 2006, the newspaper's City editor declared that from now on the paper would 'celebrate what is in this room: power, wealth and influence'. Such views seem to have survived the economic crisis. At the height of the downturn in October 2009, a debate was held at St Paul's Cathedral on the subject of 'The place of morality in the marketplace'. One of the speakers, Brian Griffiths, the Vice-Chair of Goldman Sachs and a former adviser to Mrs Thatcher, defended inequality 'as a way to achieve greater prosperity for all.'

Although these views remain at the heart of today's continuing economic orthodoxy, some global opinion leaders have been questioning the economic impact of rising inequality. In January 2011, Dominique Strauss-Kahn, the then head of the International Monetary Fund pointed to the destabilising impact of rising inequality as one of the explanations for the 2008-9 crisis. 'The distribution of income is another important issue. The consequences of rising inequality and its effects on social cohesion can no longer be ignored. Rising inequality may also have increased vulnerability to crisis.'[47]

Similar views were aired at the 2011 World Economic Forum, the influential gathering of the world's political, economic and business elites held each year in the small Swiss ski resort of Davos. Here the question of the growing global divide became something of a theme in an agenda crowded with topics from stalling recovery to the tackling of mounting budget deficits. 'Inequality is the big wildcard in the next decade of global growth', Kenneth Rogoff, a leading authority on the history of financial crises, told one gathering at the Forum. At another session, Min Zhu, former Deputy Governor of the People's Bank of China and a special adviser at the International Monetary Fund, told his audience: 'The increase in inequality is the most serious challenge facing the world.'

Martin Sorrell, the chief executive of the advertising company WPP, and a self-made member of Britain's super-rich, warned another group that policy leaders had to address inequality. 'The concentration of wealth is a big issue,' Sorrell said, reminding his audience that inequality peaked in the US on the eve of the Wall Street crash in 1929 and again on the eve of the financial crisis of 2007.

For the half a century until the late 1970s, wage-earners—in nearly all rich nations—shared more or less equally in rising prosperity. This sustained the demand that fuelled the long period of post-war growth. But as the bargaining power of labour slumped from the early 1980s, real wages for most began to fall behind the growth in productive capacity while profits surged. Although this process was at its sharpest in those countries like the United States and the United Kingdom that most embraced the free-market experiment, similar, if shallower trends occurred across much of the globe.

This book will argue that the squeeze on wages, the boost to profits and booming fortunes at the top have greatly upset the natural equilibrium essential to economic stability. These shifts have encouraged the growth of an economic tumour, one that has been slowly eating away at the wealth and job-creating foundation stones of national economies. While sapping strength from domestic economies, this cancerous growth has also moved across national boundaries, undermining resilience against shocks, weakening international defences against instability and bringing economic imbalance, greater turbulence and ultimately, malfunction.

As wage rises slumped, purchasing power fell short of the extra output being produced. If this slump in consumer demand had been allowed to continue, economies would have ground to a halt. The political solution to this problem, especially in the US and the UK where the wage squeeze was greatest, was to license huge increases in lending to private individuals, to finance every day living expenses as well as house purchases. From the mid-1990s, rising economic prosperity was being secured only by an unprecedented explosion of private debt on both sides of the Atlantic, a process that underpinned the rise in the size of the finance sector and an acceleration in its profit flow.

While ordinary consumer purchasing power was slipping, another malignant factor came into play—the creation of giant surpluses off the back of high and rising profits. These created an additional set of economic imbalances. A tidal wave of footloose global cash caromed around the world in search of the fastest returns, most of it landing in London and New York.

Little of this circulating pool of hot money ended up in sustainable, wealth and job-creating investment. Money poured into hedge funds, private equity houses, takeovers, commodities and commercial property. These mass financial spending sprees by the world's newly enriched mostly added up to large speculative bets that offered, at the time, spectacular returns. Asset prices and business values soared. Deal-making and corporate restructuring became highly complex mechanisms for transferring existing rather than creating new wealth.

Similar destructive mechanisms were also at work in the build-up to the Great Depression of the 1930s. The second half of the 1920s saw sliding disposable incomes, booming profits and a great surge in fortunes at the top, especially in the US. Then, as in the post-millennium years, hoards of speculative money poured into real estate and the stock market and debt levels boomed. An untenable economic model that benefited the few merely created the conditions for global meltdown.

The lessons of 1929 were eventually learned. For a half-century from the mid-1930s, the great concentrations of wealth were steadily broken up. Yet despite the repeat of the conditions that created the 1929 Crash, the key lesson of today's broken global economy has yet to be learned. Today, the vast income gaps that fuelled the debt surge and the multiple asset bubbles are still present in the global economy. The proceeds of growth, when it returns, are likely to continue to be very unequally shared. The 1929 Crash not only brought the Great Depression, it led to the wholesale reinvention of economics. Today, in contrast, it is largely business as usual.

2

'ZAPPING LABOUR'

Throughout her political career, Margaret Thatcher liked nothing more than to drop the name of Friedrich von Hayek—the leading, post-war, prophet of free-markets and small government. She had first read his teachings while studying chemistry at Somerville College, Oxford, just after the war. 'This is what we believe' she announced excitedly, waving a well-worn copy of his major work, *The Constitution of Liberty*, during one of her speeches after becoming leader of the Conservative Party.

Born in Austria, Hayek moved to teach at the London School of Economics in 1931. In 1947 the political philosopher helped establish the Mont Pelerin Society— an international network of ideologues committed to unregulated markets—and named after the Swiss spa near Geneva where the group of founders first met. The Society had one central aim: to build opposition to the post-war economic and welfare reforms.

In the United States, the case for free markets was promoted by organisations like the Foundation for Economic Education and the American Enterprise Association and in the UK by a small Westminster-based think thank called the Institute for Economic Affairs (IEA). Founded in 1955, the IEA set out to spread the teachings of von Hayek, awarded the Nobel Prize for

Economics in 1974, and later, the outspoken, Chicago-based academic, Milton Friedman. Friedman was another leading exponent of free market capitalism and Nobel Laureate and had also attended the first Mont Pelerin meeting.

One of the principal targets of these groups was the thinking of the British economist John Maynard Keynes. Keynes was born in 1883 and it was his theories on how to avoid recessions and minimise turbulence that came to dominate post-war economic thinking in a way which contributed greatly to economic stability for a generation. Keynes was the power economic thinker of the twentieth century. No-one has had more influence on policy and although support for his theories waned as the post-1980 era of deregulation spread through one nation after another, his ideas were at least partially revived in the immediate aftermath of the 2008 crash.

Born out of the recession of the 1930s, one of his central ideas was the need for greater control over markets. As he wrote in 1933: 'The decadent international but individualistic capitalism in the hands of which we found ourselves after the war is not a success. It is not intelligent. It is not beautiful. It is not just. It is not virtuous. And it doesn't deliver the goods. In short we dislike it, and we are beginning to despise it.'[48]

The success of the long post-war boom meant that for decades Keynesianism retained its hold over global policy makers, and these radical voices on the right stayed on the fringes of economic and political thinking. Up to the early 1970s, international post-war economic policy had, by historic standards, been highly successful. World growth between 1950 and 1973—a period dubbed the 'golden age' by historians—was double the average of the inter-war years.

But during the convulsions that engulfed the global economy in the 1970s, the post-war consensus around strong government and social solidarity began to fade while the ideas of the radical right began to take root. 'The intellectual mood of post-war Britain, still relatively homogeneous down to 1970, was changing fast', argued Kenneth Morgan, a leading British historian of the post-war era. 'In its wake was a growing disillusion with the Keynesian economists, the Fabian planners, the post-Beveridge social engineers, the consensual liberal positivists who had governed the realm like so many con-quistadors for a quarter of a century.'[49]

Although Mrs Thatcher was, at heart, a conviction politician, she quickly came under the spell of this small group of thinkers on the right. Under their influence, she came to believe that Britain had created an economic model that killed incentives and stifled enterprise, that only freer markets and personal wealth accumulation would bring a more efficient, entrepreneurial and prosperous nation. A year after coming to power she was joined in this crusade by an even more powerful soul-mate, Ronald Reagan. The new American President, who was also heavily influenced by neo-conservative thinkers, shared Mrs Thatcher's belief in the dangers of big government and the virtues of a weakened state and low taxes.

Central to this new economic philosophy was the idea that the rich should be allowed to get richer. For British advocates, improved rewards at the top, it was claimed, would correct for the failings of post-war welfare capitalism, lift Britain out of its tepid entrepreneurial culture and bring renewed economic dynamism. For the new right thinkers, egalitarianism had gone too far, while allowing inequality to rise was a necessary condition for economic success. As Ludwig von Mises, based in New York, one of the leading post-war pro-market theorists and a founding member of the Mont Pelerin Society, had written in 1955: 'Inequality of wealth and incomes is the cause of the masses' well being, not the cause of anybody's distress.... Where there is a lower degree of inequality, there is necessarily a lower standard of living of the masses.'[50] Although greater reliance on markets would mean the wealth gap might grow, all citizens would still be better off through an expanded economic cake.

It was a view echoed 17 years later by Milton Friedman, though he expressed it slightly differently. 'Few trends could so thoroughly undermine the very foundations of our free society as the acceptance by corporate officials of a social responsibility other than to make as much money for their stockholders as possible.'[51]

These ideas gelled with the thinking of Mrs Thatcher's closest advisers, especially Sir Keith Joseph, her Education Secretary. In 1974 he founded the Centre for Policy Studies, a right-of-centre thinktank committed to free-market Conservatism. As he wrote in one of the Centre's first pamphlets, *Stranded in the Middle Ground?*, published in 1976: 'Making the rich poorer does not make the poor richer, but it does make the state stronger ... The pursuit of income equality will turn this country into a totalitarian slum.' It was a philosophy embraced in full by Mrs Thatcher, though she was always careful to couch it in terms of what she viewed as the virtues of meritocracy—achievement, reward and mobility. As she told a BBC radio audience in 1980, 'Let the children grow tall and some taller than others.'

Committed to these radical ideas, the British Prime Minister and the American President subjected their economies to an all-embracing economic and social experiment. At the heart of this economic leap-in-the-dark was a switch in economic and political philosophy from the 'managed capitalism' of the post-war era to what might be called 'market capitalism'. Central to the new philosophy was a belief in efficient and self-regulating markets.

In the UK from the early 1980s, the commitments of managed capitalism to full employment, progressive taxation and inclusive welfare were dropped. Of course, the effect of this process was not a return to the much more laissez faire capitalism of the 1920s. Even by the mid-1990s, the state retained a major role in the running of the economy, with higher levels of public spending as a share of output than in the 1950s and 1960s.

Nevertheless, most elements of the post-war ideological settlement—and its belief in economic fine-tuning, greater equality and a strong state—were scaled back. State industries were privatised, regulations swept away—especially in the City—and corporate and top income tax rates axed. Markets were allowed to operate more freely than had been the case in the post-war era. Although this shift to market capitalism was applied most strongly in the UK and the US, weaker versions were eventually introduced across much of the rich world with, eventually, far-reaching repercussions for the global economy.

Allowing greater freedom for markets became the principal driver of the reversal of the egalitarian thrust of the previous 75 years. It prepared the way for an era of big money and set in train a series of economic and social reforms that were to have a profound effect on the workforce and their wages in both of these countries.

Mrs Thatcher had long harboured a profound distrust of the unions, one that had been reinforced by the industrial militancy of the 1970s. For her, private industry could not flourish under the heavy hand of the state and an excessively powerful labour movement while Britain's labour market was overly regulated, workers were too protected and too highly paid. As she had written in the early 1960s during her first term as an MP: 'Many of us on the right of the Party—and not just on the right—were becoming very concerned about the abuse of trade union power'.

Ronald Reagan was a fellow traveller. In the late 1950s, he had worked for the American giant, General Electric, touring plants to give pep talks to workers and fronting the company's in-house television drama series. From there he came to fear that companies like GE faced serious threats from the power of the unions, organisations he dismissed as no more than 'special interest groups.'[52]

This long-held hostility was reinforced by the arrival of stagflation—a lethal mix of rising inflation and unemployment—in the 1970s. Britain—where inflation outstripped all its main industrial competitors—suffered disproportionately from the economic chaos of the time. But although the country came to be widely seen, with some justification, as the 'sick-man' of Europe, inflation, collapsing output and soaring unemployment was widespread.

Western capitalism was facing its deepest, full-blown crisis since the 1930s. From the late 1960s, industrial unrest spread across Europe. In 1969 Italy lost 60 million days to strikes. In the UK, the number of days lost rose from an annual average of 3 million in the early 1960s to 24 million in 1972. Even Germany, with its traditionally calm industrial relations, saw a rise in militancy. The level of unrest was at its deepest in the United States. In 1970, it topped the strike league table of the richer nations.[53]

Although successive demands for bigger wage settlements, a series of bitterly fought disputes and the indexing of wage settlements to price movements added to inflationary pressures, the problems of the time had much deeper causes. The OPEC crisis led to a fivefold increase in oil prices in the two years from 1972. Intensified global competition brought over-capacity and reduced profit margins. While productivity rises had held firm for the first two decades of the post-war era, they started to wane in most developed economies from the first half of the 1970s. The stable post-war global monetary system built on exchange rate stability collapsed in 1971, precipitating exchange rate volatility and global currency speculation.

While industrial relations were certainly poor across some sections of British industry, and hardly helpful to economic success, it is now widely accepted by economists that the union movement played a minor role in the inflationary spiral of the time. 'In part, but mostly not' is how Adam Posen, a member of the Bank of England's Monetary Policy Committee, replied when asked if unions caused inflation at the time. 'Clearly, there was more union power at the time, but until the 1970s, union power had been mostly exercised to ensure that wages kept up with gains in productivity, that is, that labour got its share. Union power actually was not so much about price setting overall, and so did not contribute to inflation in and of itself.'[54] If anything the Thatcher/Reagan strategy had the effect of making the labour force shoulder most of the burden of tackling the surge in inflation.

Despite its multiple causes, it was to be labour forces that became the principal scapegoat for the crisis, especially in the US and the UK. President Nixon—elected in 1968—had long railed against what he saw as excessive union power. In 1974, Arnold Weber, the robust head of Nixon's Wages and Prices Board—set up to try and cap wage demands—told *Business Week* that the strategy of big business was 'to zap labor.' It was a telling phrase, one that echoed the advice given by Andrew Mellon, America's Treasury Secretary—'to liquidate labor'—just after the Wall Street Crash in 1929.

To counter the growth of union power, employers' organisations started to respond in kind. The US Chamber of Commerce, the leading American association of small and medium sized businesses, expanded its base from 50,000 firms in 1970 to 250,000 a decade later. The Business Roundtable, a powerful group of Chief Executives of the country's largest corporations founded in 1972, spent an annual $900 million on lobbying through the decade.[55]

From the mid-1970s, US employers launched a campaign of virulent anti-unionism, later described by

Business Week as 'one of the most successful anti-union wars ever'. Ronald Reagan played his own role in this war. Soon after he became President, he embarked on a bitter battle with PATCO—the air traffic controllers' union. A technically illegal strike, Reagan eventually sacked 11,000 of the strikers—only 2000 had stayed in their posts—in August 5, 1981, and banned then from ever returning to work. It took years before the service could hire and train enough professionals to replace them. It was an early taste of what was to come.

America's war on the unions has been so successful, the proportion of private sector employees that are unionised has fallen from a quarter in 1979 to just seven per cent today. There are 50 million Americans who say they want union representation but can't get it. The impact on the workforce has been stark. The Federal Minimum wage, which stood on a par with the official poverty line in 1980, had fallen to 30 per cent below it a decade later. Along with rising unemployment during the 1980s, the bargaining power of American labour began a long period of decline. One US study has found that the weakening of organised labour and the decline in union membership accounts for between a fifth and a third of the rise in American inequality over the last thirty years.[56]

In the UK, industrial unrest from the early 1970s sent a wave of panic across Whitehall, government and business, with the organised workforce coming to be viewed as a threat to future prosperity. A few months after Heath lost the election in 1974, Lord Chalfont, a former Labour Defence Minister wrote of 'the massive power and often ruthless action of the great industrial trades unions'. Headlined 'Could Britain be heading for a

41

military takeover', the article went onto warn that 'Large industrial concerns are beginning to talk in terms of a co-ordinated defence against industrial action or wholesale nationalisation'.[57]

With Britain scarred by a series of high profile and highly damaging strikes—especially during the 'winter of discontent' in 1979, Mrs Thatcher made trade-union reform one of her top priorities. From 1979, employment rights were removed, strikes made much more difficult and wages councils abolished. In 1984, the year long, set-piece battle with the National Union of Miners—badly led by the most combative of all the union bosses, Arthur Scargill—led to an historic and devastating defeat for the miners. The organised labour movement in Britain never really recovered from the strike—the third miner's dispute in 12 years.

In 1979 trade union membership in the UK stood at a post-war peak of 13.5 million, more than half the workforce. By 2009 it was down to 6.7 million, a quarter of its potential. The number of days lost to strikes fell sharply from 29 million in 1979 to just over one million in 2007. In the 1960s and 1970s, trade union leaders, from Hugh Scanlon of the Engineering Workers to Jack Jones of the mighty Transport and General Workers' were regulars for beer and sandwiches at No 10 Downing Street. They were household names amongst the public and on first name terms with the country's business leaders. In one Gallup poll in 1977, a majority said Jones was more powerful than the Prime Minister. Thirty years later, even the leaders of the biggest unions had faded largely into obscurity. Today only one-in-seven private sector workers is a member of a trade union.

The 1980s was to become a key turning point in the balance of advantage between the workforce and employers, precipitating a key shift in the way the economy functioned. The switch in economic philosophy not only brought weakened union powers. As labour bargaining power waned, the priority given to fighting inflation triggered much higher levels of unemployment.

The continued taming of the workforce may well have met the immediate interests of both British and American business. Employers quickly regained the upper hand they had lost during the militant 1970s. But while it would not have been in the interests of either nation to return to the stand-offs of that decade, making the labour force pay disproportionately for the international crisis, one that was only in small part of their making, was to have dramatic repercussions. Far from stimulating economic dynamism, as its architects hoped, the strategy helped sow the seeds of economic weakness and instability that was to dog the American, British and the global economy for the next twenty-five years.

One of the most important effects of the empowerment of employers and the erosion of union power was on the course of wage settlements. Fuelled by lengthening dole queues, real wage rises faltered. The share of national output being paid in earnings, a key measure of balance in the economy, began to slip and kept doing so. For employers, the weakened bargaining position of labour eased wage costs and boosted profits and in turn, the bank accounts of business owners and executives.

Figure 2.1, for the UK, shows the impact of this shift in the balance of power. The share of national output

The UK's long wage squeeze, 1955 to 2008 (Figure 2.1)
Wages (gross) as a proportion of GDP.[58]

going in wages had held firm at between 58 and 60 per cent during the period of relative industrial harmony in the 1950s and 1960s. It then jumped in the crisis of the early 1970s, peaking in the middle of that decade at 64.5 per cent. Although this was a sizeable and unsustainable jump, the wage share fell back almost as quickly as it soared. It settled at 59 per cent at the end of the 1970s, before beginning a three-decade long descent. By 2008, it was down to 53 per cent. This was not much higher than the share enjoyed by labour at the height of the industrial revolution in the second half of the nineteenth century.

What this fall means is that from the early 1980s, a declining proportion of the value of the nation's output was accruing to wage-earners as a group. This decline occurred in two quite separate ways. First, each year, a proportion of the benefit of *existing* output was being transferred upwards from wages to profits. Secondly, a declining share of *new* growth—of the annual addition to national output—was going to the workforce. How these shifts occurred is explained in more detail in later chapters. By 2008, the net effect of these changes was that wage-earners as a group were receiving around seven per cent less of national income—the equivalent of some £100 billion a year—than they were in the post-war decades. It is this shift that has been one of the principal drivers of the increasing economic polarisation of recent decades.

How to divide the spoils of the economy—between employees (through wages and salaries) and the owners of business (through profits)—is one of the oldest issues of political economy. Indeed, the division of what economists call 'factor shares' has crucial implications for private enterprise economies. As one of the founding fathers of classical economics, David Ricardo—who made his own personal fortune from speculation—wrote in 1821, 'The principal problem in Political Economy ' is to determine how 'the produce of the earth … is divided among … the proprietor of the land, the owner of the stock or capital necessary for its cultivation and the labourers by whose industry it is cultivated'.[59]

The division of the national wealth between earnings and profits is in part an issue of social balance. While excessive wages can threaten the future of firms, excessive profits mean unacceptable levels of inequality. Indeed, the profit share and the level of inequality tend to track each other over time. Because the income that derives from profits (through executive pay, share dividends, capital gains, interest and rents) is much more unequally distributed than pay itself, benefiting rich and higher income groups more than those on middle and lower incomes, high profit shares mean more extreme levels of inequality. The key beneficiaries of the politically orchestrated boost to profit levels from the early 1980s were mostly a tiny group of society—those who already stood at the top of income and wealth leagues.

But this balance is not just a matter of acceptable levels of social division. It is also a key factor in ensuring that economies work. If aggregate wages and profits get too out of line, in either direction, the implications for the economy can be highly damaging. On the one hand, the level of profits determines the long run sustainability of the capitalist model. Profits are the lifeblood of business—the engine of growth, both for individual firms and capitalism collectively. A predominantly free enterprise economy relies on profits for the investment that brings expansion and hence future prosperity. Low, falling or non-existent profits will reduce the rate of investment and lead to stalled growth or stagnation. They will also eventually put individual firms out of business. If the share of profits sinks too low, the very survival of the capitalist system would be under threat.

On the other hand, excessively high profit levels generated by the contraction of wages can bring a quite different set of distortions. Since consumer spending is the largest component of demand in most economies—in the decade before the recession it accounted for about 63 to 64 per cent of GDP in the UK—falling wages has a sizeable impact on demand in the economy. As the wage share started to fall well below 60 per cent, a growing gap emerged in how to maintain levels of consumption. It is

46

no more sensible for the national wage bill to add up to significantly less than the volume of available consumer goods than it is to greatly exceed it. While the latter contributes to inflation, the former brings recession. Stagnating wages suck purchasing power out of the economy and can prevent growing national output being sold.[60] Excessive profits also feed higher incomes at the top, create financial surpluses and concentrate economic power. These imbalances upset the processes of economic equilibrium necessary to prevent instability.

Although the division of the national cake between profits and wages has ebbed and flowed over short periods of time, the long run trend for the profit share from the beginning of the twentieth century to the mid-1970s was downward. The nineteenth century was the high point for both American and British capitalism. In the United States, the titans of the Gilded Age were able to amass colossal fortunes because the economic climate was biased heavily in favour of the industrial and commercial barons. Industry was highly profitable while the lack of labour muscle meant that wages were kept low. The 'robber barons' were renowned for the hard conditions they imposed on their employees. In 1883, John D Rockefeller faced demonstrations both from his own staff, who had had their wages cut, and from protestors working for competitors he had driven out of business. The demonstrators burnt an effigy of him while chanting 'the most hated man in America'.

In the UK, with labour relatively unorganised and firms unregulated, wages accounted for a little over half the total of the country's national income in 1870.[61] In the 1880s, less than three-quarters of a million workers were members of a union. Despite some successful strikes, such as the match-girls in 1888 and the dockers in 1889, improvements in pay and working conditions were mostly slow in coming. While a sizeable proportion of profits were ploughed back into the economy to enable a steady expansion in the industrial base, they were sufficiently high to fuel the growth of industrial and commercial fortunes as well.

While high profits were the main means by which the industrial revolution was financed and the British economy grew, they also meant a massive wealth and income gap between the top and the bottom. For most of the nineteenth century, wealth was heavily concentrated in the hands of a very small industrial, commercial and aris-tocratic elite, the owners of capital, property and land—at most a few thousand individuals. The great majority of the population owned nothing, poverty was rife and the economy was highly turbulent. As the biographer of John Maynard Keynes, Robert Skidelsky, has written: 'A radically unequal distribution of income was sustained by a bluff or a deception, by which the workers were subjected to an enforced abstinence on the tacit under-standing that the capitalists "saved" most of their profits.'[62]

This deception gradually receded during the course of the next century. With the election of reformist governments and the spread of unionisation, the imbalance between wages and profits began to correct, albeit slowly. Business eventually had to live with lower profits and a better paid workforce.[63] It was a highly significant economic trend that was common to most developed economies. During the 1950s and 1960s, the wage share in the UK settled in the narrow range of 58 to 61 per cent, up from a figure that hovered at just over a half in the half century to the start of the First World War. Far from undermining capitalism, the boost to wages was consistent with sustained economic success. The boom of the 1950s and 1960s brought greater industrial harmony, rising prosperity and decent profits, a virtuous circle that began to fracture from the end of the 1960s. Over the next few years, the wage share surged reaching its record high in 1975.

As industrial unrest spread, and the number of strikes mushroomed in the early 1970s, firms found it increasingly difficult to hold the line on wages, not just in Britain but across Europe and in the US. Amongst the leading industrial nations, real wages rose by 4 per cent a year in the early 1970s.[64] Already suffering from intensified global competition, international financial uncertainty and slipping productivity, rocketing wage settlements added another headache to this list—deteriorating profits.

Falling profits were a near universal phenomenon amongst developed economies. Between 1965 and 1973, the rate of profit in US manufacturing fell by 43.5 per cent. The manufacturing sectors of the G-7, the world's seven biggest economies, (the US, Germany, Japan, UK, Italy, France and Canada) suffered an average decline in profitability of some 25 per cent.[65] For good reason, this period became known as the era of the 'profits squeeze'.

Declining profits added to deepening economic problems, stifling both business investment and productivity growth. For some on the left, the crisis was seen as a sign of the inherent instability of global capitalism and its endemic internal contradiction—the difficulty of marrying decent universal living standards with the profits needed to secure expansion. Certainly a profits squeeze on the scale of the mid-1970s was never going to be sustainable. Either labour would have to accept a decline in wages and a return to the post-war norm, or the capitalist model would face a growing risk of collapse.

'The consequence of a strategy which attempts to obtain wage increases or to resist wage cuts in a period when capital faces increasing competition, is that capitalists find it harder and harder to meet those demands and to remain profitable at the same time', argued the radical political economists, Andrew Glyn and Bob Sutcliffe, in their influential book, *British Capitalism, Workers and the Profits Squeeze*, published in 1972. 'Sometimes, therefore, capital and labour are bargaining not only about wages, but about the survival of the capitalist system'.[66]

The global economic problems of the time were much more significant than just another of the periodic crises endemic to the history of capitalism. The steadily rising living standards of the 'golden age' gave way to near stagnant output. What one economist called 'disorganised capitalism' was not well enough equipped to cope with the external oil price shock of 1973, the end of cheap energy and the surges in other commodity prices and the rise of industrial militancy, while the tools of economic management, so successful for the previous twenty five years proved less able to cope with inflation than stagnation, let alone both.[67]

To settle the crisis and the weakening of private capital what was needed was a modest correction in the wage share, and the restoration of profit levels, returning them to the norm of the post-war decades. It was this level that had delivered equilibrium between the maintenance of demand and the necessary rate of capital accumulation. In the event, such a modest correction is exactly what happened *before* the market revolution that was implanted from the early 1980s began to take effect. In most advanced western nations by the early-to-mid 1980s, the wage share had slipped back from its historic high, mostly in little more than a handful of years.[68]

The profits squeeze of the mid-1970s proved to be short-lived, a blip triggered by an exceptional set of circumstances including the oil price shock, the collapse of the international monetary system and the near-peak power of trade unionism. By 1980, the wage share in the UK had already fallen to well below its peak of 65 per cent—the result of economic retrenchment and the lengthening dole queues from the mid-1970s. By the time the Conservative government launched its crusade against union power, the wage share was already back to around 59 per cent.

If the wage share had been allowed to settle at this level—the average of the 1950s and 1960s—the future course of the economy would have been very different. But the move towards market capitalism ensured that the fall in the wage share from the late 1970s proved much more enduring than the temporary fall in the profits share in the mid-1970s. Indeed, the share of national output accruing to wage-earners continued to fall from the early 1980s.

It was a similar story in the United States. In 2006 wages and salaries made up the lowest share of the nation's economic output since the government began recording the data in 1947. In contrast, corporate profits had climbed to their highest share since the 1960s. UBS— the global investment bank—described the post-millennium period as 'the golden era of profitability.' In the first quarter of 2006, wages and salaries represented 45 percent of gross domestic product, down from almost 50 percent in the first quarter of 2001 and nearly 54 per cent in the first quarter of 1970.[69]

Far from returning the wage share to its post-war norm, the policies of the 1980s brought a return to the levels of the nineteenth century. The economic revolution launched by Margaret Thatcher and Ronald Reagan, aimed in part to deal with the perceived excessive power of labour, turned out to be overkill.

Moreover the scale of the squeeze on wages for most of the workforce was greater than suggested by the headline figures shown in figure 2.1. This is for two main reasons. First, the salaries of top business executives are included in the official wage share figures used to construct the figure, yet such 'salaries' are, as the late Andrew Glyn has argued, 'really part of profit incomes masquerading as wages' and should be transferred from the wage to the profit figures.[70] Since top executive salaries have been rising much more rapidly than the average, the effect of such transfer would be an even sharper reduction in the wage share for the great bulk of the workforce.

Secondly, even below the tier of top executives, earnings have become increasingly concentrated at the top in the last thirty years. Figure 2.2 shows that between 1978 and 2008, *real* gross earnings doubled for those at the 90th percentile (the earnings point exceeded by ten per cent of earners). In contrast they rose by 56 per cent at the median (the middle earning point, and representative of the typical worker) and by only 27 per cent at the 10th percentile (the earnings point below which the poorest tenth of earners fall). As a result, the falling wage share has not been evenly distributed across the earnings range but has been borne almost entirely by middle and lower paid employees. The bottom three-fifths of earners have thus faced a sustained double-edged squeeze—a shrinking share of a diminishing pool.[71]

The economic policies of the last two decades have led to the emergence of a broadly two-speed wage economy. Leading the race in the super-track of earnings growth has been a small group of financiers, bankers and

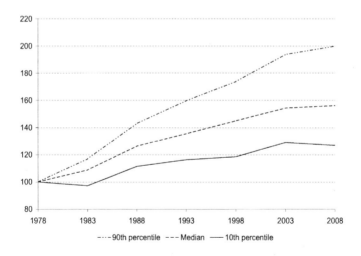

How earnings have become more unequal over the last 30 years, UK (Figure 2.2)
Index of the rise in gross weekly real earnings, full time males, 1978 to 2008. 1978 = 100. The earnings figures have been adjusted for inflation using the retail price index.[72]

company executives. Below them sits the rest of the working population. Some of these have done much better than others—especially those working in well paid white collar professions outside of the corporate and City super-elite—such as lawyers, accountants and medics. But most have ended up in the slow lane of earnings growth, with earnings that have fallen way behind the growth of the economy.[73]

While incomes continued to rise sharply amongst the very top income groups in the decade before the credit crunch, real income growth amongst those lower down the income scale started to slow and at an accelerating rate. During Labour's first term in power, much of the workforce enjoyed faster rises in take-home pay than in the previous 15 years. As a result, the wage share recovered some of its lost ground between 1996 and 2001. But the party did not last for long. The 'feast' years of the late 1990s gave way first to the 'lean' years of Labour's second term and then the 'famine' years during its third. As shown in figure 2.2, earnings growth slowed sharply, especially at the median and tenth percentile, from 2000.

From the mid-2000s, real income growth for a large body of the workforce was at best static. In the two years to 2007, wages barely kept pace with rising inflation so that median incomes rose by a mere 0.4 per cent a year—around £1 a week. Between 2002 and 2007, real hourly wage rates grew by a mere 0.1 per cent per annum amongst median earners.[74] It is this that accounts for the resumption of the falling wage share from 2001 shown in figure 2.1.

Although the 'crisis of pay' has been especially sharp

in English-speaking countries—the UK, US and Canada—there have been similar, albeit shallower, falls in wage shares in most developed and middle income economies. 'In 51 out of the 73 countries for which data are available, the share of wages in total income declined over the past two decades' according to a 2008 study by the Geneva-based International Labour Organisation.[75]

One of the most important economic consequences of these trends has been that real wages for most of the working population have been falling behind the growth in productivity (the increase in economic capacity), and at an accelerating rate. This is especially true in the case of the UK and the US, though there has been a similar if weaker trend in other rich nations. Between 1980 and 2007, real wages in the UK rose by an annual average of 1.6 per cent while economic capacity grew by 1.9 per cent. Figure 2.3 shows that this decoupling began in the 1990s and accelerated from 2000. Since the turn of the century, productivity has been rising at almost twice the rate of

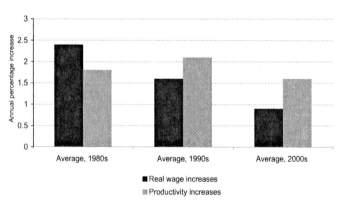

The UK's growing wage-productivity gap, 1980 to 2008 (Figure 2.3)[76]

real earnings, so that living standards for most have been rising much more slowly than overall prosperity.

In the US, wages have been falling even further behind productivity growth. Until the end of the 1970s, real wages for most of the population moved, as in the UK, in line with economic growth, doubling roughly every thirty-five years. As a result each 'successive generation lived twice as well as its predecessor.'[77] As shown in figure 2.4, that progression first started to falter from the early 1980s when the incomes of middle and low earning families stopped keeping pace with productivity rises, and, as in the UK, at an accelerating rate. From then, they started to fall well behind. While productivity rose by 71 per cent in the 27 years to 2007, median real wages grew by only 9 per cent. Since 2003, real wages have been falling.[78] Various studies have shown the way incomes for typical Americans, adjusted for inflation, have done little better than stagnate over the last 30 years.[79] As a result,

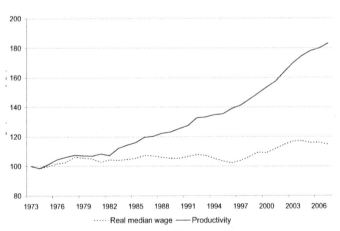

America's growing wage-productivity gap, 1973 to 2008 (Figure 2.4)
Index, 1973 = 100.[80]

college-educated workers today earn barely more than their less-educated counterparts a generation ago.

This decoupling of wage and productivity growth has been a big flashpoint for the balance of the domestic economies most affected. In the post-war era, the gains from growth were broadly equally shared. Earnings, across income groups, moved upwards in line with profit levels. Such sharing enabled economies to maintain a degree of economic equilibrium that brought sustained stability. As real wages rose broadly in line with productivity during the 1950s and 1960s, the demand for the nations' goods and services—from cars and washing machines to leisure pursuits and holidays—kept pace with their supply. There was sufficient purchasing power to ensure that economic output would be bought, and sufficient profit to maintain investment levels.

The shrinking of the relative wage pool across many leading industrial nations over the last two decades has fractured this equilibrium. Purchasing power in a domestic economy is determined heavily by the course of real wage growth. If productivity—which determines the scale of output—grows more quickly than real wages, then a dangerous productivity-wage gap develops, one which acts as a powerful deflationary force. Ultimately, this gap is likely to lead to supply rising faster than demand, overproduction, unemployment and recession.[81] The increasingly uneven division of the spoils of growth that has triggered the growing gap in many mature economies has led to a slowdown in the purchasing power of large sections of the workforce, generating a new structural imbalance in the economy.

The significance of the wage-productivity gap has now

been recognised at the highest levels. 'The build up of widening income inequality and a reduced share of wages in national income in most countries in the decades before the crisis distorted economic growth', the Director General of the International Labour Organisation, Juan Somavia, told the annual meeting of the IMF in October 2010. 'Wages did not keep pace with rising productivity. In many countries growth produced too few good jobs, too little decent work. With household incomes squeezed for all but the very wealthy, growth became dependent on an unsustainable credit bubble in some countries and on exports in others.'[82]

So what has been driving the rising earnings gap and the falling wage share? Academic economists have attributed them mostly to a mix of the steady shift in jobs from mature to developing economies and to the impact of technical change. These are important factors. With the emergence of global markets labour became much more plentiful internationally, strengthening the bargaining power of domestic employers.[83] All advanced economies have experienced intensified competition from low-wage economies in the last two to three decades, though some, such as Germany, have withstood this pressure better than others.

By increasing the demand for skill and depressing it for those without, technical change has also played a role. These largely external factors certainly help to explain the widening earnings gap between more and less educated workers and to some extent the growth of unemploy-ment.[84] But they are only part of the picture. All rich countries have faced these external pressures, but the impact on wages and the earnings gap has been very different across countries, largely because governments have adopted very different policy responses. Key has been the extent of the shift to more market-led economies and the rise of a much more aggressive business and capitalist model, a move some have described as a shift from 'good' to 'bad' capitalism.[85] Countries such as the US and the UK which have gone furthest down this road have also experienced the deepest falls in their wage-share and the widest growth in the pay-productivity gap.

3

THE VANISHING MIDDLE

In his first speech after defeating his better-known brother to become Labour's new leader, Ed Miliband made a pitch for the votes of what he called the 'squeezed middle'. There is nothing especially new about Britain's political leaders attempting to woo the central layer of British society. Mrs Thatcher won the 1979 election by spotting the importance of the aspirational working class, targeting what she called 'middle England'—those in the middle of the class and income structure—with a promise of better opportunities. Eighteen years later, the political battle for the centre ground was won by Labour, again with a carefully targeted appeal to what the popular press dubbed 'Sierra Man' or 'Worcester Woman'.

Although the origins of the phrase 'middle England' go back to Lord Salisbury in 1882, the term was not popularised until Mrs Thatcher borrowed it from the United States. She adapted it from the term 'middle America' first used by Richard Nixon on his Presidential campaign trail in 1968 to describe the country's 'silent majority'.

The irony of these appeals is that what has happened under all British and American governments, right- and left-of-centre, of the last thirty years has been policies that have had a largely negative effect over the livelihoods and opportunities of the very groups that won them the elections. There is it seems, little gratitude in politics.

It was broadly the bottom 50-60 per cent (those with low to middle incomes) of both American and British society that became the principal victims of the medicine applied in both countries to try and revive what was seen as the flagging capitalist patient. Along with the war on the unions and wages, there were two other ingredients in this medicine. The first was a fundamental shift in macro-economic priorities away from maintaining employment to fighting inflation. The second was an attempt to engineer a wholesale restructuring of the economy, to move Britain more quickly down the road of a finance and service-driven economy. It was to prove a lethal cocktail, unleashing years of unrelenting upheaval on American and British workforces, contributing to the widening gulf in incomes and bringing dramatic changes in social structures along the way.

To tackle inflation—which became the overriding goal of economic policy—both the UK and US governments greatly tightened the policies of mild fiscal restraint and monetary discipline already introduced by the Callaghan and Carter administrations. During Reagan's first Presidency, inflation fell from 12 to four per cent. In the UK, the policies were slower to work. Inflation fell, though it was not until the early 1990s that it was brought back to the levels of the early 1960s.

The medicine may have worked, but not without subjecting the patient to a series of deeply unpleasant and prolonged side-effects. The strength of the austerity programmes plunged the US, UK and the global economy into its second recession in a decade. The measures also brought bad news for companies, at least initially. At the trough of that recession in 1981, the aggregate valuation of the top 100 UK companies was lower than it had been, adjusted for inflation, at the time of Dunkirk. Andrew Glyn—who died in 2009—used to joke to his Oxford students that British capitalists had been more optimistic about the future of UK companies on the eve of the expected invasion of Britain by Hitler than they were during the early years of Margaret Thatcher's government.

For a significant minority of the workforce, the strategy brought their first taste of the dole queue. By 1981, unemployment in the UK had soared above the 3 million mark for the first time since the 1930s. By the end of 1982, real GDP in the US was lower than it had been three years earlier. Its unemployment rate had risen to nearly 11 per cent, its highest rate since the Great Depression.[86] There were similar rises across the industrialised world.

For the new economic strategists, unemployment was inevitable, but they believed it would be a merely short-term side-effect of the monetarist medicine necessary to get rid of inflationary pressure and steer the economy into a stronger wealth- and job-creating future. As the then Chancellor of the Exchequer, Norman Lamont, told the House of Commons in 1992 during the second recession triggered by the economic strategy of the 1980s: 'Rising unemployment and the recession have been the price we've had to pay to get inflation down.... That is a price well worth paying.'

This might have been the case if unemployment had turned out to be a temporary phenomenon and the costs

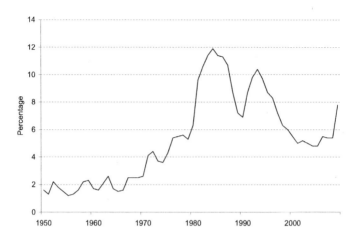

The UK's lengthening dole queue (Figure 3.1)
Unemployment Rate, 1950-2009, UK.[87]

of the contractionary policies had been evenly shared, but neither was true. Unemployment levels remained stubbornly high. In the two immediate post-war decades, the problem of the mass unemployment of the 1930s had been largely cracked. In the era of 'managed capitalism' from 1950 to 1973, the UK unemployment rate averaged 1.6 percent. As shown in figure 3.1, unemployment under 'market capitalism' has, despite the falling wage share, been much higher. It has averaged 7.8 per cent, nearly five times that of the earlier period. In the United States, unemployment rates also rose between the periods, though not by as much as in the UK.

As unemployment has soared, it has also become increasingly concentrated, hitting some areas, regions and individuals much more heavily than others. As a result, the jobless are typically out of work for longer than in the past. In the UK the proportion unemployed for more than a year since 2000 has been nearly three times the level of the 1950s. At the end of 2010, it stood at close to 30 per cent.[88]

Another characteristic of the modern labour market, with its weakened trade unions and workplace rights, has been the growth of poor quality, insecure work. The level of shift working has become much greater, The greater emphasis on markets has led to what one expert has described as the 're-allocation of risk' from companies to the workforce with workers bearing a higher cost of industrial restructuring bringing 'reduced job security, lower wages and job intensification'.[89]

A comparison of employment conditions in the UK between 1992 and 2002 found that, because of a deterioration in pay, job prospects, training and hours worked, and a greater emphasis on shift-working—or 'flexible rostering'—the 2002 'world of work is much less satisfying to employees than the one they were experiencing ten years ago.'[90] A more recent study has estimated that, although employment rights improved under Labour, in 2008 some 2 million people in the UK worked in 'vulnerable employment'—precarious work often characterised by unsocial hours, exploitative working conditions, a lack of training, pervasive job insecurity and minimal employment rights.[91]

Such characteristics are particularly prevalent in low pay sectors like care, industrial cleaning, factory packing, hospitality, security, construction and food processing, where there is heavy reliance on agency work which offers much poorer conditions of work.[92]

As with the rising wage gap, these higher levels of

joblessness and deteriorating work conditions are in part down to globalisation and the shifting pattern of skill requirements. But they are also deeply embedded in the policy switches arising from the move to more market-orientated economies. It was later admitted by one of Mrs Thatcher's key economic advisers that one of the intended consequences of the new government's economic strategy was the taming of labour. 'The nightmare I sometimes have about this whole experience runs as follows... there may have been people making the actual policy decisions ... who never believed for a moment that this was the correct way to bring down inflation. They did, however, see that it would be a very, very good way to raise unemployment' is how Sir Alan Budd summed up the multi-layered assault on inflation and the unions. Budd was appointed chief economic adviser at the Treasury in the 1980s and later became Provost of Queen's College, Oxford. 'And raising unem-ployment was an extremely desirable way of reducing the strength of the working classes', he continued, '... what was engineered there, in Marxist terms, was a crisis of capitalism which created a reserve army of labour and has allowed the capitalists to make high profits ever since.'[93]

While the dole queues remained stubbornly high, business fortunes began to revive quickly after the state-induced recession of the early 1980s. The initial slump in share prices turned, after 1987, into the longest bull run in history.

Economic and social disruption was also an inevitable consequence of the wider attempts to hasten the move to a service- and finance-based economy. The government believed that Britain's comparative advantage lay in finance not manufacturing. Britain's industrial base had been in slow decline ever since the early 1960s—the product of intensified competition from the developing world and a deteriorating record on productivity. Despite this erosion, manufacturing in 1979 remained at the heart of the economy. Ford Motors in Dagenham employed more than 40,000 workers while a significant proportion of the workforce in the West Midlands worked in local car and motorcycle factories or steel mills. In that decade, Stoke-on-Trent was still the pottery capital of the world and Royal Doulton had 18 local factories. GEC was one of the world's leading electronics companies and Raleigh's Nottingham factory was still producing 100,000 bicycles a year.

A decade later, large parts of the industrial landscape had been turned into a wasteland. Of course some decline in manufacturing was always inevitable while the process of de-industrialisation and the expansion of the service sector is in many ways a desirable hallmark of economic maturity.[94] Some industries in which Britain once had a comparative advantage such as steel, textiles and coalmining were in historic decline unable to compete with newly industrialising countries with cheaper labour. It is generally desirable for economies to adapt to changing global patterns by shifting low value production to areas which can produce the same goods more cheaply, replacing them with higher value production.

Indeed, all industrial nations have experienced a fall in the role played by manufacturing. Between 1974 and 2001, manufacturing employment fell by a third across the nations which make up the Organisation for Economic Co-operation and Development. What is significant is that the falls in the UK and the US have been much steeper.[95] In Mrs Thatcher's first term alone, as the number of bankruptcies exploded, manufacturing output fell by a third.

It is no coincidence that in both these countries finance became an increasingly dominant force as the process of de-industrialisation accelerated. Indeed the fortunes of these two sectors have been moving in opposite directions—as finance has triumphed, manufacturing has slumped.

The economic policies pursued by both Mrs Thatcher and Ronald Reagan—from a high exchange rate to financial and labour market de-regulation—were highly favourable to finance. One of the effects of Reaganomics was an overvalued dollar, hardly dream conditions for exporters. William Benedetto, head of corporate finance for Dean Witter Reynolds—one of America's largest stock brokerage and securities' firms—called Ronald Reagan's eight-year Presidency 'an investment banker's dream world.'[96] But while Wall Street flourished, key industrial sectors from timber and steel to chemicals and high-technology, sweated.

Between 1970 and 1990, American employment in manufacturing shrank from 27 to 17 per cent of the workforce. This was mostly the product of finance initiated industrial restructuring, including the shift of production centres abroad by American corporations.[97] The fall in manufacturing employment continued after 1990, with the mild recession of 2000-2003 accelerating the long term trend.[98]

In the UK, globalisation, the abolition of international control over exchange rates and the pursuit of a strong pound all hastened the decline of manufacturing. For the City, the end of exchange controls (the rules that had restricted movements of money between nations since the Second World War), high real interest rates and the appreciating pound from 1979 produced what one commentator described in 1981 as 'dream conditions for London's financial apparatus.'[99] Hot money flowed into London and bankers enjoyed, for the first time since 1939, complete freedom over where to invest these increased inflows.

While high interest rates and a strong exchange rate favoured finance, they were bad news for manufacturers and exporters. Yet for most of the period since the end of the 1970s, the pound has been held at a higher rate than justified by Britain's economic strength. It had risen by 50 per cent in real terms against the dollar in the two years to 1981. This over-valuation was initially due, in part, to the discovery of North Sea Oil which made Britain an exporting nation. But the persistently high pound has also been the result of explicit government policy to give preference to financial services and its need to attract global footloose capital. These huge capital inflows were always going to push up the sterling exchange rate.

When, in 1990, after years of pressure, Britain finally joined the European Exchange Rate Mechanism—which meant keeping sterling at a fixed position to other currencies in the scheme—it did so at an inflated and unsustainable level. It was only after Britain was dramatically forced out on 'black Wednesday'—in November 1992—that its economy eventually started to recover from the contractionary policies of the 1980s.

The Conservative governments from 1979 knew that

their policies would be damaging to manufacturing. A more regulated labour market and a less laissez-faire approach to industrial policy could have softened the impact of economic change, slowed the rate of decline and preserved more manufacturing jobs. But leading sections of the Conservative Party had an in-built prejudice against industry. The party's electoral strength lay in the Home Counties and the South rather than in the non-metropolitan industrial heartlands. While manufacturing was seen as strike-ridden, finance was largely union free.

Central to the government's economic strategy was the construction of a post-industrial society built around services and finance. According to one cabinet member at the time, the leading 'wet' Sir Ian Gilmour, the Thatcherites displayed a 'systematic belittling of manufacturing industry's importance. They always put the interests of finance and commerce well before those of industry.'[100] The view that manufacturing was dispensable also chimed with the views of the leading new right economists. As Milton Friedman said in 1980, Britain's manufacturing should be allowed to fall to bits.[101]

When Labour came to power in 1997, they took no action to slow the pace of de-industrialisation. After its fall in 1992—one that proved the key to economic recovery—the pound strengthened again and stayed high for the duration of Gordon Brown's Chancellorship. Even during the relative boom conditions from 1997 to 2007 a further 1.5 million manufacturing jobs were lost in the UK, as fast a rate as in the 1980s.

Throughout the last twenty five years, industry has proved a largely powerless force. During the 1980s, Sir

Terence Beckett, Director General of the Confederation of British Industry and the Chair of ICI, offered Mrs Thatcher a 'bare-knuckle fight' over the impact of her policies on manufacturing. As he warned, Britain would have to 'entertain another six million or 40 per cent more tourists' to make up for the loss of his company.'[102] It was a fight lost by manufacturing.

Such lobbying has proved largely in vain against the growing power of the City. Political leaders talked down manufacturing. Labour's love-affair with the City led to a huge influx of foreign funds which helped keep the pound at uncompetitive levels. While manufacturing output and employment continued to shrink, finance and the service economy prospered. In the three decades to 2008, the number of jobs in manufacturing fell from just over 7 to just over 3 million.[103]

As shown in figure 3.2, by 2007, manufacturing in the UK accounted for nearly 13 per cent of national output, down from a third in 1979. The share of output accounted for by finance, in contrast, doubled from around 5 per cent in the mid-1970s to slightly over ten per cent by 2008.[104]

The expansion of finance accelerated from the second half of the 1990s. In the three years to 2007—before the onset of the credit crunch—financial services accounted for a third of overall GDP growth (another third came from residential and commercial property) and had grown to play a bigger role in the economy than in any other comparable nation.[105] Thus financial services accounts for 7.5 per cent of the US economy, 6.7 per cent in Japan, 4.6 per cent in France and 3.8 per cent in Germany. As became clear in the turmoil of 2008-9, it is not good for

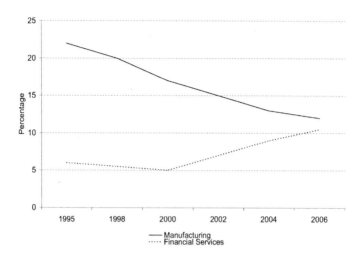

Finance closes the gap on manufacturing, 1995-2006 (Figure 3.2)
The percentage share of manufacturing and financial services in the UK
economy.[106]

resilience to have such a heavily skewed pattern of
economic activity.

One of the most important consequences of these
trends has been a big shake-up in the economic and social
composition of Britain. The replacement of factory by
clerical and white-collar service jobs has led to an
apparent upward shift in the class structure. As shown in
figure 3.3, in the four decades to 2007, the proportion of
the population classified by sociologists as 'working class'
fell from 70 to 44 per cent, while the proportion defined
as 'middle-class' rose from 31 to 55 per cent.

These are big changes in a short span. After the War,
Britain was widely seen as a 'pyramid- shaped' society
with a small and privileged group of the rich at the top, a

71

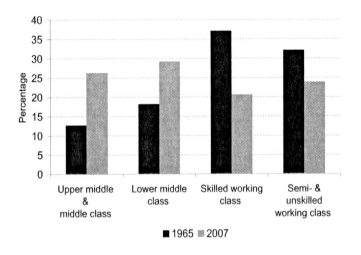

Figure 3.3: The rise of middle-class Britain, 1965-2007.[107]

larger but still small and comfortable middle and a large majority at the bottom. With rising affluence and the changing composition of work, Britain, it is claimed, has become an increasingly middle class society, better paid, educated, more affluent and with a much stronger set of upward aspirations. In 1996, the former editor of *The Times*, William Rees-Mogg, wrote of the rise of the 'classless middle-class', calling them the largest group in Britain.[108] In the same year, the writer John Mortimer talked of the contemporary class system as one with a ' "fat-cat" upper class, a huge middle class and an underclass. There's no working class anymore.'[109] At the beginning of Labour's rein, John Prescott declared 'we are all middle class now.'

The reality of the social structure of Britain is rather different. The four million service jobs created since the late 1970s have certainly changed the social, economic and geographical pattern of work. Many of these new jobs have been in well-paid professional and managerial occupations in areas such as health, education, finance, business and administration.[110]

On the other hand, because of the long term trends in wage patterns, a significant proportion of these new service jobs, especially in growth areas like cleaning, caring, security, data entry, hotel portering, customer services and retail pay less, sometimes much less, than those they replaced. These jobs—mostly those that cannot be replaced by machines or computers—may be defined as white collar but have proved far from glamorous, well paid and secure.

The effect of these trends is that, over the last thirty years, the British labour market has become increasingly polarised between higher paying, secure jobs requiring high levels of education and experience, and lower paid, less secure, more routine jobs requiring limited skill and training. In contrast there have been sharp falls in the number of jobs paying 'middling wages' and requiring middling skills.

The scale of what has been called the 'hollowing out of the middle' is shown in figure 3.4 which charts the change in employment by 1999 in jobs ranked by their position in the 1979 wage distribution. This shows a growth in the number of jobs at the top tail of the distribution—business executives, senior managers, consultants, data processors, software engineers; a smaller rise in the number of low paid jobs in the lower tail— cleaners, hairdressers, shop assistants and call centre workers; and sharp falls in the number of jobs paying

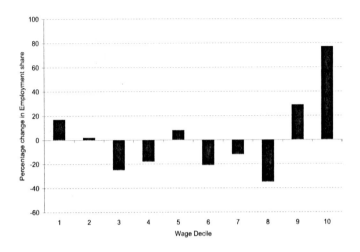

The 'hollowing out of the middle' (Figure 3.4)
Percentage change in employment share by wage decile, Great Britain, 1979 to 1999.[111]

middle wages in 1979—machine setters, foundry labourers, plant and rail signal operatives and a range of routine clerical jobs that have become automated.[112]

In the immediate post-war decades—across mature economies—there used to be more of a continuum in jobs, wages and opportunities with more intermediate, middle-skill, middle-paying work that filled the gap between semi- and unskilled blue-collar and higher paying professional jobs. These provided work for a sizeable group once described by Philip Gould, Labour's chief pollster under Tony Blair, and one of the leading advisers to the New Labour project, as 'neither privileged nor deprived'.[113] Steadily this group has been shrinking in size, eroded by 'job polarisation'.[114] The result is a country increasingly divided between the 'privileged' and the 'deprived' with a much smaller group who are 'neither'.

The effect of this 'vanishing middle' is that, if people are ranked in order of their incomes, the social shape of Britain looks very different than if they are ranked by their nominal class position. This is because the rise up the class ladder has not been matched by rising relative wages and opportunities. As low and middle earnings have fallen in relative and in some cases, absolute terms, there has been a sharp rise in the extent of low pay and of work-related poverty. Indeed, *real* earnings in some occupations—forklift truck driving, packing and bottling, and baking, for example—have actually fallen since 1978.[115]

The proportion of employees with hourly wages below two-thirds of the median nearly doubled from 12 per cent in 1977 to 22 per cent in 2009.[116] In that year 5.3 million people earned less than £7.28 per hour.[117] The proportion of poor children living in working households has been rising sharply and stood at 61 per cent in 2009. While the introduction of the National Minimum Wage in 1999 has built a floor into this sinking process, it has mitigated but not halted this broader trend.[118]

This trend has added another twist to the opening gulf between the very top and the rest. While the richest have been pulling away, the rest of society has become increasingly bunched in the bottom half of the income distribution. In the 1970s, society conformed to an 'egg' or 'diamond-shape' with a small group of the rich and the poor and a large middle. Today, the pattern looks much more like a distorted hour-glass in shape, one with a small bulge at the top, a thin stem in the middle, and a much larger bulge at the bottom.

The pattern has changed because although more people are defined—and define themselves—as middle class, many of those moving up a class rung have not progressed very far in income or opportunity terms. Many of those who have risen through the class hierarchy to swell the ranks of the 'lower middle class' (clerical and administration workers, supervisors, lower-tier managers) have ended up in a lower position in the income distribution than where they would have been as members of the skilled working class a generation earlier.

A very similar development has occurred in the United States, a country that has long had a much bigger middle class than in the UK. Here too, de-industrialisation and the sinking of wages has led to a similar 'hollowing out of the middle'. Whole swathes of American society, especially in the so-called Sun Belt, the prosperous southern states stretching from Florida to California, which were once the bedrock of conservatism, have been left behind by the economic forces of the last thirty years.

As in the UK, there has been a decline in the income position of the middle class, while as the British economist George Irvin has written, 'a large number of American families live above the poverty line but below the middle-class "threshold"; ie, have a family income of between $20,000 and $40,000.' The American sociologist, Katherine Newman, has called this group the 'missing class' or the 'near poor' and estimates their size at 57 million, a group at high risk of poverty caused by job loss or illness.[119]

As in the UK, it is a trend that has been underway since the early 1980s. There has been a continuing growth in jobs that pay well and require high skill, and in low-wage, low-skill jobs, but thanks to de-industrialisation, off-shoring and the impact of technology, 'middle-tier' jobs have been on the wane.[120] Some former industrial heartlands like Detroit, the once thriving metropolis where Henry Ford built his first mass production plant in 1913, is now little more than a ghost town with row upon row of derelict factories and street after street of abandoned homes.

In the UK, the vanishing middle is especially apparent in the once prosperous industrial heartlands in the Midlands, the North East and South Wales, areas which have been shorn of decently paid, secure work. In some parts of Britain—outside of the prosperous belts like London and the South-East where the top part of the hour-glass is concentrated—the move from industry to services has brought decaying communities with whole generations denied much of an economic purpose in life.

In some former industrial areas factories have been replaced by little more than car parks, cut-price retail outlets and warehouses. In Stoke, the once thriving Staffordshire Pottery is now a B&Q. In the Brierley Hill area of the West Midlands, the Marsh and Baxter's meat processing plant, once the biggest in Europe, is now a shopping centre. In these areas, the jobs that are on offer are often poorly paid, dull and insecure.

One of the important consequences of these wider labour market trends—the rise of unemployment, the vanishing middle, the earnings squeeze, the spread of low pay and the weakness of the labour market in many parts of Britain—has been a rise in downward occupational and social mobility. The post-war era was a period of improving pay and opportunity for most of the working-age population. As income growth and job opportunities for middle and lower income groups has slowed, that upward mobility has been petering out, a trend that has been fuelled during each of the three recessions of the last thirty years.

Britain is riddled with examples of downward job mobility—of former skilled factory workers cleaning cars, joiners working as airport baggage handlers, trained draughtsmen and IT specialists forced into temporary work in retail and customer services or taxi-driving, often with long gaps of unemployment in between.[121] Those most vulnerable to such downward mobility are those over 50 and include professionals as well as the skilled working class. The Institute of Education has found that, even before the downturn of 2008-2009, up to a third of graduates end up in permanent non-graduate jobs. The squeeze on job opportunities has brought rising levels of skills under-utilisation with significant numbers unable to find work appropriate for their skills and experience and having to moderate their job and pay aspirations, taking less skilled work on lower pay rates than in the past.[122]

Such downward mobility also applies between generations. In February, 2010, the Labour leader, Ed Miliband, accused the coalition of pursuing policies that endangered what he called the 'British promise', the expectation that children would have greater prosperity and more opportunity than their parents. One of the implicit assumptions of the post-war years was that economic and social policy should ensure each generation enjoyed better living standards and life chances. The children of blue-collar workers would become white-collar. The grandchildren would become professionals.

Incomes would rise for all. The fact is that this 'promise' was effectively broken from the early 1980s. Although living standards and opportunities have improved on average, a significant and rising section of the population has been left badly behind by economic and industrial change.

In a 2009 Yougov survey for the TUC, respondents were asked how they think their job 'compares with the one your father had when he was the same age as you are now'. As many as 27 per cent said it has a lower or much lower status, with 36 per cent saying higher.[123] Respondents were also asked to compare their own living standard with those of their parents at 'around the same age'. Despite higher material living standards, only just over a half think that their own living standard is higher than their parents 'at the same age'. In contrast, 23 per cent think it is about the same and 17 per cent lower.

Moreover, although today's middling jobs are paid relatively less well than in the past, they mostly require much higher qualifications than their equivalents a generation ago. Over time the returns to education for a significant proportion of the workforce have been falling. Obtaining better qualifications has become a necessary condition for getting work but is no guarantee of a decent or rising wage. The danger is that education and the pursuit of skills will become increasingly devalued, as awareness spreads that low level or middling qualifications buy very little in the way of opportunity.

Politicians of all persuasions have talked up the virtues of creating an aspirational culture. Yet many of those on low and middle incomes have been denied the opportunity to fulfil these extended ambitions. Successive governments have fuelled aspirations without willing the means.

The usual response from successive governments—Conservative and Labour alike—to the process of de-industrialisation has been that the rise of a finance driven-economy would help speed the evolution to a more successful post-industrial economy. Finance and services, it is argued, would more than compensate for the inevitable decline in Britain's manufacturing base. It is a theory that has, as historian Harold Perkins has argued, 'proved to be a tragic illusion'.[124]

Although there has been a rise in the numbers employed—of some 3.7 million—since 1979, most of them in service industries, the size of the labour force has also risen, with the result that the employment *rate* has fallen over the last thirty years. Of these extra jobs, only a fraction over a half have been full-time. While many of those working part-time do so by choice, just over a million working part-time would prefer a full time job.[125]

Despite its growing importance in the economy, financial services has hardly generated any net new jobs in the last thirty years. Between 1979 and 2009, as shown in figure 3.5, the number of jobs in finance rose by 140,000, a rise of only 16 per cent, despite its much faster growth as a share of output.[126] Nearly all of these new jobs came in the 1980s with new banks being set up in London. Since then, the number employed has shrunk. Indeed, it fell by 17,000 during the boom years of 2000 to 2007, largely because of the shedding of staff to boost profits. The growing profits of recent times have been used to reward existing staff, especially those at the top, rather than create jobs that benefit society more widely. Indeed, it has been shown that each unit of extra output in manufacturing generates one and a half times more than jobs than finance.[127]

The decline of the social and economic centre of gravity has opened up serious gaps in the balance of the

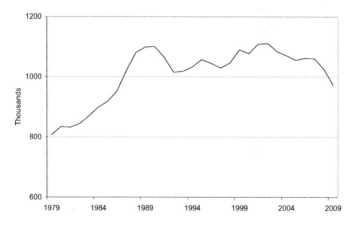

Number of employees working in financial services, 1979-2009 (Figure 3.5)
Thousands, UK, seasonally adjusted.[128]

economy with a growing minority of those of working age outside the prosperous belt consigned to a spiral of low pay, joblessness and disillusionment.[129]

Many of the key jobs in the economy, those vital to its effective functioning and on which the better-off depend—transport, street cleaning, hotels, restaurants—have become increasingly low skilled and low paid. The decline has capped opportunities, wasted talent and frustrated politically-fanned aspirations. For significant sections of the workforce it has imposed a near-permanent lid on the ability to rise. It has also fuelled the geographical concentration of work and unemployment.

In some towns such as Hartlepool, Knowsley, Blaenau Gwent and Glasgow, the real level of unemployment stood at more than twice the national average even before the onset of the recession. In May 2008, nine towns, headed by Liverpool and Nottingham, had more than a fifth of the working age population in receipt of benefits.[130]

Sinking pay has also meant a weakening skill base, a process that risks becoming re-inforcing. A low wage economy dictates the type of jobs that are created. As skills disappear, so do the jobs. One of the consequences has been that while some skilled workers can't find work, in other areas, Britain now has real skill shortages, often the sort of skills that would once have been held by those in the middle. Despite the level of unemployment, employers regularly report vacancies that are hard to fill. There is it seems, a shortage of technicians, skilled butchers, care workers and electrical supply workers.

These trends have also had important implications for the role of the state and for the state of public finances. Income has been transferred from tax-paying wage-earners to individuals and areas of the economy where tax avoidance has become increasingly rife, contributing to the shrinking of the tax base. The same process has forced an extension of the social and economic obligations of the state. In some areas purchasing power has shrunk to a level that cannot sustain much private sector activity, limiting opportunities and leaving the state with the lead economic role. There are many parts of Britain—from Hastings and Swansea to Dundee, Barnsley and Plymouth—where more than 35 per cent of jobs are in the public sector. In 2007 Barnsley had 274 VAT registered businesses per 10,000 adults; Liverpool had 241 and Plymouth 233. This compares with a national average of 415.[131]

Without state intervention, the problem of low pay and the vanishing middle would have been even more serious. A study by Manchester University's Centre for Research on Socio-Cultural Change has found that in the Midlands the state, directly and indirectly, accounted for three-quarters of all new job growth in the decade to 2007. In the North of England it was 64 per cent. Only in London and the South did the private sector outstrip the public.[132]

The state has not only had to help compensate for the weakness of the private sector across many parts of Britain. It has also had to do more of the heavy lifting to mitigate the effects of deteriorating wages in more market-led economies. The state has had to face a worsening in what economists have called 'pre-distribution', the way rewards are distributed by markets before state income support comes into play.

Faced with the impact on living standards of a rise in the extent of low pay, governments have had two options. First to let relative incomes sink and poverty rise. This was broadly the policy response of Conservative governments from the late 1970s. As a result, the level of relative poverty doubled between 1979 and the mid-1990s. When Labour came to power in 1979, more than one in four children lived in poverty compared with one in eight in 1979.[133] One of the main causes of this increase was the sinking wage share and the decline in relative pay below the middle.

83

The second option is to intervene to soften the impact of market forces on income levels. This was the one adopted by Labour. From 1997, Labour made tackling poverty one of its primary social goals. As a result, the level of poverty fell slightly over the next 12 years.[134] Yet because pay inequality continued to rise under Labour, successive governments had to work much harder merely to hold the line. Just to stabilise the level of poverty, Labour poured public money into anti-poverty programmes, raising the incomes of the low paid, notably through the introduction of a generous tax credit system.

Without this extra support, the level of in-work poverty and inequality would have risen even more sharply. Yet, far from being born most heavily by the richest groups in society, most of the burden of the extra tax required has fallen on middle income groups.[135]

These policy responses have inevitably had wider implications for the management of the economy, not just in the UK. At least part of the ballooning fiscal deficits causing mayhem across the globe in the aftermath of the crash can be traced to the need for governments to compensate for the failure of markets to deliver decent livelihoods for their workforces. In the UK, the combination of the loss of taxes and the rising cost of anti-poverty and state job creation programmes has put greatly increased pressure on public finances and may well have contributed to a structural fiscal deficit, albeit one that was largely hidden in the artificial boom of the post-millennium era.

The trends have also changed the pattern of work incentives and added to the rise in the level of public spending that took place from the millennium. In effect, the sinking wage share and rising pay inequality has meant that minimising the impact on poverty has required a degree of income redistribution and a level of public spending and taxation close to the limits of economic and political acceptability.

While joblessness and low pay has spread, the biggest winner of the last 30 years has been finance. Crucially, it became the single most important force behind the growing income gulf at the heart of the American, British and global economy.

4

A FAUSTIAN PACT

In early January 1998, a large group of London traders, fund managers and financiers braved the pouring winter rain to gather at the Mansion House, the grand official residence of the Mayor of the City of London. The group—gathered in the very heart of the old financial sector known as the Square Mile—had been invited to debate the motion 'This house believes that City salaries are totally fair and justified'. Most of the 200 at the debate would have been amongst the highest paid in the land.

Supporting the motion was George Cox, a director of LIFFE, the London International Financial Futures Exchange, established in 1982 to trade in 'futures', essentially bets about the future course of share prices, currencies and commodities. As he argued in the motion's defence, 'if you cut City remuneration tomorrow there will be less available for society at large and we would all be poorer as a result.' Andrew Winckler, former chief executive of the Securities and Investment Board—the body set up in 1984 to supervise the financial markets—spoke against the motion. The Square Mile had become 'smug and complacent' about salaries and bonuses, he told the audience. 'The current bonus system encourages a degree of speculation that is not warranted and is rewarding failure.' In the event and to the surprise of the audience, the motion was lost—with 52 per cent against, 45 per cent in favour and 3 per cent undecided.[136] It did nothing to stop top pay in finance continuing to rocket.

For the previous decade Britain's financial services industry had been on a roll. Business had flourished, profits and bonuses had soared. In just three years from the start of 1995, the FTSE 100—the index of leading UK company shares—had risen by nearly 70 per cent. But eight months before the Mansion House debate, the Major government had been ousted by the electorate, and Labour had been returned with a record post-war majority.

The City had once been apprehensive about the return of Labour to power. But following the loss of the 1991 election, the Party's leaders set about winning friends in the City. Members of the Shadow Cabinet, led by the shadow Chancellor, John Smith, toured the dining-rooms of the City meeting senior finance figures in what became known as the 'prawn cocktail offensive'. Stuart Bell MP even went to New York on a trip paid for by Kleinwort Benson Securities to reassure Wall Street that the financial markets would be safe in Labour hands. In opposition, Tony Blair had, for a time, been Labour's spokesman on the City while Brown immersed himself in the detail of banking.

In power, the political love-affair with the City launched by the Conservatives continued. Brown and Blair struck a Faustian pact with the City. The new government wanted finance to continue to play the vanguard role in the economy. To help make finance the engine of growth and prosperity, Labour promised to continue the policy of light touch regulation and turn a blind eye to some of the seedier activities of the business elite. New Labour embraced the new market experiment launched by Mrs Thatcher more or less in full. The government introduced some changes to moderate the more extreme aspects of the labour market—with measures such as the minimum wage and greater workplace protection. Despite this, a decade later, according to the OECD, Britain continued to have one of the least regulated labour markets of all developed economies.[137]

Labour was also relaxed about the greater concentration of income and wealth that had occurred under the Conservatives. The Party's leaders took the view that while it was important to tackle poverty, reducing inequality was not a priority. In his introduction to the 1997 Labour manifesto, Tony Blair wrote that he had 'no time for the politics of envy'. This was more than a symbolic gesture or vote-seeking rhetoric. It was a key turning point in Labour's central philosophy.

The three Labour governments from 1997 took extensive measures to try and build a firmer floor at the bottom, to prevent those on the lowest incomes from sinking still further. But they left unchallenged—indeed, encouraged—the process of personal enrichment by the nation's bankers, financiers and corporate executives that had begun under previous Conservative governments. Labour had no interest in capping soaring City fees and bonuses.

As Blair once put it, he didn't care what David Beckham earned, and wanted a society that encouraged 'levelling up' rather than 'levelling down'. Stephen Byers, trade secretary from December 1998, said that Labour needed to switch its priorities from redistribution to wealth creation. Peter Mandelson put it more crudely. He told business leaders at the Confederation of British Industry that New Labour was 'relaxed' about people becoming 'filthy rich'. Labour's strategy was clear. Rather than intervene to limit the inequalities generated by markets, they would allow market forces to operate relatively freely in the hope that this would promote growth.

Not only did Labour no longer care about wealth levels at the top, and tolerated a higher income gap, they also had no intention of taxing large and growing fortunes more heavily. If anything, the rich were made a special case for tax. During the 1980s, the tax system had moved from being progressive to regressive. For the first time since the tax system had been restructured after the War, the tax burden fell more heavily on lower than higher income groups. Labour did nothing to reverse this trend.[138] The gaping loopholes that enabled the very rich to pay proportionally less tax than low earners were mostly ignored and tax havens were left largely untouched.

In return for this favoured treatment, the government believed Britain would benefit in two ways. First, the City would ensure that the increasingly finance-dependent economy would flourish under its watch. Second, as the economy boomed, the government would rake in money to spend on public services. In effect the financial sector was to become the cash cow for an improved welfare state. Some of this cash was then to be used to compensate for the rise in earnings inequality resulting from a less regulated labour market by sharp rises in spending on means-tested income support.

Before finance grew to take an increasingly dominant role in the economy, it had, during most of the post-war era, played a largely secondary, intermediary function. The financial institutions mobilised savings and channelled them into investment, handled share dealings and organised the financing of government debt. They assisted the process of international trade by enabling currency conversions, managed the portfolios of the very rich and serviced the financial requirements of companies.

Most of this activity took place within the confines of the nation state. The proportion of investment that ended up overseas was historically small. Moreover, the most powerful economic players in the two decades after the war were the big global corporations, national governments and the new global economic institutions set up to bring order to the world economy, the IMF and the World Bank. This was the era when City grandees would fume about the influence of the political classes.

Finance was still a highly lucrative business. Profit margins were good. Salaries on Wall Street and in the City were high. But finance in the first two post-war decades played a lesser role compared with the past. Up to the First World War, the main financial institutions were much bigger players in the economies of the big industrial nations. In the United States the most powerful businessman of the time was the banker JP Morgan. He was not just one of the world's richest men at the turn of the nineteenth century, he controlled assets equivalent to some two-thirds of the nation's output, giving him a stranglehold over American business. The banking crisis of

1907 was solved not by the intervention of government, but by a handful of private bankers led by Morgan.

In the UK, the nineteenth century was the golden age of financial imperialism. Although the banks funded, through credit, the building of the nation's infrastructure—notably the canals and railways—the lion's share of financial investment went into overseas markets and a mix of speculative activity. The City funded world trade, organised large loans on behalf of the British government to pay for wars from the Napoleonic to the Boer War and funded economic expansion in the British Empire.

Commerce was also exceptionally profitable. Despite Britain's role as the pioneer of industrialisation, it was bankers, merchants and financiers who dominated the rich leagues at the end of nineteenth century. Non-landed wealth was more likely to be found amongst City financiers than amongst northern industrialists and manufacturers.[139]

After the First World War, the world's financial centres—dominated by New York and London—continued to enjoy a pretty free hand. There were few restrictions on capital flows and on the activity of banks and other credit institutions. During the 1920s, Wall Street and the City took huge advantage of this freedom. Credit flowed, share prices surged, financial fortunes soared.

The 1929 stock market crash, triggered by the failure of financial restraint and the property and share price bubbles created by excessive credit, brought the partying to an abrupt end. President Franklyn D Roosevelt curbed the freedoms of corporations and imposed much tighter restrictions on Wall Street bankers aimed at limiting the speculative banking activity that had preceded the economic upheavals of the inter-war years. Such was the strength of popular antagonism towards bankers, Wall Street lost most of its former political clout.

This first systematic attempt to forge a new era of regulated capitalism was strongly, but unsuccessfully, resisted by most American business leaders at the time. It was so unpopular that in August 1934, a series of clandestine meetings took place to discuss the possibility of a plot to overthrow Roosevelt's administration. A group of wealthy businessmen had secretly raised close to $300 million to finance a veteran's army and seize the White House. The plot failed when the General selected to lead the coup revealed the approaches to the House Un-American Activities Committee in a secret session in New York.[140]

After the Second World War, a new, comprehensive system of international finance was born. It had been brokered at the Mount Washington Hotel in Bretton Woods, New Hampshire in 1944. The main architect of the new system, and Britain's representative at the conference, was John Maynard Keynes. Although Lord Keynes—he had been awarded a peerage in 1942—died two years later at the age of 63, the global system of finance was part of his remarkable intellectual legacy. On his death—from a heart attack on Easter Sunday, shortly after returning from the inaugural meetings of the International Monetary Fund and the World Bank—even his critics joined in the accolades. Friedrich von Hayek, one of the key players in the subsequent attempts to discredit the Keynesian revolution called him 'the one really great man I ever knew.'

The conference agreed to a set of new measures

designed to prevent the competitive currency devaluations and the financial instability that marked much of the 1930s and which had helped prolong the Great Depression. Amongst its measures was a new system of exchange rates pegged to the dollar, while controls over capital movements and foreign transactions introduced at the start of the War were retained. These constraints on the inward and outward flow of money brought an end to the failed laissez faire policies and economic freedoms of the inter-war years. Firms and individuals were heavily limited in depositing funds in overseas banks, purchasing foreign shares or even the setting up of factories overseas.

Exchange controls—designed to support currency levels—and other limitations on financial services greatly constrained the role of finance. Capital controls and other regulations ushered in a new era of 'boring banking'. After the War, with the weakness of sterling and the strength of the dollar, the City ceded its once pre-eminent status as the world's international finance centre to New York. Globally, commerce took an increasingly back seat, wider controls kept a lid on the international concentration of wealth while the rich—on both sides of the Atlantic—were less concerned with building their wealth than hanging onto it. In the UK, those making money were more likely to be industrialists and retailers than financiers while their fortunes were a fraction of the value of the biggest fortunes of the past.[141]

But this back stage role was to be but a temporary phase in the history of finance. Parts of the City slowly devised ways around exchange controls, while the beginning of the City's revival can be dated to its development of the highly lucrative Eurodollar market from the mid-1960s. These were dollars accumulated by foreigners arising especially from the US's growing external deficit which were mostly deposited outside the US to avoid American regulations. The City grabbed the opportunity to manage this growing pool of externally held dollars, helping to re-establish its position at the centre of international finance and fuelling the growth of offshore business in the process.

By the end of the 1960s, the international monetary system was facing increasing signs of strain. When the fixed exchange rate system finally broke down in the early 1970s, it opened the way for the relaxation of global controls. By the beginning of the 1980s, most industrial nations had signed up to open or near-open markets, allowing their citizens to invest their money where they wished.

The liberalisation of global capital markets and the sweeping away of domestic controls over credit enabled global finance a gradual return to the supremacy it had last enjoyed in the nineteenth century. In the post-war era, the international finance industry was a highly regulated system with largely fixed exchange rates and heavy restrictions on capital flows. By the mid-1980s, it was marked by lax regulations on lending, the free mobility of capital and for most countries, freely floating exchange rates. Moreover the other pillars of the market experiment adopted in the US and the UK—the weakening of unions, the axing of business regulations and the switch from maintaining employment to fighting inflation—also served to re-concentrate power in the hands of the leaders of the global finance industry.

Nowhere was this dismantling of the post-war

financial and state economic apparatus more welcome than in the offices of the City, Wall Street and the other financial centres. Although the pillars of the post-1979 pro-market economic experiment were embraced most strongly in the UK and the United States, the ripple effects were felt globally. The adoption of what became known as the 'Washington consensus' by the IMF and the World Bank—the belief in liberalised trade and labour markets—ensured that, throughout the 1990s, financial and trade liberalisation policies spread across the world economy—rich and poor nations alike.

From the early 1980s, cross-border financial flows accelerated. To enable London to compete on equal terms with New York in the race for the world's expanding pool of mobile capital, Mrs Thatcher set out to transform the City from a cosy, insular club into a global leader, able to win the race for the spoils of the new open borders. The rules governing City transactions were eased and the City opened up to foreign banks in a bonfire of regulations known as 'Big Bang'.

Through Big Bang, the City became less tightly regulated than its main competitors, including New York and Frankfurt, while the traditional barriers to foreign ownership of London-based firms were removed. Eventually, the giant American investment banks—from Goldman Sachs to Merrill Lynch—which poured into London to take advantage of the freer rules, swallowed up most of the smaller and less aggressive British merchant banks. From the mid-1990s, the increasingly Americanised City had become a country within a country, 'a global stage located in Britain, rather than a British stage in the global arena.'[142]

The City was not just an increasingly global economic force, it became the centre of gravity of the international financial system. As the City historian, David Kynaston, has written, London emerged as 'a far more international centre than New York or Tokyo, whose financial centres in large part live off servicing their domestic economies.'[143] Steadily London secured a larger and larger share of global financial business and now has more cross-border financial flows than any other financial capital.

By 2007, the switch in fortunes from New York to London was complete. In March of that year, research house Z/Yen announced that the crown for the world's principal financial centre had passed from Wall Street to the Square Mile.[144]

In the months before the onset of the credit crunch, the City led the world in several complex financial areas holding a 40 per cent share of global equity trading, nearly a third of international foreign exchange and a fifth of international bank lending.

Labour's pact with the Square Mile appeared to have worked. Under Blair, London became the world-beating financial centre. As finance flourished, so did the economy. Unlike other countries, Britain even passed through the mild global downturn caused by the 2000 dot-com bubble relatively unscathed, without a single quarter of negative growth.

On the surface, finance appeared to have played a key role in national and global economic success. The City— as its lobbyists liked to boast on a regular basis— undoubtedly made a significant and growing contribution to the nation's export drive. As the City's profits boomed—at a much faster pace than other sectors—money poured into the Treasury.[145] The City could claim it had fulfilled its part of the bargain, having become a vital national asset.

Labour allowed the City a loose rein and, it seemed, the country had benefited. A grateful electorate gave Tony Blair three successive election victories, largely off the back of a booming economy, a record for the Labour Party. Brown, the longest serving post-war chancellor of the exchequer, was never shy about the apparent success achieved on his watch. He rarely missed an opportunity to proclaim the 'end of boom and bust'.

In return for their apparent contribution, the chancellor poured praise on the City. In April 2004 he accepted an invitation to open the sparkling new European headquarters of the American investment bank, Lehman Brothers, in Canary Wharf, paying a warm tribute to the bank's contribution to British prosperity. Brown's adulation of the City reached its high point at the annual Mansion House lecture—one of the traditional set piece occasions in the City's calendar—in June 2007.

'I congratulate you on these remarkable achievements, an era that history will record as the beginning of a new golden age for the City of London', Brown told his audience of leading figures in the Square Mile. The occasion was the eve of his elevation to Prime Minister, and was just eight weeks before the world economy was to implode in dramatic style. 'I believe it will be said of this age, the first decades of the 21st century, that out of the greatest restructuring of the global economy, perhaps even greater than the industrial revolution, a new world order was created.'

The renaissance of finance was in part the product of the changing political climate. Finance from Thatcher and Reagan onwards came to enjoy an unprecedented degree of freedom granted by government. Under Labour's pact, as long as the City delivered a booming economy, it would remain unpoliced, free to retain the extraordinary power and influence it had only previously enjoyed in the pre-First World War era before the onset of regulation.

But political patronage was not the only factor behind the extraordinary growth in the economic dominance of the City. An equal if not more important force was the impact of the huge international financial surpluses being generated by the intensified concentration of wealth.

The squeeze on wages, rising profitability and soaring personal fortunes all meant the accumulation of big corporate and private cash reserves across the globe. These swelling surpluses arose out of the rising wage-productivity gap with productivity gains being steered increasingly in favour of corporations and super-rich individuals. The first effect was on profits among the big global corporations. The profit revival took a while to get going, and was interrupted by the downturns of the early 1980s and the early 1990s. But from the mid-1990s, profitability across western capitalism had been restored to levels last seen 30 years earlier. Moreover, the profits flow was at its greatest outside of manufacturing, especially in the UK and the US, where much greater returns could be had in the business of lending and growing money and in corporate restructuring than in the traditional productive sectors of the economy.

By the turn of the twentieth century, finance had greatly grown its share of total corporate profits, accounting in the five years before the credit bubble finally burst, for thirty per cent of all FTSE 100 company's profits.[146]

In the United States, the financial sector's share of total corporate profits was even higher as it expanded from 14 per cent in 1981 to between 21 and 30 percent in the 1990s and then to an average of 40 per cent during the 2000s.[147] The size and turnover of finance companies—from investment banks to hedge fund houses—surged. By the mid-2000s, America's biggest banks from Goldman Sachs to Merrill Lynch all enjoyed rates of return on equity of over 20 per cent. In the two years to 2006, both earnings and profits amongst investment banks grew by almost two-thirds.[148] Finance was taking a share of global profits that greatly outstripped, size for size, that available in the productive sector of the economy. By 2004, the stock market valuation of US financial companies (a reflection of expected long-term profits) stood at 29 per cent of the value of non-financials. Twenty-five years earlier it had been a mere 7 per cent.[149]

The explosion of international financial surpluses also led to a surge in the volume of cash held in the private bank accounts of the world's super-rich. Although some of these huge fortunes were being accumulated by new industrialists and entrepreneurs engaging in traditional business activity, a rising number were being accrued by a new business elite—corporate executives, investment bankers, private equity barons and hedge fund operators, who owe their enrichment mostly to an explosion of financial deal-making, aided by more generous tax policies.

Although some of this personal wealth was held in relatively non-liquid assets, such as property, most—some 84 per cent—was held in a liquid or relatively liquid form, in equities, deposits, cash, bonds, hedge funds and private equity houses. According to the annual *Wealth Reports* by Merrill Lynch Capgemini, the value of funds invested by the global rich with investable assets of over $1 million more than doubled between 1997 and 2009 from $19,100 to $39,000 billion.[150] What does this mean? Well, $39,000 billion is a sum equivalent to slightly more than three times the size of the annual output of the world's largest economy, the United States. It is also around three times the output of the European Union.

These individual fortunes were being accumulated across the world, not just in the richest nations. Some of the biggest belonged to Middle Eastern oil sheikhs, Indian industrialists and Latin American mining magnates. Many, like Carlos Slim Helu of Mexico and the Russian oligarchs, had become rich through the great state sell-offs of the 1990s.

Although this money was mostly being generated within national boundaries, these financial surpluses rarely stayed in the countries where they originated. The oil barons, global monopolists and Russian and East European oligarchs have ploughed little of their new wealth back into investment in their own countries. Oil money has mostly flowed out of the Middle East, one of the explanations for the political upheaval across the region in 2011. During and following Russia's privatisation process—one of the most flawed economic reforms in modern history—vast amounts of money poured out of the country.

Some of these surpluses were used to finance higher levels of personal consumption which helped fuel the global economic boom from the mid-1990s. The new oligarchs, oil sheikhs and international financiers snapped up football clubs, built mass property empires and created surging demand for luxury mega-yachts. Long waiting lists grew for the world's fastest private jets and specialist cars. In London, where much of the new wealth was concentrated, jobs and new businesses were created in industries as diverse as property development, security and chauffeuring off the back of the personal wealth boom.

The main effect of these surpluses, however, was to flood the world's financial markets with capital. This capital was then multiplied many times over, through the use of what bankers call leveraging, leading to a huge expansion in the level of international liquidity—the volume of money flowing around global markets. Between 1989 and 2007, the stock of global financial assets held by banks—loans, financial derivatives and credit advances rose four times faster than the growth of world output.[151]

As credit became the world's greatest growth industry, the might of global finance was displayed in the heightened skylines of the world's financial centres—London, Manhattan, Tokyo, Frankfurt, Hong Kong and now Shanghai. Behind the glass frontages of these towering edifices, traders sitting in front of electronic screens masterminded a massive increase in financial turnover.

In the 1980s, global financial assets held by the world's banks were about the same level as total world output. As

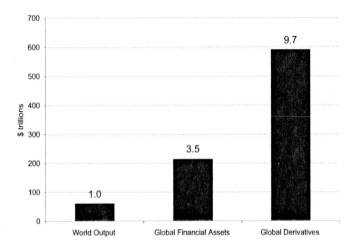

Global liquidity in relation to global output, 2008 (Figure 4.1)[152]

shown in figure 4.1, in 2008, these assets—a mix of
equities, bonds and other assets—stood at $214,000
billion. This was 3.5 times the value of global output. At
the height of the crisis, the outstanding claims on banks
thus outstripped the value of the whole of global output
by almost four times.

Some of this money flow found its way into
productive investment, financing new industries in the
developed world, the building of factories in Taiwan or
improved transport infrastructure in southern Africa. But
gradually the finance process became increasingly
divorced from the national productive base as the cash
surpluses came to be associated with the transfer of
existing rather than the creation of new wealth.

Most of this rising flow of money ended up back

where it often started—in bank deposits, private wealth management companies, hedge funds and private equity companies. From the early 1990s, the big international banks found themselves awash with cash, most of it the product of soaring global inequality, as the volume of financial flows grew to magnitudes that greatly exceeded anything that had been seen in history. The main role of capital markets had once been to finance the expansion of real trade flows and rising capital spending on infrastructure and investment. But financial trading has come to greatly exceed the level needed for these roles. As a report by Manchester University has put it, banking became a 'great transaction generating machine' leading to 'ballooning balance sheets'.[153]

An inadequate amount of this great expansion was linked to productive activity, encouraging investment in new or expanded business activity. As Paul Volker, the Chairman of the Federal Reserve for most of the 1980s and currently adviser to President Obama, once described the process: 'It seems to be easier to make money in some sense, with paper chasing paper, than in investing in real goods and services'.[154] Too much money came to swamp a system whose primary role should have been providing credit for innovation. Instead most financial trades have taken the form of secondary activity that is marginal to the proces of real investment. This growth was also largely u chartered territory. As Peter Drucker, the managem nt guru, reflected in 1987, 'We have no theory for an in ernational economy that is fuelled by world investment rather than world trade. As a result, we do not understand the world economy and cannot predict its behaviour or anticipate its trends.'[155]

In 2010, the daily turnover in foreign exchange markets, for example, stood at around $3500 billion—three times the level of 2001 and seven times that of 1990.[156] This turnover—most of it conducted in London—greatly exceeds the level needed to finance the global flow of imports and exports.[157] It is an excess accounted for largely by an increase in aggressive currency speculation, much of it carried out by hedge funds. While money flows at the right level are essential to the health of the global economy, financing investment and oiling the wheels of commerce, these surpluses rose to levels which were ultimately to prove poisonous for the international economy.

Up to the mid-1970s, the world's wealthiest individuals along with pension and other institutional funds had a limited number of homes for their cash. Financial flows were much more closely tied to the nation state, indeed much more so than before the First World War. As finance was freed from the constraints of the past, money became nomadic. Surpluses, dividends and profits arising in one country could be recycled across the world, mostly through offshore intermediaries, to any of the world's burgeoning number of financial ports.

Not only have capital controls been abandoned, 'we have now taken a full step again beyond that, into a world where capital is not only free to flow across borders, but is actively and artificially encouraged to move,' writes Nicholas Shaxson in his study of the power of the offshore tax industry, 'lured by any number of offshore attractions: secrecy, evasion of prudential banking regulations, zero taxes.'[158]

Soon international capitalism—'financial liberalisation

on steroids', as Shaxson has described it[159]—was being driven by the demands of a tsunami of global footloose capital looking for the most lucrative home. In this new borderless world, money poured into the global financial centres, especially London and New York. From there it spiralled round the world often at speed creating wave after wave of hot money flows. The super-rich owners of this money might once have been more closely tied to their own nation, and had a genuine identification with the country where they were born and lived.

Today the super-rich are rarely tied to a particular place or nation. Five-thousand Britons have relocated to Monaco, a tiny mini-state the French like to call 'le rocher Anglais'. The Egyptian-born Mohammed al-Fayed, the billionaire owner of a Scottish estate and Fulham football club, had been resident in Britain from the mid-1970s before fleeing into tax exile in Switzerland in 2003. As one of the world's new super-nomads, Roman Abramovich, once said in one of his rare interviews, 'I live on a plane'.[160]

En route, most of this financial tidal wave has passed through secretive offshore accounts. According to Middle East experts, Egypt's former President, Hosni Mubarak, has accumulated a family fortune close to £40 billion. Most of this has been siphoned offshore and into accounts in Swiss and British banks. Some is invested in property in London, Manhattan and Beverly Hills. Mohammed al-Fayed, the former owner of Harrods, has deposited tens of millions of pounds into an offshore trust in Bermuda.

When the controversial Russian oligarch, Boris Berezovsky, fled Russia and settled in London in 2000, he sold most of the assets he had acquired in the controversial privatisation deals of the mid-1990s. The hundreds of millions of pounds from thee sales were first deposited in an offshore trust fund held in Gibraltar and then transferred to accounts at the Clydesdale Bank.[161]

Such 'capital flight' became one of Russia's most debilitating economic problems, eroding the country's tax base, reducing domestic investment and destabilizing its financial market. Most of the money was being ferreted out by highly paid British lawyers and accountants, employed to arrange their clients' finances in a way that made them fireproof from investigation, either by the Russian or the British authorities.[162] According to Russia's Economic Development and Trade Ministry, between $210 and $230 billion left Russia during the reforms. Other sources suggest that around $300 billion of assets in the West belong to Russian citizens.[163] Capital flight is not unique to Russia. Lured by the prospect of much higher returns, money has poured across borders, much of it coming from the world's poorest countries.

Since the 1970s, the number of offshore tax havens has more than doubled to over sixty while offshore companies are now numbered in the millions.[164]. The capital of the Cayman Islands, George Town, is the world's fifth largest banking centre, with nearly 600 banks and trust companies, though only fifty have a physical presence and just thirty-one are authorised to trade with the local residents.[165] The country has a population of 35,000 but it is home to some 48,000 corporations and trusts. Most are no more than a nameplates on a local accountant's door. The London-based Tax Justice Network has estimated that wealthy individuals alone hold some $11,000 billion offshore. These funds generate $860 billion in income a year while the loss of global tax exceeds $255 billion annually.[166]

The extraordinary rise in the role of the offshore haven—a huge headache for the tax-raising ability of governments across the globe—has been made possible by the globalisation of money flows, the liberalisation of

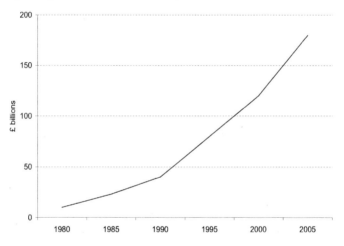

The explosion of tax havens: the case of Jersey (Figure 4.2)
Growth of bank deposits in Jersey, 1980 to 2005.[167]

capital markets and the blind eye policies of national governments. Figure 4.2 shows the rapid acceleration in the amount held in bank deposits in Jersey alone following the removal of capital controls from the early 1980s.

With the opening up of capital markets, the world's

financial centres found themselves in a new global race. Huge profits were to be made from acquiring, managing and investing these footloose funds. Together, the City and the British authorities set out to woo the world's super-rich and with such success that the lion's share of this financial tidal wave was washed up on Britain's shores. This was a further element of the Faustian pact, to ensure the wave continued to flow.

Successive British governments didn't care how these international capital flows ended up in Britain as long as they did. For decades, London had been the preferred base for the fortunes of super-rich foreign nationals. Some simply parked their cash. Many not just relocated their money and assets but also themselves to the UK. Since the 1970s, there has been a steady wave of foreign money landing in the UK—from the Middle East, Greece, Nigeria, Japan, Russia and Easter Europe, Hong Kong, India and China. Some of it has been used to colonise parts of London, some has merely been passing through. 'The British have found a new vocation', says William Cash, the well-connected publisher who founded *Spear's Wealth Management Survey*. 'That is being the financial bag-carriers of the world... the fee-earning servants, servicing the global financial elite.'[168]

In part, it is geography that has helped London— where it is possible to talk to Tokyo in the morning and Los Angeles in the evening—beat the competition for the world's global liquidity. But location is only part of the story. British governments embarked on an explicit process of seduction. In 1996, the Major Government introduced a new 'investor visa' for those wanting to make the UK their main home and able to invest a minimum of £1 million, of which at least £750,000 has to be invested in either government bonds or UK-registered companies. Those investing in this way are, after five years, allowed to apply for permanent residency and eventually UK citizenship. 'Essentially, if you are coming to the country with money to spend, you're very much welcomed with open arms', said John Tincey, vice-chairman of the Immigration Service Union, in 2007.[169]

The second weapon was a compliant banking system and a set of generous tax breaks. The UK boasts an unrivalled tax avoidance industry with an abundance of highly paid accountants able to devise labyrinthine ways of hiding wealth. The country is increasingly seen as one where large corporations and rich individuals can legally treat tax as a largely optional obligation. In 2007 the International Monetary Fund ranked London alongside Switzerland, Bermuda and the Cayman Islands as 'an offshore financial centre'.

While Britain has maintained only loose controls over the City, New York was forced to respond to a series of high-profile financial and business scandals, from Enron to WorldCom, by passing the controversial Sarbanes Oxley Act in 2002. This imposed much tougher corporate tests on the disclosure of information, on accountancy procedures and on the process of listing on the New York Stock Exchange, making New York less attractive to the world's business rich and contributing to London's eventual seizure of the global crown.

London has long attracted the extravagantly rich, but the recent flood of foreign wealth is unprecedented. For those who make money out of money, it has been a golden decade. As *Forbes* describes it, 'London attracts the elite of the world's rich and successful. It can lay claim unchallenged to one title: it is the magnet for the world's billionaires.'[170]

5

THE INCESSANT PRESSURE TO TRANSACT

The evening of 6 October 2005 proved a night to remember for several hundred MBA students at Oxford University's prestigious Said Business School. The School had invited two businessmen renowned for their money-making skills to address the audience of students and business leaders on the future of private equity. One of them was the swashbuckling, controversial and multi-billionaire retail magnate Philip Green. The other was David Bonderman, an American financier specialising in buying up companies and co-founder of the Texas Pacific Group, then owner of a number of British firms from Burger King to Punch Taverns. Their reputations had filled the large modern lecture hall and overflow rooms had to be hastily arranged.

At the end of their talk, the speakers were grilled by the 500-strong audience. One of the students asked the two men if they would be willing to consider investing in any of the students' ideas for new businesses, a question which brought a ripple of laughter throughout the lecture hall. Looking uncomfortable, Green threw it back to the audience. Could he have a show of hands to give him some idea of how many present thought they had a backable idea. A forest of arms shot up.

In an almost throwaway manner, Green suddenly announced that he would be willing to invest not £10,000, not £100,000 but £500,000 of his own money in the best idea. The audience had not expected such generosity and broke into spontaneous applause. A grinning Green turned to Bonderman and invited him to match his generosity. Although he initially appeared to back off from the idea, the stubborn American financier eventually agreed and the fund was established as a ten-year programme.

For Green, among the top ten richest Britons, the sum was largely pocket money. A few months earlier, he had splashed out £4 million on his son's bar mitzvah, the Jewish coming of age, at a specially built synagogue constructed on a private peninsula overlooking the Mediterranean between Nice and Monaco. The 300 guests were put up at the £1000-a-night Grand-Hotel du Cap-Ferrat, a favourite celebrity haunt, while the musical highlight was provided by Beyoncé and her platinum-selling group Destiny's Child. Three years earlier, he had spent £5 million flying out 200 guests to a five-star Cypriot hotel to celebrate his fiftieth birthday. Highlights at the three-day event included a special edition of *This Is Your Life* presented by Michael Aspel and a solid gold Monopoly set complete with diamond-studded dice from his wife, Tina, with the properties representing all his high street assets.

Bonderman, a fellow billionaire, came to business after a career in law and retains the air of an American corporate lawyer. Like Green, he is no stranger to big spending and certainly not shy about flaunting his wealth—he blew a reputed $7 million on his 60th birthday party three years earlier, hiring the Rolling Stones to front it in Las Vegas.

Neither Green nor Bonderman are entrepreneurs in the traditional sense. Green had a twenty-year string of failed retail ventures behind him before he joined the big wealth league. What brought him his multi-billion pound fortune and a jet-fuelled lifestyle, was a series of hostile and highly lucrative takeovers. For the first, in 1999, Green pocketed £250 million for a few months work by seizing and dismantling Sears, the once mighty high street consortium that owned retailers as diverse as Warehouse, Dolcis and Freemans. With the profit from this deal, a new nickname, 'Conan the Barbarian', and a new reputation as a hit-and-run financier, Green snapped up the high street chain, BHS, and later the Arcadia group of shops that encompassed outlets like Top Shop and Miss Selfridge. In a handful of years from the breaking up of Sears, Green had become one of the richest individuals in Britain.

Bonderman also became rich by buying up existing companies. He founded Texas—now called TGP Capital—in 1992 to specialise in leveraged buy-outs. Over the next 15 years he bought and sold hundreds of companies across the globe, from the US to Asia. At the time of the Oxford talk, he was estimated by *Forbes* to be the 334th richest person in the world with a $3.3 billion fortune.

Moreover, the two are not just rich. Their wealth stands shoulder to shoulder with some of the pioneering industrialists and retailers of the past. Green is as rich—in terms of his wealth as a share of the economy—as many of the pioneers of the industrial revolution.[171] His wealth is many times that of earlier path-breaking retail moguls such as Jack Cohen who created Tesco or Simon Marks and Marcus Sieff who built Marks & Spencer into Britain's largest fashion retailer.

The two private-equity barons are typical of the new breed of financiers and business operators to have joined the ranks of the world's super-rich, largely by feeding off the growth of huge global surpluses. Once this highly exclusive club would have been open only to more traditional entrepreneurs, building companies from scratch, creating jobs and new wealth, or adding value to existing companies. The industrialists of the nineteenth century mostly took decades to build their companies, often using their own or family money to do so. They often took big personal financial risks to help build the foundations of Britain's industrial success. For all their faults—and there were many—the American robber barons turned America into the biggest economy in the world, a position it has kept for over a century.

Green and Bonderman have become billionaires not by the patient route of creating and building new successful companies, but, like most rich financiers, by trading in existing companies. They are not the first to have done so and are merely the latest in a long line of financial storm-troopers to make money, big money, by shaking up British and American industry. The difference is one of scale. Such activity has come to play an increasingly dominant role in the economy.

The history of business since the war can be seen as an often bitter struggle between two essentially contradictory models of capitalism. In the immediate post-war era, a model emerged that broadly signed up to the idea that companies have a wide range of responsibilities, to employees and the local and national community as well as shareholders. This more moderate, regulated model became the dominant form in richer nations. New norms emerged about acceptable corporate behaviour, including executive rewards.[172] According to Paul Krugman, top executives in the 1950s and 1960s behaved 'more like public-spirited bureaucrats than like captains of industry'.[173]

In his 1967 book, *The New Industrial State*, the American economist, JK Galbraith—the author of the global bestseller, *The Affluent Society*, and who held office under both John F Kennedy and Lyndon B Johnson—gave a description of typical executive behaviour at the time, 'Management does not go out ruthlessly to reward itself—a sound management is one expected to exercise restraint'. He went on, 'With the power of decision goes opportunity for making money… Were everyone to seek to do so… the corporation would be a chaos of competitive avarice'. At the time the cultural climate operated to prevent such 'chaos', a kind of hidden and accepted social code that was pretty effectively abided by, partly through fear of public outrage of overt excess.

But via the deregulation of financial and labour markets from the end of the 1970s, the capitalist model evolved into a much more aggressive business model, a new, de-regulated super-capitalism—all embracing, short-term and cutthroat—first taking hold in the Anglo-Saxon nations.

The central driving force of this model was the chase for what came to be known as 'shareholder value'—that companies should be run primarily or solely for the interests of their owners, subordinating all other goals. The pursuit of shareholder value meant maximising the short term rise in the share price, while linking executive rewards to shareholder interests. The concept was pioneered in the United States in the 1980s by companies like the giant General Electric, run by one of the most ruthless company bosses of the decade, Jack Welch.

In Britain, the first company to embrace the new model was Lloyds Bank. At a board meeting in 1985, the Bank set itself a single, overriding new goal, '... of doubling our shareholder value every three years.'[174] One by one, even companies long wedded to the 'stakeholder model' such as Cadbury Schweppes, with its strong Quaker and paternalist traditions, fell under its spell. By the mid-1990s, what one commentator has described as an 'almost unassailable mantra' had become almost universal in British boardrooms.[175]

To encourage managers to take this direction, a new form of remuneration package was introduced, one in which executives were paid increasingly in stock options. This was, at least initially, seen by the American management gurus who promoted the idea as a way of linking executive pay to company success as measured by changes in the share price. Stock options—which operate by giving an executive the right to buy a given amount of stock at a certain price at a later date—provided a very strong incentive to top executives to maximise the share price as that was the mechanism by which they would be paid. By 2001, more than half of America's top 200 chief executives had 'mega-options', which by now had grown to an average value of more than $50 million. In this way, executives were able to build personal fortunes on a scale previously enjoyed only by entrepreneurs.

The rise of the stock option in both the US and the UK and the pursuit of 'shareholder value' had a dramatic effect on the way executives ran companies. As the decade progressed, evidence of abuse started to emerge. Many companies began to re-price their senior executive's stock options at a lower level when the stock price fell. As one commentator put it, 'it is hard to think of a better example of what is wrong with corporate America. When the firm's stock price does well, the people in charge make out like lottery winners. When it plummets, they get another set of chances to win.[176]

It soon became clear that one of the most successful ways of maximising the increase in share prices, at least in the short run, was to 'downsise'. Although downsizing was sometimes driven by technological improvement, the prime motivation was to shed labour. Industry could cut costs sharply by shrinking payrolls. Jack Welch at GE led the way in the 1980s, shutting down factories and ruthlessly eliminating jobs. Unionised plants were closed with the work transferred to non-union facilities elsewhere in the country or to low-wage havens such as Mexico. Although GE was far from unprofitable, the company began to demand wage and benefit concessions or work-rule changes from those unionised workers who were not dismissed.

Between 1980 and 1985, Welch—or 'Neutron Jack' as he became known—cut the payroll from 411,000 employees to 299,000. In return, GE's profits boomed, and its market valuation soared. Welch's strategy was copied by other CEOs across corporate America. 'It was clear that the quickest way to add 5 points to your stock price was to lay off 50,000 workers.'[177] There is little doubt that the sustained bull run of the 1990s—the Dow Jones index of leading American shares rose from 3000 in April 1991 to 9000 in May 1999—was in part the product of a decade of lay-offs.

Under the mantra of shareholder value, labour, instead of being seen as an invaluable asset, became a mere cost of production, an essentially expendable commodity, to be hired and fired according the needs of the companies and the whims of their executives. Business had no intrinsic social dimension. The key to success lay in keeping wages low and workforces small. The weakening of the unions had paved the way for a revolution in workforce size and pay.

The policy continued after the millennium and during the 2008-2009 recession. One study, by the Washington-based Institute for Policy Studies, found that during the downturn 'slash and burn' executives were by far the best rewarded. Bosses of the top 50 US companies that sacked the most staff earned 42 per cent more than their peers, while chief executives shared little of the pain felt by their workforces. According to the report, such lay-offs often involved sacrificing long-term prosperity for short-term profits. 'You see really long-term consequences of layoffs. You get lower staff morale in the workforce which can turn into lower productivity over time. You have the cost of having to rehire and retrain people when things pick up.'[178]

With bankers let off the leash, most of this change was driven by a rejuvenated global finance industry. Finance came to exert an increasingly powerful grip on the global and British economy. 'Here is an elite of the elites' according to the *Financial Times*, 'whose power has grown to a dimension that is truly imperial in the modern world'.[179] It is London—which spread its wings from the Square Mile to much of Canary Wharf, built, symbolically on the site of the old Thames docks, and to chic office space in Mayfair—where most of this imperial power is concentrated.

Figure 5.1 shows that in 1960, the assets held by the ten largest UK banks were equivalent to 40 per cent of national income. By 2010, they had grown to nearly five times the size of the economy. That is proportionately higher than any other country bar Switzerland and Iceland, and a twelve-fold increase over 1960. Although the banks are smaller in relation to the economy in the US, the trend has been similar. The US banking sector has

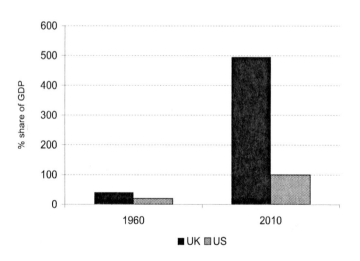

The explosive growth in UK and US banks, 1960 to 2010 (Figure 5.1)
Assets of the banking sector in each country as a share of GDP.[180]

risen from a fifth of the economy in 1960 to around 100 per cent today.

Once the regulators had taken a back seat, the banks seized the chance to take a much more direct role in the shaping of the economy and in the development of individual firms, a process academics have called 'financialisation'.[181]

Corporate financiers, investment analysts and fund managers came to exercise an increasing stranglehold over the captains of industry in even the largest boardrooms on how they could maximise the increase in share prices, and swell their personal bank accounts in the process.

The pull of big money quickly transformed boardroom ethics and corporate values. Today's chief executives have been nurtured in a business culture that values buying and selling above the organic growth that can be too slow to bring success in today's frenetic climate. Companies sought to grow not through innovation but through acquisition. This may have helped to cut costs and improve immediate returns but did little to improve economic vitality. In the process, many company bosses and boards have become more distant from their businesses, much less focused on long term strategy and much more on delivering improvements in the short term share price.

This is well expressed in an interview with a City analyst in a study by Manchester Business School: 'When I talk to the corporate managers of large German and Japanese companies, they speak of products, quality, customers and costs. They assume that if they produce innovative, attractive high quality products at a competitive cost, they will do well and be profitable. With

UK and US managers, the opposite applies. Many of them seem to be a million miles away from the real business.'[182]

Chief Executives found themselves under increasing pressure to sign up to the new 'slash and burn' policies being encouraged by management consultants and investment bank advisers. Having tasted the towering rewards that followed from the introduction of stock options in the booming share market of the 1990s, most executives were only too happy to fall into line. Matthew Barratt, who became chief executive of Barclays Bank in early 2000, announced the wholesale closure of high street branches and the transfer of former face-to-face customer services to call centres. While this was deeply unpopular with staff and customers, its potential to cut costs and improve profit margins 'went down a storm' in the City.[183]

The other retail banks soon joined in the aggressive pursuit of shareholder value, shedding staff in an ongoing cost-cutting drive. The number of bank branches halved in the 20 years to 2009. The UK now has 197 bank and building society branches per million inhabitants compared with 500 in Germany and over 1000 in Spain.[184] Rapid growth in the banking sector coincided with a shrinking of staff. In the five years to 2008, Abbey, Lloyds and RBS cut their staff levels by 39,000.[185]

Although shareholder value was initially shunned in those nations most wedded to a 'social market', notably Germany and Japan, a weaker version of the new super-capitalism spread, if gingerly, elsewhere. Parts of Asia—from Hong Kong to Singapore—embraced the new capitalism in full. Milton Friedman once described Hong

Kong as the world's best example of laissez faire capitalism in action. Most richer and developing nations embarked on at least some degree of deregulation and privatisation.

The German model has been distinguished by fewer takeovers, a greater emphasis on investment from retained earnings and lower dividend payments. But even Germany, the spiritual home of the social, stakeholder model, with its greater emphasis on collective success, consensus and the long term, found itself being drawn in the direction of the greater individualism and short-termism of the Anglo-Saxon model.

In November 2000, the Chief Executive of Siemens, Heinrich von Pierer, talked of 'shareholder value' in an address to 3000 staff in Munich. Previously he had been careful to use the phrase 'value-creation'. Since then German stakeholder capitalism has been in mild retreat. Today in Germany, there are now more German share-holders than trade unionists.[186]

Nevertheless, full-blooded financial capitalism remains far from universal. Some countries, especially on the European continent, have maintained a regulatory framework which requires companies to accept wider social responsibilities while, even in the US and the UK, many companies continue to accept that good business practice and profitability depend on at least a degree of social responsibility.

It was the chase for short-term share value and personal wealth that fuelled the boom in corporate restructuring. It was masterminded by a small group of international executives who ran the British and American investment banks and a mix of hedge funds, private equity houses and wealth management companies.

The new breed of financiers was hardly unique. Even before domestic and global markets were liberalised, a handful of buccaneering financiers with their controversial methods and seething disregard for tradition had blazed a trail for the explosion of industrial restructuring that came a decade and a half later. In the 1960s and 1970s, a small group of British financiers from Charles Clore to James Goldsmith built sizeable fortunes through predatory corporate raiding—the often highly controversial takeover, dismantling and reconstruction of mostly medium-sized, vulnerable companies. In 1973, Edward Heath denounced one of the controversial new money barons—the outsider Tiny Rowland—as the 'unpleasant and unacceptable face of capitalism'.

The craze was soon to be repeated in the United States, when a number of financiers—including Goldsmith—spotted the potential created by deregulation to make big money out of hostile corporate raiding. The most notorious of these hostile deals was the buy-out of RJR Nabisco, the giant tobacco and food conglomerate in 1988 and documented in the international best-seller, *Barbarians at the Gate*. The winner of the bidding war, a nail-biting game of corporate poker played for immensely high stakes, was the buy-out specialists, Kohlberg Kravis Roberts (KKR), founded in 1976. The $25 billion deal—then the most expensive in history—involved a river of money so great that for a month it greatly distorted the American money supply figures.

Nevertheless, the takeover boom of the 1980s was merely the prelude to an avalanche of lucrative financial deal-making on both sides of the Atlantic, one that has delivered fortunes that came to greatly outclass those made by these earlier predators. The total value of such activity (a mix of mergers and acquisitions) in the US had reached over $2000 billion by 2000, more than forty times its 1980 value.[187] These deals involved some of America's highest profile companies. They included the acquisition of Warner Lambert by Pfizer in 1999 to form the world's fastest growing drug company and the $180 billion takeover of Time Warner, the world's top media conglomerate, by the US's largest internet service provider, AOL, a year later.

There was a similar boom in acquisitions in the UK. The total value of deals in the opening years of the twenty-first century stood at twenty times the level of the early 1980s, most of them hostile.[188] Some of the largest deals include the 1999 acquisition of Amoco by British Petroleum, the bitterly fought and titanic £112 billion Vodafone takeover of Mannesman in 2000 and the Glaxo Wellcome takeover of SmithKline Beecham in the same year. In 2007, a consortium led by RBS landed the $100 billion takeover of the Dutch bank, ABM Amro, beating a number of rival bids in the process.

Increasingly, such acquisitions have involved the foreign takeover of national companies. In the last five years, these have greatly outstripped, in value terms, the takeover of foreign by British companies.[189] A third of Britain's largest companies are now foreign owned, among them Scottish Power, Asda, Hanson, Pilkington, British Energy, BAA and Cadbury.

As the opportunities for financial dealing-making accelerated, the fates of companies came to be determined by the new generation of international bankers, financiers and corporate lawyers. These new power-brokers were mostly barely connected with the companies they were restructuring, had any knowledge of their workings and rarely went onto get their own hands dirty running the companies they refinanced. Typically interventions were driven less by improving the health of the companies they targeted or their employees, but how much money could be made. They had taken a lesson from Lord White—one of the pioneering British corporate raiders of the 1970s and 1980s. White used to boast that he had never stepped foot on the shop floor of any of the companies that he had bought. As his business partner, James Hanson, later acknowledged, the name of the game was to get hold of 'tomorrow's money today'.[190] It was a philosophy embraced in full by this new breed of corporate raider.

In the UK and the US, the great majority of mergers have occurred as a result of pressure from investment banks which both advise the boardrooms and raise the finance to fund the deals. Investment banks would warn companies that if they made no acquisitions they risked being downgraded by analysts for 'having no strategy'. City and Wall Street investment bankers and advisers do not wait for client companies to seek their advice. 'The cold-calling of companies with merger advice is commonplace. They point out how the prospect's competitors are merging. They calculate the possible synergies of a merger and entice companies with the prospect of a soaring share price.'[191] This 'incessant pressure to transact' as former senior investment banker Philip Augar has described it, explains the increasing emphasis on merger and acquisition activity, financial engineering and the big top-down cost reduction strategies which have brought big short-term rewards but mostly limited, if any, benefit for long-term performance.[192]

All this was made possible by the huge cash surpluses being generated across the world. Once cautious pension-funds and endowment trusts deposited, along with oligarchs and monopolists, an increasing proportion of their funds into the highly risky investments being made by the racier end of the City. To these funds could be added some of the state surpluses being generated in China, parts of Asia and the Middle East, the latter used largely as the personal bank accounts of the oil sheikhs.

These new clients demanded one thing—faster and bigger returns. More and more of this money—seismic levels compared with the past—found its way into essentially speculative investment. From the mid-1990s such investment mostly offered succulent returns to the world's newly enriched multi-millionaires and billionaires. The private client divisions of the big investment banks like UBS, JP Morgan or Citibank increasingly offered more adventurous homes for their money. As *Newsweek* put it in 2006, 'Consider how UBS, the world's largest private banker, has evolved over the past decade. Its clients, increasingly entrepreneurs and self-made financiers with a web of multinational investments and homes in several countries, want 24/7 global access to every imaginable asset via bespoke trading platforms (highly encrypted for privacy, of course).'[193]

Not only were banks sitting on much bigger deposits. With the new blind-eye regulators, they upped, in bankers' speak, the level of leverage. Throughout history, the banks had usually lent more than their capital base, financing the difference by borrowing. During the 1950s and 1960s, this ratio was relatively modest, typically around four or five to one, and rarely more than ten to one. In the 1970s, wealth management was a relatively straightforward business. The clients' wealth would be invested in a set of simple options—stocks, bonds and property.

To bring these heightened returns—in 'a wild chase for yield'—financial institutions lent huge multiples of their deposits. Leveraging meant the banks could, apparently miraculously, turn money into more money, inflating returns along with fees and bonuses. Banks would turn deposits of a few billion pounds into lending parcels worth twenty or thirty times this amount, or in some cases even more. 'The essence of the contemporary monetary system is the creation of money, out of nothing, by private banks' often foolish lending', wrote *Financial Times* columnist, Martin Wolf in 2010.[194]

In 1974, new rules had been drawn up by global finance regulators meeting in the historic Swiss city of Basel about the level of capital banks were required to hold. Under Basel 1, as it was called, banks were required to keep liquid capital reserves of at least eight per cent of their lending and investment. Yet banks soon found a set of obscure devises for by-passing these rules, mostly through the creation of more and more exotic, and highly risky, financial instruments called derivatives. In the summer of 2008, as shown in figure 4.1, the value of these derivatives stood at close to $600,000 billion—almost ten times the world's output on real goods and services.

The Royal Bank of Scotland, a small regional bank in the 1990s that grew to become one of the world's top five, was lending up to 40 times its deposit base in 2007, way above the Basel limit. The giant US investment banks—Goldman Sachs, Morgan Stanley and Merrill Lynch—had 'leverage ratios' of between 30 and 50 to one. Such was the level of borrowing, most of it very short-term, the banks had to keep refinancing their outstanding debt every few months. Once the regulators might have taken a closer look at these mass lending hikes, but by the late 1990s, Wall Street and the City had been canonised, handed freedom and a license to make money by manipulating their expanding cash bases at will.

As a result, the level of liquidity in the global economy exploded. It was this leveraged explosion that financed the boom in the acquisition and restructuring of existing companies. When the American businessmen, Malcolm Glazer, bought Manchester United in 2005 for £790 million, only a third of the money came from his own pocket. The rest was borrowed from a mix of investment banks and hedge funds. In 2007, the Americans Tom Hicks and George Gillett bought Liverpool Football Club, again with a large loan for most of the £174 million cost, most of it provided by the Royal Bank of Scotland.

Others to benefit from the largesse of British banks were a number of Russian oligarchs. In the years before the economic meltdown, Oleg Deripaska, one of the wealthiest Russians and a man close to the Vladimir Putin, built a mammoth international business empire. By 2007 he enjoyed stakes in a diverse range of overseas companies from the Birmingham-based van manufacturer, LDV to the German construction firm, Hochtief, and the Canadian car parts manufacturer, Magna. Although his holding company, Basic Element, enjoyed annual revenues in excess of $2 billion—mostly from the aluminium giant Rusal he had acquired in the 1990s—Deripaska financed these purchases largely through borrowing from a mix of British, Russian and European banks.

One of the early beneficiaries of this soaring money flow was Sir Philip Green. When he bought the BHS chain in 2000 for £200 million, a move which helped pioneer the post-millennium boom in retail public-to-private deals, he put less than £20 million of his own money into the deal, only a fraction of the profit he had secured from the break-up of Sears. The remaining 90 per cent came almost entirely from two investment banks—the German banking group WestLB and the investment banking wing of Barclays. When, two years later, he bought Arcadia, the parent company of a string of retailers, Green's own contribution was again modest. The lion's share of the near £1 billion purchase price came from HBOS, the Anglo-Scottish bank formed from a merger between Halifax and the Bank of Scotland in 2001.

The process of leverage financed, corporate re-engineering was a huge personal gravy-train for the top participants. Among them were the wealthy investors, company chief executives and above all the 'marriage brokers'—the City financiers and their banking and legal advisers who arranged and executed the deals, while avoiding any risks with their own money. In the 1970s City and Wall Street fees were much more modest. Top bankers would be well paid but not enough to join the super-rich class. The 1980s changed all that. The fees charged in the takeover of RJR Nabisco, for example, outstripped anything that had previously been seen on Wall Street. In the quickest and largest of the 'quick bucks' of the time, the firms involved—from Drexel Burnham Lambert to Merrill Lynch—pocketed between them some $800 million in fees.

As bankers were given the political license to make money, fees and bonuses headed skywards, especially in the case of corporate finance transactions such as acquisitions, as both sides—bidders and defenders—have to hire investment banks for advice. When Vodafone acquired Mannesman in an extended hostile bid in 2000, the investment banks masterminding the takeover earned advisory fees in excess of £400 million. Chris Gent, Vodafone's chief executive was voted a £10 million bonus for the deal. Mannesman directors, who switched from their initial opposition to supporting the deal, were paid $77 million between them, with the Chairman of the Board, Klaus Esser, pocketing $40 million alone. The size of the payouts caused outrage in Germany and became the subject of a high profile trial on criminal breach of trust charges in 2004 during which the defendants were acquitted.

The post-millennium boom years brought a frenzy of global deals. When the Royal Bank of Scotland acquired NatWest in 2000, fighting off a similar challenge from the Bank of Scotland, the deal generated £300 million in fees. In 2004, the merger between Glaxo and SmithKline involved fees of £112 million. In 2007, the investment bank Merrill Lynch pocketed the lion's share of the estimated £300 million fees paid out by the consortium led by Royal Bank of Scotland for its successful bid for ABN Amro.

It was the surge in deals and fees that enriched a generation of investment bankers, largely as a result of the bonus policy operated by the banks. Before Big Bang, UK merchant banks paid bonuses averaging 3-4 per cent of salary. In some firms, the annual bonus would take the form of a Christmas turkey or food hamper. It was only from the early 1990s that giant bonuses started to become common practice inside the American investment banks which had now come to dominate the industry. In 1993, more than 100 partners at the London offices of Goldman Sachs—or 'Goldmine Sachs' as it was known— were paid year-end bonuses of more than $1 million each. In 1996, it was estimated that there were at least 1000 dollar millionaires working in the City—double the number four years earlier.[195]

By the middle of the 1990s, 'the guaranteed bonus', a curious oxymoron, had become commonplace. In 1997, the City bonus pool hit the £1 billion mark for the first time. A decade later, at the height of the post-millennium economic boom, it had soared to £9 billion—equivalent to half the UK's transport budget. The lion's share of this sum went to a tiny proportion of the City's 350,000 staff: some 4,000 received bonuses of over £1 million, a few hundred over £5 million and twenty or so in excess of £10 million. The latter included 46 year old Richard Gnodde, co-chief executive of Goldman Sachs International and the lead banker for Lakshmi Mittal's £17 billion takeover of Europe's largest steel-maker, Arcelor, in 2006. Other beneficiaries were Michael Zaoui, Chairman of Morgan Stanley's European M&A division

131

who represented the board of Arcelor, and Bob Wigley, Chairman of Merrill Lynch for Europe, Middle East and Africa, and the mastermind behind several large deals in 2006.

Over the last twenty years, the pay premium for working in the City has soared. In the 1970s, the average City employee would earn around a fifth more than the average professional. Today it stands at more than 100 per cent. The banking industry has been raising the 'compensation ratio'—the proportion of net turnover returned to staff in the form of bonuses—closer and closer to a figure of 50 per cent.[196] Almost 30 per cent of the best paid 0.1 per cent of the population work in financial intermediaries.[197]

The City and Wall Street is so marked by frenzied competitiveness, that bonus day has become known as the 'Valentine's Day Massacre'. As one insider put it, 'By the time bonuses are paid, most salesmen and traders are so infused with greedy, revolutionary fervour that no matter what amount the firm actually pays them, they automatically think they have been screwed'.[198] The issue became so publicly sensitive that in December 2010, as pressure mounted on banks to show restraint, Morgan Stanley boss, James Gorman, told his 500 top traders that he would 'personally escort' anyone caught leaking bonus details out of the bank.

Pay and bonuses have risen to such heights because of the escalating fees—typically between five and eight per cent per deal in recent years—finance charges companies and institutional investors for its services. How has this happened? First, big business has become increasingly dependent on the banks and rarely queries charges for advice. Secondly, the City's clients—who mostly handle other people's money and whose own salaries are high by the standards of other professionals—have had no incentive to query the fees being charged. Indeed the top executives of companies often stand to make big personal gains from deals such as mergers and takeovers while the costs are paid for by the company and ultimately share-holders, customers and sometimes taxpayers.

Although individual deals are toughly negotiated, finance directors in Britain's biggest companies rarely haggle over the fees for services from underwriting and organising new share offerings to managing acquisitions. As the *Evening Standard's* City editor, Anthony Hilton, has put it, 'While the City is ferociously competitive, the competition between firms rarely extends to price.'[199] Some parts of the City in effect operate an informal cartel charging what most independent observers believe to be excessive fees (known as 'the croupier's take') for activity that is often only marginally associated with improving economic performance.[200]

The process of financial and corporate enrichment has not been confined to investment bankers. Others to have joined the fast upward-moving escalator include corporate executives, private equity barons and hedge fund operators. Boardroom pay has been escalating at such a rapid rate that becoming a director of a FTSE 100 company guarantees multi-millionaire status. Pay even continued to soar in the eighteen months after the global downturn despite a collapse in share values. In 2009, three FTSE 100 chief executives earned more than £30 million each. Outstripping them all was Bart Becht of Reckitt Benckiser who earned £90 million after cashing in share options, on top of £37 million in 2008. Although running a major international company is a more difficult job than it might have been thirty years ago, these rewards bear little relationship to performance. Indeed, there is now a large body of academic literature that shows that executive compensation is only weakly correlated with a company's success.[201]

Rewards for those running private equity companies—who are free to pay themselves whatever they like from their companies—have been even more inflated. In July 2005, Richard Desmond, the proprietor of the *Express* newspaper titles (worth £950 million in 2010), announced that he was paying himself a 'chairman's remuneration' of some £52 million. It was a few months later that Philip Green paid himself—or more strictly his wife Tina—a mighty dividend of £1.2 billion from his Arcadia group of shops. This was the equivalent of the annual pay of 54,000 people on average earnings. Green may have rolled up his sleeves to try and improve the fortunes of his companies, but with only partial success. Apart from Top Shop, few of his outlets could be sold for more than he paid for them. Indeed, the dividend was paid not out of revenue but from a £1.3 billion bank loan agreed by Peter Cummings, deputy chief executive of HBOS, and a long standing financier of Green's business deals.[202]

As escalating fees, pay and bonuses became embedded in the small print of finance capitalism, they became an increasing source of controversy, even within the industry. In 1998, the chief executive of the giant investment bank Credit Suisse First Boston admitted, 'OK. If I am being honest with you then yes, let's whisper it, but the truth of the matter is that all of us are overpaid.

There is nothing magical about what we do. Anybody can do it.'[203]

As pay mounted so did the outcry. One insider has called the money earned by the banks 'supernatural'.[204] As one senior trader has said: 'What the vast majority of people in the City get paid is much too high. I have no issue with a genius trader making £100 million but most people, whilst being talented are doing roughly the same kind of job that they could do in any other industry yet seem to get paid 2-3 times as much.'[205]

But the hike in rewards available to financiers is not just a matter of proportionately. Just as important is their impact on the performance of the economy. The soaring personal fortunes available in finance may have fed the rising concentration of wealth, but, it was argued, this would have a positive effect on economic ambition. By unlocking the gates to riches, the new fortune hunters would forge a new era of entrepreneurialism and more dynamic and wealth creating economies.

So has the enrichment of a small financial elite delivered the promised crusade to re-energise American and British capitalism? Has it delivered more stable global and domestic economies?

6

THE AGE OF TURBULENCE

When the first signs of the credit crunch emerged in early August 2007, no one was more shocked than the British Prime Minister. Gordon Brown—who had been in number 10 for barely six weeks—had long argued that Labour's economic strategy had ushered in a new era of economic stability. Up to that point, Britain and most of the world had been riding a wave of economic success which had brought rising average prosperity, falling unemployment and in the three years to 2007, an extended bull-run for the London stock market. For Brown and the Treasury, this success was viewed as the product of astute economic management and was predicted to continue well into the future.

Such optimism was widely shared. By the turn of the twentieth century, the market experiment had achieved a widespread ascendancy. Following the recession of the early 1990s, the world economy boomed and growth in both the United States and the United Kingdom picked up.

Some talked of an 'economic miracle' while company chief executives—viewed as key players in the resurgent American economy—started to be treated as superheroes. In 1980, only one issue of *Business Week* featured a chief executive on its cover. In 1999, the number was nineteen. Few turned an eye as the executives started to translate that new public reverence into personal reward, and at a staggering rate. 'We are fortunate to be alive at this moment in history' is how President Clinton summed up the prevailing mood in his State of the Union Address on January 27, 2000. 'Never before has our nation enjoyed, at once, so much prosperity.'

Despite a series of economic, business and financial crises in the immediate post-millennium years—from the bursting of the dot-com bubble to the collapse of the energy-trading giant, Enron—the belief in markets proved remarkably resilient. Across the globe, regulators, politicians and financiers had come round to the view that, after a shaky decade and a half, the market model had finally triumphed. According to Kenneth Rogoff, chief economist at the IMF from 2001 to 2003, 'the policy community has developed a smug belief that enhanced macroeconomic stability at the national level combined with continuing financial innovation at the international level have obviated any need to tinker with the (international financial) system'.[206]

The prophets of market ideology made grand claims for their beliefs. The medicine of the markets had at last overturned the failings of post-war welfare capitalism. The rise of finance to a more central place in the economy had lowered financial risk. The de-regulation of financial and labour markets had brought greater economic stability and dynamism. Countries like the United States and the UK which adopted extensive dereg-ulation were set to experience less economic turbulence.

The new theories on the virtues of freer markets were

developed from the 1960s mainly by a group of American economists, many of them based or trained at the University of Chicago. In essence, this group—including Milton Friedman, Robert Lucas, Gary Becker, James Buchanan and Gordon Tullock—wanted to turn working economies into textbook models. Most were fierce opponents of Keynes and had some influence in turning the economic turbulence of the 1970s against his ideas. 'At research seminars, people don't take Keynesian theorising seriously anymore; the audience starts to whisper and giggle to one another' declared Robert Lucas as early as 1980.

Using the tools of advanced mathematics, the new high priests of the market school constructed highly sophisticated and rigorously tested economic models that claimed to demonstrate that free and flexible financial and labour markets deliver greatly superior economic outcomes—on employment, productivity and growth—than regulated ones, that government failure was much more likely than market failure. They also welcomed the personal wealth booms that accompanied the birth of the free-market era. Greater inequality was interpreted as a healthy sign that markets were working. According to their economic models, markets were self-regulating, economic shocks would quickly be reversed while any tendency to imbalance would be quickly corrected provided markets were free to adjust.

The Chicago-based Robert Lucas, one of the most influential of the new thinkers with his 'rational expectations' theory of boom and bust, demonstrated that, with rational individuals, perfect capital markets and full information—assumptions at the heart of economic theory—governments would be unable to deliver economic stability. In 2003, Lucas, who won the Nobel Prize for Economics in 1995, gave the Presidential Address at the annual meeting of the American Economic Association. 'The central problem of depression-prevention', he momentously explained to his audience, 'has been solved, for all practical purposes.'

By this he did not mean that the economic cycle had disappeared, or the economy would not suffer occasional setbacks, just that the days of severe recession were over and that economic fine-tuning was of no value. A year later, in February 2004, Ben Bernanke, a former Princeton Professor and soon to be appointed Chairman of the Federal Reserve, gave a speech called 'The Great Moderation', that made a similar point. Bernanke claimed that because of the apparent decline in the variability of both output and inflation from the mid-1980s, modern macroeconomics had largely solved the problem of the business cycle. According to these accounts, from two of the leading economic theorists in the US, the disaster of 2008-2009 should not have happened.

So what about the record of the thirty-year long era of market economics? Have markets delivered greater economic prosperity and stability than in the more inter-ventionist post-war era? Have successive waves of economic and industrial restructuring brought a hike in the level of value creation? Has rising inequality brought the promised improvement in economic performance?

For a decade from the mid-to-late 1990s, it seemed that the new prophets might be right. After serious birth pangs in the 1980s and early 1990s—when restrictive macroeconomic policies blunted growth rates—the more open and globalised world economy entered a period of sustained growth. Although this upward path faltered slightly in 2000 and 2001 with the collapse of stock markets following the bursting of the new economy bubble, average growth rates across the world and the richer nations were higher in the period 1997-2007 than they had been in the earlier period 1981-1996.[207]

Growth in both the UK and the US—an annual average of 3.0 and 3.3 per cent respectively in the decade to 2007— outstripped that of the other G7 nations less wedded to markets (Japan, Germany, France, Italy and Canada) which averaged between them only 2.4 per cent.[208] These figures lent some support to the market school.

But we now know that this apparently promising economic performance, a solid improvement compared with the 1980s and early 1990s, was an illusion. It was built on shaky foundations and was to prove unsustainable. One study, by the City brokerage firm, Tullett Prebon, has estimated that, after stripping out what they call 'the Brown bubble borrowing', the UK's real growth from 2000 to 2008 was half its headline rate. Half the much vaunted growth over this period was artificial. Moreover, while the contribution to the economy made by financial services (the 'bubble effect') more than doubled over this period (rising by 123 per cent), manufacturing shrank by a quarter and mining by more than a quarter. During the UK's post-millennium boom years, the money and productive sectors of the economy were moving in opposite directions.[209] That this was the case is anything but a coincidence.

Worse was to follow as the world economy plunged into the deepest recession since the 1930s. In the UK, economic output fell by over 6 per cent in 2008-2009. In the US, it fell by 4 per cent. Across the world, unemployment levels soared.

There was no economic miracle. Freer markets and escalating rewards at the top failed to deliver the sustained improvement in economic performance that had been promised. For their advocates, the new economic orthodoxy and its acceptance of soaring inequality, was to be judged above all on its impact on the real economy, on whether it delivered more productive, efficient and innovative economies.

Yet the evidence is that market capitalism has been weaker on most key measures of economic performance than the period of managed capitalism. This is clear from dividing the post-war era into two distinct periods. The first—the 23 year period of 'managed capitalism'—dates from 1950 to 1973, the year of the first OPEC oil shock and the one which perhaps best marks the end of the post-war boom. The second period—the 29 years of 'market capitalism'—covers the period from 1980 to 2009, beginning with the first full year of the new economic experiment.

Although this comparison misses 1974-1979, this period was a special case which saw the first serious recession of the post-war era, one ushered in by the OPEC shock. Moreover, the application of market principles did not start until Margaret Thatcher and Ronald Reagan were in power. However, if the period of 'managed capitalism' was extended to take in the period 1974 to 1979, the comparisons would not be significantly different.

On only one count—curbing inflation—can the post-1980 era be judged a clear success. Inflation rates tailed off during the 1980s and have remained lower ever since. On all other counts, the economic record of market capitalism has been inferior to that of managed capitalism. Growth and productivity rates have been slower, unemployment levels higher. As the proceeds of growth have been very unequally divided, the wealth gap has soared, without the promised pay-off of wider economic progress. Financial crises have become more frequent and more damaging in their consequences.

At 3.2 per cent, the annual rate of real world growth was significantly lower from 1980 to 2009 than the 4.8 per cent from 1950 to 1973.[210] This pattern holds for all the major economies. The US, UK, Japan, Germany and France all experienced slower growth after 1980 than during the post-war era.[211] Figure 6.1 for the UK shows an average annual growth rate of 3 per cent from 1950 to 1973. The figures are low by international comparisons—Germany, Japan and France all did better—but high by historic ones. Since 1980, in contrast, the growth rate has fallen to an average of 2.2 per cent a year.[212]

Of course, the golden age of the post-war era with its high growth rates was aided by several factors in addition to the introduction of managed markets and Keynesian fine-tuning, notably the programmes of post-war construction and a rapid period of technical change. Nevertheless, controlled markets, capital controls and steady demand were important factors driving success. The period was, above all, evidence of how managed economies with a mix of national and global controls over markets and the free flow of capital can be highly successful.

One of the most important measures of changing dynamism is what has happened to labour productivity.

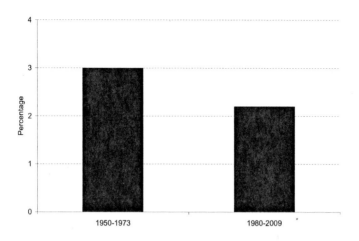

The record on growth, UK (Figure 6.1)
Average annual growth rate per period.[213]

As the American Nobel Economics Laureate, Paul Krugman, has said, 'Productivity isn't everything, but in the long run it's almost everything.' And it is the record on productivity that lies behind the slowing growth rates of the last thirty years.

As Andrew Glyn has shown, productivity—the growth of output per job—in the US and Europe has grown much more slowly since 1979 than from 1960 to 1973.[214] The slipping in the productivity rate during the 1970s and 1980s in the world's most advanced nations can perhaps be explained away by the economic difficulties of the 1970s and a delayed reaction to the impact of the dramatic switches in direction—deflation, privatisation and deregulation—of the 1980s. What is less easily explained by the orthodox school is why there was not an improved performance from 1990 to 2004 arising from

143

the freeing up of markets and lower inflation.

Despite leading the pack of rich nations when it came to deregulation, the US displayed a poor record from 1990. The country enjoyed a boost to productivity in the years of the late 1990s to the early 2000s—when it reached 2.5 per cent a year—success which came to be viewed at the time as a justification for the opening up of markets. Nevertheless, the longer performance from 1990 cannot be described as outstanding. Productivity rose by an annual average of 1.9 per cent in the fourteen years to 2004 compared with just over 3 per cent from 1960 to 1973.[215]

In the UK, the architects of deregulation preached that liberated markets would unleash a new spirit of enterprise, and close the nation's gap in productivity with the US and leading European nations. Yet the evidence is that freer markets, hands-off government and soaring corporate pay at the top have failed to engineer a significant improvement in Britain's productivity and innovation record.

In some ways Britain is more entrepreneurial. Business schools are booming and entrepreneurial aspirations have grown. Yet these aspirations have yet to be translated into a noticeable improvement in the quality of entrepreneurship. New business-start up rates have marginally improved and there has been a steady rise in the number of small businesses. But the rate of business failure has remained pretty static in recent years while the UK's record on patent applications has been slipping. The UK fell from 7th in the world competitiveness rankings (compiled by the World Economic Forum) in 1997 to 13th in 2009.[216]

144

Britain's weak record on enterprise is reflected in its productivity performance. Although productivity rates improved sharply in the 1980s in parts of manufacturing, this was largely because of the mass shedding of jobs at the time. Privatisation of state owned firms also led to improved productivity in several industries such as steel, which lost close to half its workforce.[217] Overall, however, as shown in figure 6.2, productivity growth has deteriorated since 1980, averaging 1.9 per cent a year to 2008 compared with an annual average rise of 2.95 per cent from 1961-1973.

Internationally, the UK has slightly closed the productivity gap with its main international competitors over the last two decades, but still lags well behind the US, Germany and France. According to a study by the

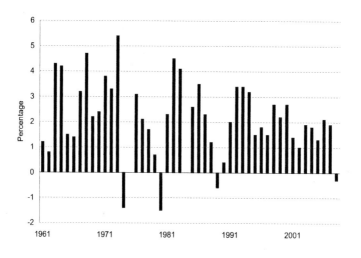

The UK's deteriorating productivity record, despite deregulation (Figure 6.2)
Growth in productivity per annum, UK, percentages.[218]

145

Economic and Social Research Council, the reasons
include 'a relative failure to invest, failure to innovate,
poor labour relations, trade distortions attributable to
Empire, antagonism towards manufacturing, "short-
termism" among business leaders and financial
institutions, technological backwardness and lack of
entrepreneurship.'[219]

Britain's weak record on productivity is in part down
to the failure to translate the rising profit share into
productive investment. Because of the low level of
investment, Britain's infrastructure remains poor
compared with her main competitors. Too many plants
operate with antiquated systems while levels of training
have lagged behind other countries. Despite the introduction of freer markets, funding for training, research
and development and innovation has slowed.[220]
Manufacturing entrepreneurs like James Dyson who
invest in engineers are the exception.

The evidence is of a strong link between R&D and
related capital spending and added value and eventually,
profitability.[221] Yet, apart from a handful of industries
such as defence, pharmaceuticals and mobile phones,
UK companies invest less in R&D, innovation and
capital equipment than their international competitors.
In most industries the levels of capital expenditure by
foreign companies in Britain greatly exceeds that of
indigenous companies.[222] In the 1960s and 1970s, the
UK's spending on R&D as a share of GDP was
comparable to its leading competitors. Since then, the
UK has slipped badly behind and in 2005 spent a lower
proportion than in 1973. In contrast, most leading
economic nations increased their share of GDP spent on

R&D.[223] As one former leading industrialist has complained. 'The British tragedy is that we have moved from a system of high R&D spend, accompanied by rotten management, to one of low R&D spend, accompanied by a different form of poor management!'[224]

The slowing of growth and productivity since 1980 amongst the world's leading economies has also been a central factor in the onset of domestic and global instability. The downturn of 2008-2009 was merely the most acute of a series of global crises. For the generation after the Second World War, active intervention to moderate the business cycle was largely successful. As the American economist Hyman Minsky observed in 1982, 'The most significant economic event of the era since World War II is something that has not happened: there has not been a deep and long-lasting depression'.[225] Despite claims that the injection of market forces would reduce the capitalist tendency towards instability, the world became a more turbulent place in the next three decades than in the immediate post-war period.

The IMF has generally been reluctant to use the word recession, but when forced, its chief economists have defined a 'global recession' informally as a year with less than 3 per cent growth. This is because while 3 per cent would be a strong rate for rich countries, emerging market economies have much higher 'normal' growth rates. In these countries a fall in growth to below a figure of 3-4 per cent is similar in impact to negative growth in advanced economies.

On this definition, the world has experienced no less than five recessions since 1980—notably in the early

1980s, early 1990s and 2008-2009. Moreover, the busts have been getting steadily larger. In contrast, as shown by the political economist and biographer of Keynes, Robert Skidelsky, in his book, *The Return of the Master,* there were no global recessions in the era of managed capitalism—the world did not record a single year from 1950-1973 when growth fell below 3 per cent.[226]

On the alternative, more conventional definition of a recession—negative real growth in two successive quarters—this pattern still holds. There have been more and deeper recessions since 1980 than between 1950 and 1973. This would be true even if the period was extended to take in the 1974-5 global recession. Take the UK economy. Although it experienced a number of exchange rate and stop-go crises in the two decades from 1950, there were only three shallow and short-lived recessions in this period. As shown in figure 6.3, there was one in 1956 when output fell by 1.4 per cent over three quarters, one in 1957, when output fell by 0.9 per cent over two quarters, and then in 1961 when it fell by 0.7 per cent over two quarters.[227]

In contrast, the period since 1980 has been distinguished by more frequent, more prolonged and more severe economic shocks than the first, with three deep-seated recessions. Specifically, in 1980-1981 when output fell by 4.7 per cent (over five quarters); 1990-1991, when it fell by 2.5 per cent (over five quarters); and 2008-2009 when it fell by 6.4 per cent (over six quarters).

One study of the 2008-2009 recession—by the independent National Institute of Economic and Social Research—shows that Britain's experience was worse than the average for advanced countries. Their analysis

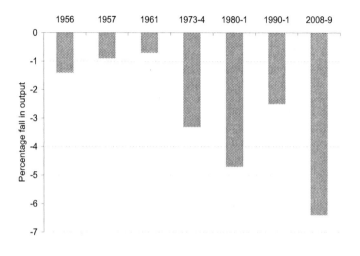

Post-war recessions in the UK: percentage fall in output (Figure 6.3)[228]
Percentage fall in output.

found that across the OECD, output fell by an average of 4 points between the first quarter of 2008 and the same period in 2009. In the UK output fell by 5 points over this period.[229]

Not only has the world experienced more and deeper recessions, the crises of recent times have had very different origins. Earlier post-war dips (mild as they were by comparison) were triggered by deflationary policies needed to get inflation under control (as was that of 1980-1982). The most recent recessions have nothing to do with inflation or soaring wage demands. They have much more to do with rising asset prices driven by excess profits and unsustainable credit, fuelled by financial deregulation.

This has also been the main cause of the upsurge in

149

financial crises, most of them associated with a torrent of currency, stock or property speculation. In the two decades from 1950 there were no banking crises and relatively few financial crises. Since the end of the 1970s, the number of such crises has mushroomed. As the *Financial Times* columnist, Martin Wolf, has put it, 'financial liberalisation and financial crises go together like a horse and carriage'.[230] In October 1987, the world's leading stock markets crashed, their largest fall in a day since the crash of 1929. A serious fall-out for the world economy was only averted by a huge injection of liquidity by the Federal Reserve and the Bank of England.

From the beginning of the 1980s, the number of banking failures in the US started rising sharply, a problem exacerbated by the impact of bank deregulation.[231] In 1989, the bursting of a serious property bubble in Japan, triggered by a series of bank liquidity crises, led to a decade-long period of deflation and a sustained collapse in Japanese shares prices. It had been preceded by a decade of rising profits (which rose to 40 per cent of output) and soaring assert prices.[232] Between 1990 and 1992, Norway, Sweden and Finland all suffered a banking crisis sparked by a similar property boom, the deregulation of financial services, and excessive lending by the banks. The economies of Sweden and Finland shrank for three years in succession. Finland's unemployment rate hit 20 per cent in 1994. Again, only decisive action by the national governments prevented a more prolonged fall-out.

Five years later, the Asian currency crisis, driven by financial over-reach, caused mayhem across south-east Asia when currency speculators pulled billions out of

Asian currency markets. In 2000, the collapse of the dot.com bubble brought world stock markets crashing once again. The FTSE 100 lost close to half its value between 2000 and 2003, with internet and new technology stocks bearing the brunt of the falls. In 2007, the credit crunch brought a surge in bank collapses and state bail-outs across the globe.

As the age of stability gave way to the age of turbulence, the chronic economic crisis that hit the global economy in 2008 provided the ultimate test of the effectiveness of the near thirty-year long experiment in market capitalism. It was one that culminated in dramatic failure. According to the market theorists, the economic meltdown of 2008-2009 should not have happened. The promise of self-regulating markets may have worked in the computerised mathematical models of the neo-liberal economic theorists, but not in the real world.

The crash of 2008-2009 has been widely blamed on a mix of excessive profiteering, reckless financial risk-taking and blind-eye supervision by the regulatory authorities. In January 2009, the *Guardian* newspaper drew up a list of 25 guilty parties, a mix of Central Bank governors, American and British political leaders, top Wall Street financiers and British bankers and credit agency bosses.

Some analysts—notably the former Chairman of the Federal Reserve, Sir Alan Greenspan, and its current Chairman, Ben Bernanke—have pinned some of the blame for the 2008-2009 crisis on what Bernanke described in 2005 as Asia's 'savings glut'. This was the surplus accumulated in a number of successful Asian exporting countries—notably China—that was then recycled via financial institutions into the main importing and deficit nations. This money derived from the increase in the foreign exchange reserves accruing to countries with large export surpluses, from China to the Middle-Eastern oil producers. As most of these surpluses ended up being invested in American Treasury Bills, this helped to allow the United States to run a large trade deficit simultaneously with a cheap money policy. By helping to perpetuate low interest rates, it is argued by some, the cash transfer contributed to the American debt bubble.

Such flows have inevitably played a role in adding to global imbalances, but are of secondary importance, small beer compared with the rise of other sources of international credit and liquidity which grew to levels that were greatly in excess of that needed to run economies productively. As shown in figure 6.4, the Asian savings glut—$2200 billion in 2007—added up to around one per cent of the stock of global financial assets (of $220,000 billion). It was this much greater growth of global liquidity that created what became a severe economic shock to the system. As the economist, José Gabriel Palma of Cambridge University has concluded, 'If this glut were in fact the "smoking gun" of the current crisis, never in the history of finance would anything have had such a multiplier effect.'[233]

Each of these were important ingredients of the global implosion. The banks were certainly reckless. The regulators failed to understand the dangerous implications of the new derivative-linked financial instruments—collateralised debt obligations, credit default swaps and special investment vehicles—that helped drive up world liquidity rates while greatly raising the level of risk in the

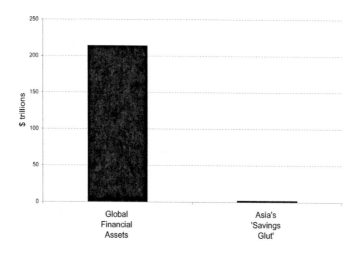

Asia's 'savings glut' (Figure 6.4)[234]

system. Amongst those individually responsible, those on watch in the US and the UK were more culpable than those in other nations.

Nevertheless, these issues only tell part of a much bigger story. Indeed, the common explanations offered for the financial crisis cannot be seen as primary causes, but symptoms of much more-deep seated trends. They deal more in epiphenomena than fundamentals. Reckless behaviour by an unregulated banking system provided the final spark, but the slow-burning fuse had been laid much earlier in the growing income and wealth inequalities that became the hallmark of market capitalism.

This is far from a widely accepted view. Indeed the idea that inequality might have been a central player in the crash has been almost entirely ignored or dismissed in the official explanations of the crisis. The findings of the bipartisan US Financial Crisis Inquiry Commission, published in January 2011 blamed pretty well everybody for what happened from politicians and regulators to Wall Street banks and credit rating agencies—'a crisis of this magnitude cannot be the work of a few bad actors'—but failed to mention 'inequality' once in its mammoth 662 page report.[235]

Outside of the official enquiries, however, a handful of academics and independent researchers have begun exploring the idea that inequality had a big hand in the crash. In December 2008, the British economist Gerry Holtham published an article in *Prospect* magazine arguing that the way profit growth had outstripped wage growth had contributed to the crisis.[236] In 2009 and 2010, I published two articles that explored the possible link between the falling wage share, the growing wage-pro-ductivity gap and the crash. The first went on to examine the likely impact on recovery of a continuing wage squeeze. It included a first attempt at a simulation that suggested that holding the wage share steady at its 2001 level would have led to 'a mild boost to consumption and growth, a weaker recession and a slightly faster recovery and lower asset prices and personal debt levels.'[237]

In the autumn of 2010, Professor David Moss, an economic historian at Harvard University, and an expert on inequality, was discussing the issue of the crash with a colleague. Moss had already noted that American recessions had followed the build up of banking crises. US Bank failures, for example, mushroomed in the 1920s in the run up to the Great Depression. These failures then ground to a halt with the greater degree of financial regulation introduced in the 1930s. For the next 50 years,

America did not face a single serious banking crisis. Then, from the late 1980s, banking failures and financial crises started to re-appear again with the advent of a new era of 'self-regulation'.[238]

Moss then compared his work on the history of US financial regulation and bank failures with the historical evidence on income inequality charted by Piketty and Saez, and shown earlier in figure 1.2. The two data sets showed a near complete correlation.[239] Bank failures and the level of income inequality both rose sharply in the 1920s. From the 1930s through to the end of the 1970s, there were virtually no bank failures while income inequality fell. From the early 1980s, the pattern of the 1920s was repeated. Income inequality rose along with the incidence of financial and banking crises. 'I could hardly believe how tight the fit was—it was a stunning correlation,' Moss told the *New York Times*. 'And it began to raise the question of whether there are causal links between financial deregulation, economic inequality and instability.'[240]

Of course, as Moss has accepted, correlation is not the same as causation. As one of his critics, R Glenn Hubbard, dean of the Columbian Business School and top economic adviser to former President George W Bush has put it, 'Cars go faster every year, and GDP rises every year, but that doesn't mean speed causes GDP.'[241] The correlation could mean that the direction of causation is from slump to inequality. Yet what is significant about this pattern is that in both the 1920s and the pre-2007 period, inequality rose sharply in the years *before* recession took hold.

There is now an increasing, if still small, body of

academics that have attributed the crisis at least in part to rising inequality. These include Joe Stiglitz, a Nobel prize-winner and a former chief economics at the IMF; Jean-Paul Fitoussi and Francesco Saraceno of the Paris-based Centre for Economic Research; Professor Raghuram Rajan, another former IMF chief economist; Gerry Holtham, a former City fund manager and co-director of the Investment Management Resource Centre at Cardiff University; the American economist Ravi Batra; and Michael Kumhof and Romain Rancière, two IMF research economists.[242]

The latter, for example, have argued that 'The crisis is the ultimate result, after a period of decades, of a shock to the relative bargaining powers over income of two groups of households, investors who account for 5 per cent of the population, and whose bargaining power increases, and workers who account for 95 percent of the population (and whose bargaining power has fallen).'[243]

Although these are the views of a small minority and remain highly controversial, they have prompted an ongoing debate. Reviewing some of the evidence, Harvard economist David Laibson concluded, 'income inequality was not a major contributor'.[244] In January 2011, in a spirited debate at the annual meeting of the American Economic Association in Denver, two economists—Daron Acemoglu of MIT and Edward Glaeser of Harvard took on Chicago's Raghuram Rajan, with Glaeser concluding that 'Inequality seems as if it was only a small part of the story.'[245] Then in February, in the first attempt at a systematic analysis of the relationship between rising inequality and banking crises, two Oxford academics, including the distinguished economist, Tony

Atkinson, concluded that 'at first sight this does not provide overwhelming evidence for the *increase* [in inequality] hypothesis'. Nevertheless they tempered this conclusion by accepting that there are several routes by which inequality could generate asset bubbles and hence instability.[246]

It is these routes which are the key to understanding the wider economic impact of rising inequality and which are explored in more detail in the remaining chapters. There are, it is argued, four principal mechanisms at work that underpin the concept of a limit to inequality, that link heavier concentrations of income—and the factors that drive it—to patterns of business behaviour that put financial and economic systems at risk. Each of these, sometimes working separately, sometimes mutually reinforcing, it will be argued, helped translate soaring inequality into the increased economic and financial fragility of recent times. Sometimes these mechanisms follow directly from excessive levels of inequality. Sometimes they follow from the causes of rising inequality.

The first mechanism arose via the shrinking global wage base and the decline in relative incomes amongst middle and low income households. This led to the stalling of demand and fuelled the rise in personal debt in a way that greatly increased risk in the financial system. As Fitoussi and Saraceno have put it: 'The widespread increase of inequality depressed aggregate demand and prompted monetary policy to react by maintaining a low level of interest rate which itself allowed private debt to increase beyond sustainable levels.'[247]

The evidence is now overwhelming that it was

increased income inequality that fed rising levels of personal debt. Examining the period from 1963 to 2003, Matteo Iacoviello, an economist at Boston College, Massachusetts, concludes that the rise in earnings inequality after 1981 was the principal explanation for this rising level of debt.[248]

While consumers were starved of cash through the suppression of earnings growth, the banks were given the political license—through deregulation—to embark on a massive expansion of lending to consumers. This both sustained the economic boom from the mid-1990s and helped generate the massive expansion in the size and role of financial institutions and in the scale of bank assets shown earlier in figure 5.1. Once increased levels of indebtedness caused by rising inequality were perceived to be unsustainable, they became 'the trigger for the crisis.'[249]

The second link arose through a steady divorce between the process of enrichment and the interests of the wider economy. The revised structure of executive rewards that emerged from the mid-1980s—especially in finance—and the chase for shareholder value were not just key drivers of rising inequality. They also led to perverse business incentives. As it became easier to make big money through business strategies that were essentially unproductive, trading, investment and restructuring decisions changed in ways that often weakened the foundations of the economy.

According to the American economist, Tyler Cowen, the author of the influential book, *The Great Stagnation*, the increased concentration at the top mattered because it had been largely generated within finance, encouraging banks to 'take far too many risks and go way out on a limb, often in a correlated fashion.' Over time, Cowen argues, the way the finance sector operates 'corrodes productivity, because what the banks do bears almost no resemblance to a process of getting capital into the hands of those who can make most efficient use of it. And it leads to periodic financial explosions. That, in short, is the real problem of income inequality we face today. It's what *causes* the inequality at the very top of the earning pyramid that has dangerous implications for the economy as a whole.'[250]

Modern economic theory predicts that pure markets work in a way that benefits the wider economy. Yet it was perverse incentives that led to banks pumping uncontrolled supplies of credit into the global economy. This enriched a generation of financiers but only by the expansion of activity which stifled the 'real economy'— the part directly producing goods and services or what Americans call 'main street'. Money poured into takeovers, private equity, property and a variety of forms of speculative activity and financial and industrial engineering that led to the accumulation of fortunes but mostly via the transfer of existing rather than the creation of new wealth, businesses and jobs.

These financial strategies might have been rational from the point of view of the individual bankers devising them, but they often had damaging side-effects which made the economy more fragile and less able to cope with external shocks.

The third mechanism arose through the impact of the soaring cash surpluses which were the counterpart of the wider wage squeeze. These surpluses came to provide an additional economic shock to that generated by falling wage shares. They became the base for the record levels of liquidity that led to a larger and larger banking sector, while injecting much higher, and ultimately unsustainable, levels of risk into the global financial system. As David Moss described it, 'The rise of these massive [American banking] institutions represented a profound change in our financial system and a powerful new source of systemic risk.'[251]

Far from improving the efficiency with which resources were allocated, as banking executives liked to claim, ballooning levels of liquidity, fed by more and more complex forms of financial innovation, merely fuelled a series of unsustainable financial and asset bubbles.

While it was the role of government to put a cap on risk, a fourth mechanism then came into play. In more equal societies, the financial sector is more circumscribed and much less able to capture regulators and politicians. As wealth became more concentrated, so did the distribution of power. From the early 1990s, the finance industry and its lobbyists were able to exercise an increasingly disproportionate degree of influence at the highest levels to ensure weak financial regulation by the state, lower taxes on the wealthy and inaction on tax havens.

Britain and the US in particular came to resemble what Ajay Kapur, head of global strategy at Citigroup in New York, called a 'plutonomy'—a society in which wealth and economic decision-making is heavily concentrated in the hands of a tiny minority.[252] This was what Britain was in Victorian times before the development of full democratic institutions and the emergence of a powerful middle class. It equally applied to the United States during the 1920s. From the 1980s, suddenly able to exercise this plutocratic power, bank bosses effectively came to write their own financial rules in a way which, hardly surprisingly, made them and their executives even richer.

In the United States, this process began under President Reagan but accelerated under all subsequent Presidents from Bill Clinton onwards. As Richard N Goodwin, former speechwriter to JF Kennedy put it as early as 1997, 'The principal power in Washington is no longer the government or the people it represents. It is the Money Power. Under the deceptive cloak of campaign contributions, access and influence, votes and amendments are bought and sold. Money establishes priorities of action, holds down federal revenues, revises federal legislation, shifts income from the middle class to the very rich'.[253]

Joseph Stiglitz, an adviser to President Clinton, claimed that even under Clinton, 'finance reigned supreme' and the President 'buckled to pressure from big financial interests' time and again.[254] Clinton may well have wanted to check the plutocratic power wielded by US businessmen but the key influences in the framing of his economic policy came not from within the Democratic Party but from Wall Street.

Commentators have likened the power trend to a return to the last decades of the nineteenth century when money power was at its height. Asked in 2002 if the wealthy had captured more political power than in the gilded age and the 1920s, the political scientist Kevin Phillips replied, 'It is a pretty close run thing between now and then. That, in itself, is damning because the conclusion… was that the rich had way too much power by the first decade of the twentieth century. '[255]

In the United States, this influence became even more direct with a revolving door between Wall Street and government. The two Bush administrations from 2000-2008 were packed with former chief executives and financiers—more than any American government in modern history. George W Bush's first cabinet—dubbed a 'junta of major corporate interests'—had a combined wealth more than ten times that of the Clinton cabinet.[256] Government was effectively captured by a group of cheerleaders for the further deregulation of finance. Thomas Hoenig, President of the Reserve Bank of Kansas City has called the American economic system 'crony capitalism ... who you know, how big your political donation is.'[257]

A similar if less direct process has been at work in the UK. Gradually an elite group of financiers came to exercise an increasingly monopolistic influence on Britain's political leaders, out of all proportion to their real economic contribution. In his book, *Britain's Power Elites,* Hywel Williams, a former adviser to the Conservative Party, wrote that '...at no previous time in British history have the financial and business elites been as dominant as they are today.'[258] In 2010, just over a half of donations to the Conservative Party came from City donors—a mix of bankers, hedge fund managers and private equity financiers. Five years earlier it was a quarter. In 2010, City donors gave a total of £11.4 million, and a total of £42 million over five years.[259]

Not that long ago, the balance of power was much more evenly shared. But gradually other interest groups with legitimate claims for a share of the influence, from trades unions and town halls to manufacturers and small businesses, became at best marginalised, at worst, ignored. The only voices that came to count, it seemed, were those coming from corporate boardrooms and City offices.

The Treasury itself became little more than an outpost of the City. A torrent of City lobbying secured Treasury support for the idea that financial innovation was good for the economy, that the City was a key generator of social value and should be the central engine of economic growth. As Manchester University academics have described it, 'The new Treasury doctrine is the impossibility of upsetting the City.'[260]

The forces that drove economic instability were not external shocks that could not have been foreseen, but ones implicit to the great shifts in policy direction instituted from the late 1970s. As the American international investor and a man who knows a little about speculation and destabilisation, George Soros, has put it, 'the salient feature of the current financial crisis is that it was not generated by some external shock like OPEC... The crisis was generated by the system itself.'[261]

7

LIVING ON BORROWED TIME

One evening in late 2004, a couple who had been living in a small council house in Bradford for ten years got an unexpected knock on the door from a mortgage salesman. The broker, working on commission, was cold calling people on the estate to see if they could be persuaded to buy their council house.

The couple, aged 53 and 58, were both unemployed and living on benefits. One suffered from chronic arthritis while the other had only one lung. Although they were hardly strong candidates to take out a mortgage, they were given the hard sell and signed the papers that evening. A few weeks later, they started payments on a 25-year £55,000 mortgage provided by a Manchester-based bank called London Scottish. The mortgage they'd been sold is what's known in America as a NINJA mortgage—'no income, no jobs, no assets.' Such loans—which offer higher commission for brokers than conventional mortgages—are a type of sub-prime mortgage, a high-interest package sold to people with low and uncertain incomes and a poor credit history.

Although the couple were told the repayments would be no more than the rent, this was only true for the first twelve months. A year on reality set in. The repayments rose sharply, the couple fell into arrears and the lender tried to repossess their home. They were only saved from eviction with the help of their family and a new payment plan which still absorbed a very large chunk of the couple's benefits.

The same year, a 55-year old lady living in a council house in Cheshire was approached in a similar way by another 'door-to-door' mortgage broker working for Home and County Mortgages Ltd, a Cheshire-based company specializing in right-to-buy-sales. The lady was a part-time cook working for the local council, with both very modest earnings and a history of credit problems.

Because her earnings were insufficient to get a normal mortgage, she was persuaded to take out a self-certificated loan, one where very limited, if any, checks are made on declared earnings. Encouraged to exaggerate her earnings, the lady was even given a script of what to say if the bank rang to check her details. She ended up with a £75,000 mortgage and monthly payments of about £600, way above her actual earnings. Within months she had started borrowing from friends and taking out credit card loans to meet the payments.

Home and County Mortgages—which sold prime as well as sub-prime mortgages—developed something of a track record in such sales. Subsequently the company was investigated by the Financial Services Authority (the FSA), the financial watchdog charged with monitoring the mortgage industry, and cracking down on mis-selling and fraud. In 2006 the firm was fined £52,500 by the FSA for 'management failures, a lack of skill, care and diligence'. The regulator also found that one of the company's salesmen had 'inflated customers' incomes' on their mortgage applications.

The small scale of the fine—little more than token—happened despite evidence uncovered by the BBC's *Panorama* programme that 'the FSA had been warned the total fraud by this company could amount to more than £7 million potentially involving around 150 customers.'[262] During the course of the investigation by the FSA, the company's most successful salesman was seen shredding vital documents at their offices. While many documents were missing, the FSA discovered that of the mortgages granted where the paperwork had survived, 40 per cent should never have been approved.

Selling such mortgages has been highly profitable—the Home & Counties' owner and managing director paid himself one and a half million pounds in the year of the investigation. But it is also a very high risk for those taking out the loans. Most sub-prime borrowers end up with 'adjustable-rate mortgages' that give a low starting interest rate—'teasers'—but which escalate sharply after one or two years. Sub-prime borrowers have also been especially vulnerable to re-possession. Although there are no official figures, it has been estimated that close to 70 per cent of repossessions granted in a 3 month period in 2007 involved banks and building societies specialising in sub-prime mortgages.[263]

In the past, low income families like these from Bradford and Cheshire would not have been the target for mortgages they would not be able to afford. This kind of lending grew out of the much greater freedom granted to the banks. It also came with political sanction. The finance industry—in both the UK and the US—has been encouraged to extend lending further and further down the income scale. As shown in the next chapter, such encouragement has been part of the wider political response to the shrinking income base amongst large sections of the working population.

Until the early 1980s, all forms of lending were tightly controlled in the UK. Before financial deregulation, the great majority of mortgages were provided by Britain's long established building societies. Most of these mutual organisations had been born in the nineteenth century in response to the Victorian self-help ethic to encourage savings and run for the good of their members. These controls involved rules governing mortgage lending from the size of deposits and interest rates to the ratio of loans to income. Building Societies operated a basic rule—that total outgoings on housing costs should not exceed a quarter of income.

The sweeping away of these controls brought great changes in the way mortgages were provided. Gradually, most building societies chose to sell up and convert into banks, abandoning mutuality in favour of profits (at least in part because of the City-style rewards available to bank executives) and making them accountable not to members but to shareholders. One by one, the biggest of the high street names—Abbey National, Halifax, Cheltenham and Gloucester, Northern Rock—converted. Although mutual building societies—from Nationwide to the Yorkshire—still exist, the majority of mortgages are now provided by banks.

Deregulation and demutualisation proved another personal gravy-train for those at the top of the finance industry bringing higher fees, commissions and bonuses. For customers, deregulation meant mortgages were easier to obtain with a much greater range of products offered to a much wider group of people. But it also meant that banks and building societies engaged in increasingly aggressive competition for customers offering a maze of mortgage offers, from endowment and interest-free to sub-prime. Such competition even extended to door-to-door selling. Sub-prime mortgages started to be issued in the UK from the early 1990s and have grown to account for around 8 per cent of the total market, covering more than a million people. While many lower income families have been helped into home ownership through such mortgages, weakened regulation has also made it much easier for unscrupulous operators determined to make easy money.

While the process of deregulation brought more choice—and more risk—for consumers, it also led to the slow build-up of a massive debt mountain. Given the profit to be made from the mortgage business, the banks had every incentive to try and capture a growing share of the market. A higher share meant bigger profits, share values and executive bonuses.

After the freeing up of mortgage restrictions, the lending institutions became increasingly innovative—some would say reckless. In the 1960s and 1970s, the typical mortgage was limited to two and a half times earnings, and rarely more than 80 or 90 per cent of the property value. Some kind of deposit was mandatory. After big bang, these restrictions were mostly axed and mortgage deals became more and more generous.

The bank leading the charge on innovation was Northern Rock, the Newcastle-based building society that had started life as a friendly society in the nineteenth century. More than a century later, it was among the last of those building societies succumbing to privatisation, converting, despite a good deal of opposition from members, into a bank in 1997. The company's newly appointed chief executive, the 38-year old Adam Applegarth, a highly-motivated and confident local man who had climbed his way up through the company, was determined to move the newly created bank, a small fish with only 76 branches, into the big league. He introduced a new corporate logo, expanded the bank's headquarters and opened up branches in Ireland, Guernsey (to handle offshore accounts) and even Denmark. Applegarth launched an audacious business strategy—to grab a bigger and bigger slice of the mortgage market.

To meet this goal, the bank had to outbid its competitors. At the heart of its burst for growth was a new mortgage concept—the 'Together Loan'—which offered young borrowers 125 per cent of the purchase price and up to a maximum of six times income. Despite raising eyebrows across the industry and being attacked by some rivals as 'too racy', other banks soon started offering more generous deals just to stay in the race. By 2006, mortgages of five times salary or more were commonplace.[264] For a while, Northern Rock's aggressive business model appeared to pay off handsomely. By 2007, it had risen to provide a fifth of all mortgages, outstripping bigger rivals like Halifax and Nationwide, while its share price hit an all-time high.

But Northern Rock's strategy was in many ways a microcosm of what had been happening to the finance and market-led British economy. By the middle of the 2000s, Britain was riding the wave of an economic boom and house prices were heading skyward. But with the national wage base continuing its long term slide, this boom was only possible because of a growing dependence on debt, not just to finance the rising cost of buying a home, but to pay for an increasing share of ordinary spending as well.

The beginnings of this growing reliance on credit can be traced to the removal of lending controls from the mid-1980s. Before that time credit was much less easy and came with tough restrictions. By far the majority of consumption was financed out of current income. Some items were bought through mail order while capital items such as cars and furniture were often bought through hire purchase. But hire purchase was always heavily controlled as part of the policy of restrictions on lending. Targets were set on consumer credit and were only dropped in the mid-1980s.

The launch of Barclaycard—Britain's first credit card—in 1966 and based on the BankAmericard that had been issued in the US in 1958, extended the opportunity to purchase on credit. Nevertheless, despite the launch in 1972 of a second card—Midland Bank's Access card— the British, whose earnings at the time had kept pace with economic growth, continued to finance most of their non-housing consumption through current income.

With the ditching of credit restrictions, the opportunities to borrow mushroomed. The retail banks extended opportunities for overdrafts, credit card companies upped their credit limits and new loan companies offered juicy deals, all forms of credit that mostly offered big margins to the lenders. Households were deluged with unsolicited junk mail encouraging them to take out loans. In the late 1980s and early 1990s, Barclaycard launched a series of popular adverts featuring Rowan Atkinson in various guises as the spy character, Richard Latham. Consumers could acquire as many credit cards as they wished, and with high street stores joining in, there were plenty on offer.

The burgeoning credit business—from store cards to mortgages—was mostly very lightly controlled. The FSA focused mainly on the big banks and financial institutions rather than the large number of smaller businesses entering the mortgage and lending market. Checks were often cursory. The regulators simply lacked the resources or the powers to keep a lid on some of the more dubious practices. Mis-selling became rife. On one occasion the FSA admitted that it had issued a license to sell sub-prime loans to a man who'd served jail time for fraud.

Credit may have become easy, but with very limited controls over charges, it was also costly. In 2006, for example, while the Bank of England base rate stood at between 4.75 and 5 per cent, the Miss Selfridge and Laura Ashley store cards provided by GE Consumer Finance both carried annual interest rates of 29.9 per cent. The B&Q store card provided by General Electric Consumer Finance carried an annual interest rate of 26.8 per cent. A Report by the UK's Competition Commission in 2006 noted that these charges 'have been some 10% to 20% above what they would have been had they reflected providers' costs across the sector.'

From the early 1990s, a larger and larger proportion of household consumption came to be funded by borrowing, not just in traditional areas like housing, white goods, cars and school fees. More and more staple areas of spending like holidays, clothing and utility bills came to be funded through credit. While earnings growth amongst middle and lower income households decelerated, personal indebtedness boomed. Between 1994 and 2007, the level of outstanding debt on credit cards rose more than sevenfold.[265] In the seven years to 2007 consumer spending by individuals grew by £55 billion more than their income. Over the same period, the Government's index of retail sales by volume grew by no less than 35 per cent in constant prices, more than three times as fast as disposable incomes.[266]

With new shopping malls and retail parks sprouting across the country, Britain appeared to be dripping with affluence. The giant Westfield Centre in West London— taking nearly ten years to build—became the biggest urban, indoor retail outlet in Western Europe. Sprawling across 43 acres, the site boasts 50 restaurants and 255 shops including all the leading designer outlets from Dior and Prada to Louis Vuitton and Tiffany. It was just one of the scores of new malls opening across Britain during the boom years.

But this apparent affluence was illusory. It was underpinned only by an increasingly indebted nation. In a telling symbol of the consumer bubble that was building across Britain, the Westfield shopping centre opened its doors in November 2008 a few days after the government announced that Britain was officially in recession. Figure 7.1 shows that in the decade from 1994, the total *real* level of lending to households (consumer credit and mortgages combined) increased four and a half times to peak at £36.9 billion in the first quarter of 2004.[267] Most of this leap took place from 2000, a period when the growth in real earnings slowed sharply to little

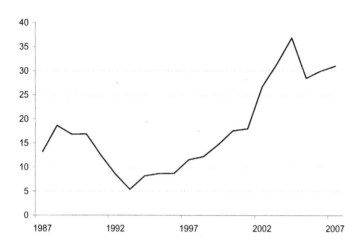

The debt binge, 1987 to 2007 (Figure 7.1)
Level of personal lending, £ billion. Lending secured on dwellings and
unsecured consumer credit, UK, first quarter of each year, adjusted to
2006 prices using the Retail Price Index.[268]

more than a trickle.

Some of this rise took the form of a higher level of
consumer credit (a mix of credit card bills, overdrafts
and other non-housing loans). The average UK
household non-mortgage debt in 2008 stood at £9,280.
A quarter of the population had unsecured debt of some
kind.[269]

Indeed the real level of such credit was seven times
higher in 2004 than the average of the early 1990s.[270]

Most of the rise—more than four fifths—was
accounted for by increased mortgage lending. Some of
this was the result of inflation-busting rises in house
prices. But a significant proportion of this mortgage
lending—as much as 43 per cent in 2006—took the form

173

of re-mortgaging, the granting of an extended mortgage then siphoned off to fund consumption other than home improvement. Increasingly banks came to allow extended mortgages with no questions asked about what the money was to be used for. In this way the mortgage became an additional pay cheque not just financing a modern kitchen or garage extension but a new car, a luxury holiday or in some cases a second home. Between 2002 and 2006, the amount of borrowing through this 'housing equity withdrawal' was equivalent to an additional 6 per cent of post-tax income. Homes became cash cows for their owners and a key source of the way consumption levels were sustained as rises in disposable income slowed.[271]

Although new lending on housing and consumer credit fell back slightly from 2004, the total level of outstanding personal debt kept on soaring. By the beginning of 2008 it stood at £1400 billion, up from £574 billion in 1993.[272] As shown in figure 7.2, in that year, families in the UK had debt levels 57 per cent higher than their income. The ratio of debt to disposable income was higher than in any of the other Group of Seven (G7) leading industrialised economies, and was sharply higher than the 91 per cent recorded in 1997. The 2007 figure represents a three-and-a-half fold increase over 1981 when the ratio of debt to income stood at 45 per cent.

As many of those turning to lending were those least able to afford to do so—from those with low pay or insecure or temporary work—growing debt soon came to leave a rising trail of individual insolvencies and debt write-offs amongst those unable to maintain repayments,

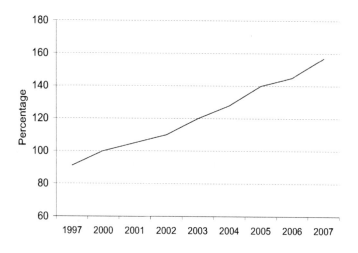

Personal debt as a ratio of disposable income, UK (Figure 7.2)
Total household debt as a percentage of disposable income.[273]

even during the boom years of the post-millennium. The number of home repossessions rose to 40,000 in 2008, double the 2005 figure, while the number of households in arrears stood at 183,000. Personal bankruptcies in England and Wales rose from an average of 22,000 a year throughout the 1990s to reach 106,700 in 2007 and 120,000 in 2008.[274]

The more fragile working environment from the early 1980s—spreading unemployment, deteriorating pay and greater earnings volatility—brought growing vulnerability to financial insecurity, indebtedness and hardship.[275] Because lending was also extended and expanded to lower income families, the level of default risk in the economy rose along with the fragility of the banking system. Indeed, an important consequence of the

175

growth of indebtedness has been the increased risk of financial hardship associated with worklessness or falls in pay. This risk is exacerbated by the fact that the poorest sections of society have few savings or little in the way of tangible assets. In 2006-2008, nearly three per cent of the population had zero or negative wealth while ten per cent had less than £7,390. The richest ten per cent was more than 100 times as wealthy as the poorest ten per cent.[276]

For two decades, Britain's economic strategy had been built on a triple-formula—high and rising consumption, a low and declining wage share and soaring levels of borrowing. This model may have helped maintain growth and employment levels, but only by stoking property values and creating a debt mountain larger than in any of the other rich nations. It was an unsustainable model that finally imploded in the autumn of 2007.

Although the UK topped the G7 nations in the rise and level of personal household debt, it was followed closely by the United States, a nation with a very similar economic model to that of the UK and one which experienced a very similar explosion in personal debt. Here real consumption rose by a fifth from 2000 to 2007 despite stagnant wages, again financed by growing debt.[277] The level of outstanding debt also rose sharply from the 1990s—from $5,500 billion in 1997 to $14,400 billion a decade later.[278] As shown in figure 7.3, debt started to exceed total household expenditure in the economy from 2000. Although borrowing and personal indebtedness reached their highest levels in the Anglo-Saxon economies, there were similar, if more muted, upward trends in the other richer economies.

As in the UK, debt levels rose much more sharply for

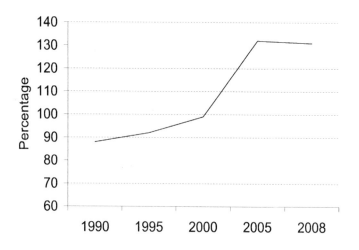

Personal debt as a proportion of household expenditure, US (Figure 7.3)[279]

lower than higher income households.[280] Bank lending was highly profitable, especially from the early 1980s. Up to that point lending had been highly regulated. To prevent profiteering, there were also controls over the interest rates that could be charged. In 1980, Delaware passed a new law lifting interest rate ceilings on credit cards and personal loans. It was another bonanza for bankers and similar restrictions in rates were soon withdrawn in other states and across America. By 2007, credit card debt had risen to close to $1000 billion.[281]

In the US, the sub-prime mortgage became the most publicised example of the great lending surge. While the two government-sponsored lending agencies, Fannie Mae and Freddie Mac, offered more conventional mortgages and were strictly controlled, the less regulated private banks found the sub-prime market a route to easy money.

The great surge in sub-prime lending was heavily driven by the high rates of return they offered to the lenders, always higher than those available on prime mortgages.

Between 2000 and 2006, the proportion of all new mortgages taken by the sub-prime sector rose from a twentieth to a quarter. At its peak the value of sub-prime lending—targeted at lower income households—reached $900 billion. 'At one point the boom was so great that people with no banking qualifications or lending experience were joining in. Tens of thousands of people enlisted in the real estate industry, working as realtors, mortgage originators and sales people.'[282] As *Newsweek* reported, the demand for mortgage brokers in Las Vegas was so strong that 'every stripper, waiter and bartender on The Strip had a broker's license'.[283]

Much of the lending was also 'predatory', aggressively sold with hot commissions and sometimes designed to trap borrowers into a lucrative debt spiral. Loans were often poorly supervised and were supplied to people with little hope of repaying, and on a much larger scale than in the UK. As sub-prime loans were risky, they meant higher charges than more conventional mortgages. New 'affordability products' proliferated, aimed at extending home ownership to more marginal groups. 'Liar loans', involving little documentation, limited or no proof of income or credit history became increasingly common, with one study finding that in a third of sub-prime loans, the brokers had failed to assess whether the buyers could afford the loan.[284]

In one case, a retired 78-year old postal worker living in New York City was persuaded by a broker to re-mortgage his home on the promise that he would pay less than he was already paying. After the new mortgage deal had been signed, the interest rate escalated sharply. The mortgage had been provided by Countrywide. Despite being one of America's large mortgage providers, they refused to cancel the deal when the worker complained.[285]

There is nothing wrong in principle with allowing credit levels to rise in excess of savings. Credit has played a key role in economic history, driving innovation and development throughout the nineteenth century. But the power to create credit has come to be poorly managed since the axing of controls.

The effect was an increasingly over-heated market in the post-millennium years and a massive credit explosion. As in the UK, much of this credit boom was being used to finance general consumption. With house prices rising sharply until 2007, the banks mounted advertising campaigns to encourage households to 'refinance' their homes. In 1995 American households extracted $106 billion of funds against the value of their homes. By 2005 this had risen sevenfold to $750 billion.[286] Much of this was spent on personal consumption or paying off credit card debt.

It was not just the middle class that turned to the prop of cheap credit. As the heavily squeezed American middle class found themselves reaching the limits of their capacity for debt, the lending institutions had to turn elsewhere to boost borrowing. Lending spread further and further down the income scale with the rapid increase in indebtedness from the late 1990s increasingly concentrated amongst poorer Americans. As David Harvey, professor of anthropology at New York's City University, describes it: 'Political pressure was put on financial institutions like Fannie Mae and Freddie Mac to loosen the strings for everyone. Financial institutions, awash with credit, began to debt-finance people who had no steady income. If that had not happened, then who would have bought all the new houses and condominiums the debt-financed property developers were building?'[287]

That taking the blocs off bankers would lead to a credit explosion could hardly have come as a surprise. There had been a similar experience in 1920s America. Britain had also lived through a much more short-lived experiment in the liberation of the credit markets that should have acted as a sign of the dangers inherent in such a strategy. In 1971, the Heath government, a year into office, took a dramatic decision to axe monetary controls through a series of measures known as Competition and Credit Control. These lifted lending ceilings and withdrew the liquidity minimums imposed on banks. Former physical and administrative controls on credit growth were axed. The level of credit would now be controlled through market forces via interest rates. 'The brakes were well and truly off', as Edward du Cann, a banker and former Economic Secretary to the Treasury, observed at the time.[288]

Heath had been guided by a number of motives. Britain was on the edge of a deepening economic crisis, with unemployment heading upwards. Giving greater lending freedom to the banks would not just prevent stagnation, it was argued, it would also lead to a smaller state. The Prime Minister also hoped that freeing up the banks would help create a much-needed investment boom. But what had been unleashed was competition without control.

The impact was both dramatic and predictable. The banks, unsurprisingly, shovelled money in the direction of customers. Credit ballooned. According to one account, '... the clearing banks began churning their files, generating credit—literally "printing money"—and not lending it to, or investing it in, British manufacturing, as Heath seems to have expected, but to domestic consumers, to the property markets and the so-called "fringe banks".'[289]

Far from the investment boom Heath had hoped for, the axing of controls—later described by Mrs Thatcher as 'monetary incontinence'—led to a near threefold increase in the money supply between mid-1970 and early 1974, a surge in property speculation and the then largest post-war boom in both commercial and domestic property prices.[290] As one account of the period described it: 'What had been created, under the eyes of the Bank of England, was a simulacrum of the lethally unbalanced Wall Street of the late and roaring twenties'.[291] By 1973, with the balance of payments and inflation spiralling out of control, the whole rush for growth was put into reverse. Hire purchase controls were re-introduced and the reforms suspended. The dash for growth lasted less than two years. While the unions came to be seen as the principal villains, opening the money floodgates played a bigger role in the inflationary spurt of the time.

The second experiment in the liberating of the banking system lasted a little longer, but with predictable effects. By 2006, the signs of strain were all too clear. Default rates grew, especially in the US. 'For sale' signs mushroomed. When American interest rates were pushed up to puncture the dangerous bubble in the housing market, caused in part by high levels of sub-prime lending, the house price boom turned into a crash and foreclosure rates escalated. The banks that led the charge found themselves with mounting losses. By 2007, the latest American dream was over.

The whole house of cards, erected with such hope, but so little caution, came tumbling down. As lending dried up precipitating the credit crunch, house prices began to slide, the first nationwide fall since the 1930s. In July 2010, US banks repossessed the second highest number of homes ever—nearly 93,000—in a single month. Across America, one suburb after another was swathed in rows of decaying, boarded up homes, un-let office blocks scarred most city centres while the glut of empty properties depressed house prices still further. As banks stopped lending to each other, within and across nations, the international wholesale markets froze. Much of the international banking system, with accumulated debts that could no longer be paid, was effectively bankrupt.

The consequences of unregulated financial and credit markets were now plain for all to see. Not only had the finance industry embarked on an unsustainable lending spree, it had abandoned all the lessons of the past. In the UK, Northern Rock—no longer able to finance its way by borrowing short-term from the wholesale money markets—faced the first full scale run on a British high street bank since the fringe bank crisis of the 1970s. Over the next year the Government was forced to pump billions of pounds of public money to shore up the sinking banking system.

In the US, even the biggest financial empires were brought to their knees. In March 2008, the giant investment bank, Bear Sterns—whose value had collapsed from $20 billion to $230 million in six months—was bailed out first by a Government loan before being rescued by JP Morgan. By the end of the year, Fannie Mae and Freddie Mac had been nationalised, and the insurance giant, AIG, which had insured many of the risky bets of American and European banks, became the biggest bail-out in American corporate history. One by one Wall Street titans succumbed to the crisis. Amidst much controversy, and with dramatic repercussions, Lehman Brothers was allowed to go to the wall by the US authorities. Meryll Lynch was bought by Bank of America while Goldman Sachs and Morgan Stanley converted to commercial banks, thereby subjecting themselves to much tighter scrutiny. The biggest financial institutions in the world that had once taken the lion's share of America's corporate profits had been brought to their knees.

In the UK, Northern Rock, Bradford and Bingley (another demutualised former building society) and the Royal Bank of Scotland were nationalised, while Lloyds was reluctantly persuaded by the government to buy out HBOS. In Iceland the country's three largest banks, Giltnir, Landsbanki and Kaupthing, were successively nationalised.

The exploding debt boom of the post-2000 years, allowed to keep economies afloat as wages were squeezed, had finally driven the global financial system over the cliff.

8

A CONSUMER SOCIETY
WITHOUT THE CAPACITY TO CONSUME

On January 5 1914, Henry Ford invited reporters from three local papers to his giant Detroit factory. The 51-year old automobile entrepreneur and one of the richest men in America was about to make a dramatic announcement. 'The Ford Motor Company, the greatest and most successful automobile manufacturing company in the world, will, on January 12, inaugurate the greatest revolution in the matter of rewards for its workers ever known in the industrial world,' he told the assembled journalists. 'Each man over 22 will receive the minimum wage of $5 a day... We believe in making 20,000 men prosperous and contented rather than follow the plan of making a few slave drivers in our establishment million-aires.'

The next morning the story topped the front pages of America's press. The *Michigan Manufacturer and Financial Record* called Ford's plan 'the most generous stroke of policy between captain of industry and worker that the country has ever seen.' The Toledo *Blade* deemed it 'a lordly gift' and the New York *Evening Post* 'a magnificent act of generosity.' Other automakers were less ecstatic. Ford's rivals resented the company setting wages—at close to double the industry standard—they felt they couldn't match. *The Wall Street Journal* accused Ford of being 'a traitor to his class'.

The Automobile tycoon's motive was twofold. First he had noticed that his workers had come to hate the repetitive assembly-line work and productivity was low. But in addition to motivating his workers, Ford was, by giving his employees more disposable income, also attempting to create a consumer base for his product. He later claimed that with the $5 day 'we really started our business, for on that day we first created a lot of customers.'

Henry Ford had come to acknowledge one of the central contradictions of a capitalist economy built on low earnings and high profits. If the workforce is not paid enough, it won't be able to afford to buy the economy's output. The issue of the level of earnings has dogged private enterprise economies heavily dependent on consumer demand through much of their history. It was a big issue facing the two largest industrial nations—Britain and America—during much of the industrial revolution. It surfaced again during the 1920s and again from the 1980s. Each of these periods was characterised by a level of earnings growth insufficient for demand to keep pace with growing output.

In both these latter periods—the 1920s and the 1990s/2000s—the political solution to slowing wage growth was cheap credit and rising personal debt. Without this debt, the mass consumption on which a private economy depends would not have been forthcoming. In the 1950s and 1960s, with wages keeping pace with productivity across the richer nations, debt was unnecessary to sustain the economy. When there were periodic shortfalls of demand in these two post-war decades, public money was boosted through the process of demand management devised by Keynes. It was a solution adopted across the developed world.

From the early 1980s, with Keynesianism discredited by the problems of stagflation in the 1970s, the declining level of demand caused by shrinking wage shares in the UK and the US would have led to economic collapse. One study of the United States from 1978 to 2000, for example, has shown that the rise in the inequality of earnings over this period had a significant dampening effect on consumption.[292] Of course, a falling wage share might have been less damaging if it had meant consumption making way for other forms of demand such as higher exports and productive investment, but this is not what happened. The solution adopted to tackle lagging demand came to lie in what has been called 'privatised Keynesianism.'[293] Consumption was maintained less by injections of public money than by higher levels of bank lending and personal credit, a process set in train by deregulation.

Although this might have appeared a politically astute solution—though one that was hardly consistent with 'sound money'—and kept the British and American economies afloat for the next 25 years, it was never sustainable. Soaring household debt became the first of the four mechanisms that translated rising inequality into eventual financial disaster.

Credit ensured that those falling behind in the economic race could at least keep up when it came to consumption. As a result, consumption inequality did not rise as fast as income inequality. Without such debt, the growing income gap would have led to a spending slump.

Home ownership rates would have stagnated and fallen. New homes would have been left unsold. Mortgage and consumer durables markets would have seized up. Eventually lagging demand would have brought companies—from car manufacturers to housebuilders—to their knees.

'An important political response to inequality was populist credit expansion, which allowed people the consumption possibilities that their stagnant incomes otherwise could not support' as Professor Raghuram Rajan has argued. 'Easy credit has been used as a palliative throughout history by governments that are unable to address the deeper anxieties of the middle class directly.'[294]

To ensure access to credit, the monetary authorities—in both the UK and the US—kept interest rates at historically low levels. In the United States, the Chairman of the Federal Reserve, Alan Greenspan, reduced interest rates steadily from the millennium—when they stood at 6.5 per cent—to an all-time low of one per cent in June 2003. Greenspan—a man lauded by bankers and ordinary Americans alike and awarded the Presidential Medal of Freedom, a British Knighthood and the French Legion of Honour—was pumping money into the economy. Low interest rates helped drive the increase in credit but what caused it was the economic necessity to compensate for low wages. Without the low interest rate strategy, credit expansion would have been more subdued, and growth would have faltered.

If growth had been more evenly shared with wages rising in line with rising productivity, as in the 1950s and 1960s, the British and American economies would have been able to grow without such a heavy reliance on debt. Just how important the rise in credit was to maintaining economic growth has been shown by the economic consultant, Graham Turner, in his book, *The Credit Crunch*. In a series of simulations conducted by Oxford Economics he examined the impact on the economy for the decade to 2007 of a slower rise in the level of debt in both the US and the UK.[295]

The effect in each country was a substantial shortfall in consumer demand, with a fall in demand of 9 per cent over the ten years in the UK and of 6.2 per cent in the US. Demonstrating just how important credit was to house price inflation, UK property prices would have risen by a third of their actual value in the decade from 1997, while in the US they would have risen by a quarter of their actual value.

The importance of the level of wage demand in the economy has long been recognised. A low wage strategy may help profitability, but in doing so it creates a new problem—how is the expanding output that underpins growth going to be bought? Before Henry Ford made his dramatic intervention, a number of economists had explored the economic consequences of a lack of working class purchasing power, a problem labelled the theory of 'underconsumption'. Such theories were developed during the nineteenth century by a range of British scholars, most notably Thomas Malthus—who developed his own theory of the insufficiency of demand as early as the 1920s—and fifty years later by John A Hobson.

Writing at the end of the nineteenth and beginning of the twentieth century, Hobson—who was born in Derby in 1858—challenged much of the accepted economic thinking of the time. He was critical of the methodology of economic science on the grounds that it abstracted from human welfare in its widest sense and developed an alternative theory of the distribution of output which linked economic surpluses to the distribution of power. Along with others, Hobson believed that the Long Depression that began in 1873 in the US and the UK and the unemployment to which it gave rise was rooted in a shortfall of demand. He saw a mal-distribution of income, and very low spending power of the working class, leading, through under-consumption and over-saving, to unemployment.[296]

The rich used their growing wealth mainly to invest in more capital goods or in unproductive speculation. As much of the population did not earn enough to consume the full output, the system was unstable. The remedy lay in income redistribution in order to build demand and sustain growth. 'If apportionment of incomes were such as to evoke no excessive savings, full constant employment for capital and labour would be furnished.'[297] Although such theories were controversial and had been dismissed by classical political economists from David Ricardo onwards, Hobson's work became influential in subsequent debates and anticipated in important respects the theories later developed by Keynes. Indeed, Keynes later described Hobson's first book (which he co-authored with Arthur Mummery) published in 1889 as 'an epoch in economic thought'.[298]

In 1926 Hobson had a big hand in a pamphlet, *The Living Wage*, published by the Independent Labour Party which called for an increase in working class purchasing power through redistributive taxation. The 1920s was a period of downward pressure on wages, while unemployment was high.[299] The risks associated with a demand shortage were also developed in the 1920s by two Americans, Waddill Catchings and William Trufant Foster in a series of books including *The Road to Plenty* published in 1928. Their proposed solution to such a shortage was to use spending on public works to restore the balance between production and consumption. Their ideas had some influence in the later attempts by Franklin D Roosevelt in attempting to pull America out of the Great Depression of the 1930s.

The views of the underconsumptionists clashed strongly with the conventional economic theory of the natural harmony of the economic system, one which dominated economic thinking as well as the mindsets of those with their hands on the policy tillers. According to the laissez faire economic orthodoxy of the early twentieth century, markets were largely self-correcting: production was seen as the driving force of economic activity and demand would adjust to its equilibrium level without any need for external stimulus to boost it. These theories held that left to themselves, competitive markets would produce more and distribute better than regulated ones. Their advocates believed in a combination of sound money and balanced budgets. Anybody taking a different view such as those arguing for active government policies and deficit financing were treated more or less as heretics.

Keynes—considered one of the heretics in the 1920s—was certainly influenced by theories of underconsumption. In a challenge to the conventional economic wisdom, he demonstrated that economies fail to automatically self-correct following an economic shock such as that of the Great Crash of 1929. His seminal work, *The General Theory of Employment, Interest and Money,* published in 1936 and drawing on the experience of the 1930s slump, showed that to prevent a recession government intervention was necessary to boost demand. His theories eventually became the new orthodoxy for managing economies, one that held for the next forty years. In his general theory of aggregate demand, Keynes laid the emphasis on sources of demand other than consumption, especially investment and public expenditure in maintaining an adequate level of demand and preventing recession. Nevertheless, consumption— which accounts for up to two-thirds of aggregate demand in most economies—was always going to be the key player in sustaining output.

During the passion fuelled debates that took place in the early 1930s about how to secure recovery, opinion divided between two sharply opposing schools. First, the economic conservatives who wanted public spending cuts to balance the budget and ensure what they saw as fiscal responsibility. As Andrew Mellon, the Treasury Secretary throughout the 1920s, once graphically put it: 'Liquidate labor, liquidate stocks, liquidate the farmers, liquidate real estate... purge the rottenness out of the system.'

The second 'reflationist' school, led by Keynes, called for a larger fiscal deficit to boost demand. It was the 'conservatives' that won the argument, at least initially. In the UK, the coalition government led by Labour's first Prime Minister, Ramsay McDonald, imposed a series of controversial spending cuts that ultimately plunged the economy deeper into recession. Though the British and American economies did ultimately recover from the Great Depression—one of the deepest and longest in modern history—recovery was slow and too weak to prevent the persistence of widespread unemployment. Keynes argued strongly in 1933 that the stimulus packages eventually applied to boost purchasing power through public works in the United States and the United Kingdom were inadequate.[300] As a result, full employment was not achieved until the end of the decade with the start of significant war spending.

There is now a strong body of opinion that attributes a good deal of the blame for the Wall Street Crash and the Great Depression that followed on the mal-distribution of income. The 1920s was a time of low wages and irregular employment for many Americans, while the middle class represented only a small group in society. The American economy was thus heavily dependent on the spending, saving and investment decisions of a tiny section of society—the wealthy and the affluent. The top 24,000 families received three times as much income as the 6 million people at the bottom.[301] It was a classic plutocracy.

Most Americans could not afford to join in the consumer society that was emerging in the post-war years. Those that did often depended on credit to do so. In 1930, an estimated 16 million families, 60 per cent of the total and representing 70 million people, received less than $2000 a year. This was the figure calculated by the Brookings Institute as the minimum necessary 'to supply only the basic necessities'.[302] Moreover, the scale of inequality rose sharply during the 1920s, with the proportion of income held by the top one per cent increasing from 15 to 24 per cent.[303] The decade was also one of rising bank profits and finance-related earnings.[304]

According to those who see the rising income gap as the central cause of the 1929 Crash, excessive inequality generated two forces that led to the economic convulsions of the time. The first of these was that demand in the American economy was insufficient to sustain the gains in productivity being made in industry and agriculture. The ten years from 1919 was a time of exceptional productivity growth, with manufacturing enjoying an annual increase of 5.3 per cent, a much higher rate than achieved in the decade before or the three subsequent decades. Farming productivity was also extremely high.[305]

As this surge in productivity was not matched by wage growth, the productivity-wage gap rose sharply. Earnings fell well behind the steady expansion in the output of consumer goods, boosting profits in the process. As a result, the gains in productive capacity were being scooped up largely by the wealthy. As one historian of the time has written, 'The increasing wealth of the 1920s flowed disproportionately to the owners of capital'.[306] While the rich were hefty consumers, there was a limit to the volume of goods and services they would buy. 'Structural poverty, irregular employment, and low wages meant that America was a consumer society without the capacity to consume.'[307]

Some of the increase in profits went into boosting capital investment—factories, equipment and warehouses. For a while this investment helped the economy to flourish. New cars and household goods poured off the modern production lines during the 1920s. But with too many Americans living at subsistence levels, and not enough of these goods being bought, the economy eventually started to falter. Inventories grew, order books were revised downwards, confidence began to fall.

Indeed, output had already slowed sharply before the stock market crash in October 1929. In June of that year the index of industrial production had peaked and started to turn down. 'By the autumn of 1929 the economy was well into a depression', according to JK Galbraith's account in *The Great Crash 1929*. 'By October, the Federal Reserve Index of industrial production stood at 117 compared with 126 four months earlier. Steel production declined from June on; in October freight-car loadings fell. Home-building, a more mercurial industry, had been falling for several years, and it slumped still further in 1929.'[308]

Nevertheless, these falls were sufficiently modest—perhaps typical of a mild cyclical downturn rather than a potentially serious depression—that appropriate corrective monetary action could have moderated the downward trend. But here the second force arising directly from rising inequality came into play—the speculative boom. While wages lagged productivity growth, the wealthiest accumulated larger and larger fortunes. The rich were greatly helped too by the policies pursued by the Secretary to the Treasury, Andrew Mellon. A multi-millionaire financier and banker, and the third richest American at the time, Mellon was appointed Treasury Secretary in 1921, a post he held until 1931. A conservative Republican, and a fully paid-up member of the orthodoxy school, he believed in a balanced federal budget and low taxes. During the 1920s, he cut the size of the national debt incurred during the First World War and also sharply reduced taxes on profits, incomes and estates. The top marginal rate of income tax, for example, which had been increased during the War, was cut over the decade from 73 to 24 per cent.

One historian described this policy as a 'notorious example of self and class interest ... saving millions for himself and his companies, and hundreds of millions for his peers in the highest circles of wealth and commerce'.[309] Looking back at the decade from the 1930s, the historian Arthur Schlesinger Sr noted that 'America, in an ironical perversion of Lincoln's words at Gettysburg, had become a government of the corporations, by the corporations and for the corporations'.[310]

As the portfolios of the wealthiest swelled, an orgy of economic extravagance followed. Money poured into assets, first property and then the stock market. The great real estate boom of the mid-1920s began in Florida but spread across much of America. A classic speculative bubble, it was encouraged by low interest rates, a reduction in lending standards, and weak banking supervision. Construction companies, property entrepreneurs and thousands of Americans tried to join in the rush to get rich off the back of appreciating land and property values.

As contemporary accounts reported, a collective madness consumed Florida investors. Speculators descended on Miami, hungry to buy land in the hottest property market in the country. Salesmen swarmed to meet them. 'Bird dogs'—youngsters trying to cash in— scanned the new arrivals at Miami's train station and steered the most promising prospects to their bosses' offices. Transactions were swift. Buyers often only had to put down a tenth of the purchase price for the lot they were buying to close a deal; further instalments were payable when the sale was legally recorded. Many new owners had no intention of waiting that long, simply selling their lot onto the next buyer through a process of 'flipping'. Some bits of land were sold and resold several times during a single day. A majority of those who bought land in Florida were able to do so without stepping foot in the state, by hiring people to speculate and buy the land for them. In many ways the property boom of the post-millennium years followed a very similar pattern.

Soaring property prices were followed by a stock market boom. In the four years to the third quarter of 1929, the Dow Jones index rose by 120 per cent, a compound annual growth rate of 21.8 per cent.[311] When the index fell on successive days in the last week in October, between the 'black Thursday" of the 24th and the 'black Tuesday' of the 30th, record numbers of shares were traded—16 million on the Tuesday—as desperate shareholders tried to minimise their losses. In September 1929, the Dow Jones had reached 381. Three years later it stood at 41.2, a drop of 90 per cent. By the end of 1930, more than 800 banks had failed, among them the Bank of United States, which accounted for a third of the total bank deposits lost during the crisis.[312] Between 1929 and 1932, the volume of US production fell by a third while unemployment rose to a quarter of the labour force.

The American 'roaring twenties' was a time of exuberance and excess. Galbraith called the decade a 'mass escape into make-believe, so much part of the true-speculative orgy.'[313] Looking back in 1931, the novelist F

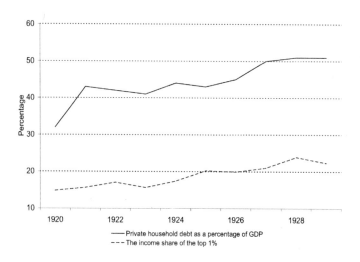

How debt levels and income concentration soared in 1920s America (Figure 8.1)[314]

Scott Fitzgerald, author of *The Great Gatsby*, described the time as the 'most expensive orgy in history... '. It was a decade that arguably gave birth to consumerism, with people seemingly desperate for cars, radios and the other trappings of the new consumer era. As was the case in the build up to the crash of 2008, there were plenty of warning signs along with a good deal of denial. Many Americans thought that, with growing prosperity, their economy had been transformed. In one advertisement backing Herbert Hoover during the 1928 Presidential campaign, the Republicans promised: 'A chicken in every pot and a car in every garage'. Irving Fisher, one of the country's most distinguished economists, opined shortly before the crash that shares had reached 'a permanently high plateau'. On the eve of the crash the financier John

197

J Raskob, in an article called 'Everybody Ought to be Rich', came out with a plan to allow the poor to make money on the stockmarket.

As in the decade leading to 2007, much of the apparent economic miracle of the 1920s had been built on an expansion of debt. As shown in figure 8.1, the ratio of household debt to national income rose by more than 70 per cent between 1920 and 1930. The rise in debt followed a very similar upward path to the share of income accruing to the top one per cent. It was another pattern repeated four decades on.

The urban consumer boom of the decade was financed largely by borrowing. There was also an explosion in rural bank credit. The boom in share prices was also paid for largely by a surge in debt. With only limited controls over lending practices, investors could buy shares from brokers with only a small down payment, often around 15 or 20 per cent. Some brokers who handled the selling of stocks operated a 'margin' as low as 10 per cent—that is they could lend as much as $90 for every $10 that customers paid them.[315] The difference would be borrowed from the brokers themselves or the banks, with the stock itself used as collateral. The level of gearing was very similar to that of the post-millennium years.

By putting only a small amount of cash upfront, the investors were effectively betting that the price of the stock would rise enough and provide sufficient profit to repay the loan when it fell due. The degree of leverage available simply fuelled the speculative frenzy as mounting stock prices seemed to offer easy profits to investors, mostly a small class of the rich and very rich, though with some 'ordinary' investors joining in. 'By August 1929, brokers had lent small investors more than two-thirds of the face value of the stocks they were buying on margin—more than $8.5bn was out on loan.'[316]

On October 7, 1929, the *Financial Times* reported that the President of the American Bankers Association was concerned about the level of credit for securities: 'Bankers are gravely alarmed over the mounting volume of credit being employed in carrying security loans both by brokers and by individuals.' When the market eventually imploded in 1929, this level of leveraging intensified the scale of the crash, as depositors defaulted on their debt, banks began to fail and there were multiple runs on the banks. President Franklyn D Roosevelt attacked the excesses of the economic elites he labelled the 'money-changers'.

Keynes likened the 1920s stock market to a casino. As he put it in the *General Theory*:

'Speculators may do no harm as bubbles on a steady stream of enterprise. But the position is serious when enterprise becomes the bubble on a whirlpool of speculation. When the capital development of a country becomes a by-product of the activities of a casino, the job is likely to be ill-done. The measure of success attained by Wall Street, regarded as an institution of which the proper social purpose is to direct new investment into the most profitable channels in terms of future yield, cannot be claimed as one of the outstanding triumphs of *laissez-faire* capitalism—which is not surprising, if I am right in thinking that the best brains of Wall Street have been in fact directed towards a different object.'[317]

But Keynes also viewed the growing income gap as a

key contributor to the build-up of financial instability during the 1920s. He argued that because lower income groups consume a higher proportion of their income than the rich (in economic jargon, they have a lower marginal propensity to consume) while the rich also have a high propensity for speculation, excessive income inequality increases the risk of financial instability and economic collapse. Because of differences in the propensity to consumer among different income groups, a greater concentration of income simply leads to a dampening of the overall level of demand. Keynes' solution to this problem of failing demand was to maintain investment and to increase the propensity to consume by 'the redistribution of incomes... so that a given level of employment would require a smaller volume of current investment to support it.'[318]

In *The Great Crash, 1929*, Galbraith also identified 'the bad distribution of income' and its impact on the pattern of demand as the first of five factors causing the crash and the great depression. Galbraith argued that the growing dependency of the American economy on the consumption of a small minority made it increasingly fragile. It's 'highly unequal income distribution meant that the economy was dependent on a high level of investment or a high level of luxury consumer spending or both. The rich cannot buy great quantities of bread. If they are to dispose of what they receive, it must be on luxuries or by way of investment in new plants and new projects. Both investment and luxury spending are subject, inevitably, to more erratic influences and to wider fluctuations than the bread and rent outlays of the $25-week workman.'[319]

The 1920s was a classic example of the 'limit to

inequality' at work. By concentrating so much of the national income and wealth in the hands of a small group of the very rich, the American economy became dangerously unbalanced. Not only did this concentration play a big role in creating the conditions for financial instability, it meant that there was a big overreaction to the crash when it came. Because the drivers of the economy were so heavily dependent on the economic power of a small group of citizens, any sudden shock, such as that of 1929, had a disproportionate impact on subsequent levels of consumption, savings and investment. When the rich cut back, sold their shares and stopped investing, the impact on the economy's income generating power was severe.

The decade that preceded the crash of 2008-2009 has many striking parallels with the 1920s. Both periods saw a substantial rise in the level of income concentration at the top. Levels of personal debt also rose sharply. In both periods, there was a high degree of economic illusion created by booming conditions, even though these were being created by debt bubbles that were always going to prove unsustainable. In both the 1920s and the post-millennium years, there was an excess of optimism about the course of the world economy with the warning signs of an impending crash largely ignored or dismissed by those who count. In both periods, leading commentators believed the elusive secret of permanent prosperity had finally been found.

There are also strong parallels between the dominant economic doctrines of the two periods, and their central belief in laissez-faire and the self-regulating nature of markets, without the need for government intervention or adequate wages to tackle shortfalls of demand. According to today's market theorists, full employment can be secured by allowing wages to fall until equilibrium and stability is restored. This is remarkably similar to the ideas that helped to intensify the recessionary pressures that stemmed from the 1929 crash.

There is also one final and particularly striking parallel. What Galbraith described as the 'inordinate desire to get rich quickly' of the 1920s returned in the decade leading to 2008-2009, bringing a range of business strategies that simultaneously undermined the foundations of the real economy.[320]

9

THE CUCKOO IN THE NEST

Since the general election of 2010, the coalition government has made their primary economic goal the elimination of the Britain's mounting fiscal deficit (the excess of public spending over tax revenue) within a single Parliament. To achieve this they are implementing, at speed, a massive £83 billion package of public spending cuts announced in October 2010. In his first budget speech soon after the election, the new Chancellor, George Osborne, justified the cuts in public spending, at least in part, by describing the state as 'crowding out private endeavour'.

It was a telling phrase but hardly new. The concept of 'crowding out'—that excessive state spending simply starves the wealth-creating private sector of resources—grew out of the debates about the condition of the British economy in the 1970s. The idea had been discussed at the Treasury but was popularised by two Oxford economists, Roger Bacon and Walter Eltis, in a series of articles published in the *Sunday Times* in November 1975. At the time, the British economy was being buffeted from one crisis to another with inflation out of control and deteriorating public finances. The Bacon-Eltis thesis—elaborated in *Britain's Economic Problem: Too Few Producers*, published in 1977—offered an apparently simple explanation and solution for Britain's growing economic plight. Make the state smaller and the private sector would thrive.

The economic problems of the 1970s had many roots, but, according to the academic studies of the period, excessive state spending played only a minor role. Even simulations of the Treasury's own model could find no crowding out effect. Although there were some difficulties with financing the deficit, these seem to have derived 'from the much enhanced role played by the financial markets once Britain abandoned a fixed exchange rate in 1972, and the new circumstances occasioned by much higher levels of unemployment.'[321]

Despite the lack of evidential backing, the idea was embraced with enthusiasm by Mrs Thatcher and became a key guiding principle of her economic strategy. Her hope was that by capping public spending and reducing taxes on the rich, the private sector would thrive. It was a strategy that largely failed. Far from the promised private sector renaissance, the only part of the economy to do well in the 1980s was finance. Other parts of the private sector did not start to show solid signs of life until 1992 when the pound fell against competing currencies as a result of Britain's ejection from the European Exchange Rate Mechanism.

The problem of 'crowding out' is also largely marginal to the situation of the British economy today. Crowding out can only occur under very specific conditions, especially where a budget deficit leads to a hike in interest rates. Yet interest rates are currently at historic lows while the public sector deficit could be funded many times over. The issue is one of inadequate, not surplus demand.

A much more fundamental problem with the British economy is its highly skewed economic structure. The fragility of its economy has less to do with the size of the state and more to do with the imbalance within the private sector. The growing dependence on a finance-driven business model has played a big role in the failure to build a productive and sustainable economy. Britain—and the United States—does suffer from a crowding out problem, but one that stems from the way an excessive reliance on finance has stifled other parts of the private economy.

Although there has always been something of a tension between finance and productive sectors, the interests of these two limbs of the economy have grown increasingly at odds. This is well illustrated by the impact of the boom in financial and industrial deal-making. Private equity takeovers, mergers and downsizing have mostly delivered much higher cash returns for much lower risk than could be obtained by providing long-term capital for new plants, business development or designing new products. This is because the patient building of new companies or expansion of existing ones—on which enduring companies and long-term wealth are founded—may not deliver returns for many years, sometimes decades, if at all. It was much easier for the world's financial surpluses to be siphoned off, before the crash, into different forms of financial and industrial re-engineering.

The world's most successful economies are those which have ensured an adequate flow of funds for long term wealth creation—building capital infrastructure and investing in new technology and business development. For many industries—from pharmaceuticals to electronics—the fruits of investment take many years to deliver a return. Nokia, now the world's largest manufacturer of mobile phones is only successful because it was given sustained long term financial support by the Finnish government to support its electronics division. In South Korea, the giant POSCO steel company and Hyundai shipbuilders were set up and sustained by government initiative over many years.[322]

During the last twenty years, the UK banking system has been on something of a lending rampage. This has been driven by three factors: by the expansion in the volume of international footloose funds, with most of this flowing in the direction of the banks and boosting their assets in the process; by the increase in the share of total profits taken by global finance, especially in the US and the UK and also by sharp rises in leveraging.[323]

Yet this lending hike has not been translated into a rush of spending on infrastructure, new enterprise and developing the productive base of the economy. Investment for long term success has been outpaced by a surge in short-term, fast-buck, deal-making. Booming surpluses have financed a property and takeover boom, the purchase of financial instruments and a very mixed bag of financial activity much of which increased the fragility of the financial system.

As shown in figure 9.1, in the eight years leading to 2007, institutional lending was heavily skewed towards property. In that year, around 45 per cent of all bank and building society lending went on residential or commercial property, some of it to finance an office building expansion in London and other cities, but most to finance the purchase of existing housing and offices

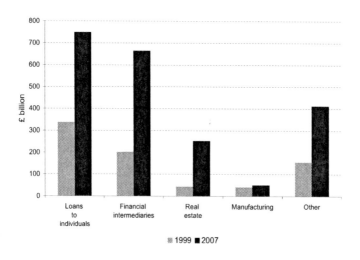

UK Bank Lending to UK residents and businesses, 1999-2007 (Figure 9.1)
£ billion.[324]

and thus a change of ownership, especially through the expansion of 'buy-to-let'.

This amounted to little more than a highly misguided bet that property prices would continue to rise much faster than prices. A further 31 per cent went to intermediaries—other financial institutions like banks. While the total of domestic bank lending rose almost threefold between 1999 and 2008, the value of loans to manufacturing stayed roughly constant. As a share of all lending they more than halved settling at a mere 2.4 per cent in 2007. While banks invested some £50 billion in manufacturing, nearly $1000 billion went on property investment of one kind or another.

In the decade to 2007, an increasing share of bank lending was also being swallowed up by the boom in corporate buy-out and takeover activity, greatly outstripping that spent on Research & Development. In 2005, the top 750 R&D-intensive companies in Britain spent £17 billion between them. By comparison, UK companies spent an average of £86 billion a year between 2000 and 2008 on mergers and acquisitions—home and abroad—activity which merely flips the ownership of existing companies and has a mixed record on creating value.[325] In October 2007, the Royal Bank of Scotland borrowed most of the $100 billion cost of its takeover of the Dutch bank ABM Amro. To buy EMI, the private equity specialist, Guy Hands, borrowed £3 billion from Citigroup (nearly three-quarters of the purchase cost) in 2007. It was a disastrous deal that landed Hands with a $2 billion loss and a failed court action.

'Buy, not create', as Don Young, a former director of the FTSE 100 building materials company, Redland plc, described Britain's industrial strategy.[326] 'The financial sector has become almost completely detached from the real world.' declared Angus Tulloch, partner at the global fund manager, First State Investment, in an address to members of the Scottish Parliament in February 2010.

By 2010/11, the pre-recession lending boom had been turned into a lending strike, with recovery being threatened because smaller companies unable to issue bonds were being starved of credit. Yet the banks managed to find the cash to fund a number of controversial takeovers. When the American firm Kraft bought one of the UK's iconic companies, Cadbury, for example, it borrowed close to £11 billion, much of it from British banks and hedge funds. At the end of 2010, a number of American buy-out specialists had raised multi-billion dollar war chests from investors, much of it to be targeted at UK acquisitions.

Industrialists have been sounding off for decades about the increasingly short-term priorities of finance, mostly with little effect. 'The demise of British-owned companies in advanced service and high technology industries has been spectacular over the last 20 years or so' wrote Don Young in his 2004 co-authored book, *Having Their Cake,* which presented an extraordinary catalogue of the impact of the growing power of finance on large and medium sized British companies. 'Some companies have been destroyed, some have retired (hurt) to the relative quiet of the lower reaches of the FTSE 350, some have moved out of the equity markets to private ownership and many have been acquired by foreign competitors.'[327]

It was not until after the crash that those in authority began to echo such concerns. 'While the financial services industry performs many economically vital functions, and will continue to play a large and important role in London's economy', Adair Turner, the chairman of the Financial Services Authority, told a business audience in September 2009, 'some financial activities which proliferated over the last ten years were "socially useless", and some parts of the system were swollen beyond their optimal size.'

Turner had said nothing that was not common currency amongst the City's critics, but he carried weight in senior government circles. A week later, Peter Mandelson, Secretary of State for Trade and Industry, and once a cheer-leader for finance, told the Labour Party Conference that what Britain needed was 'less financial and more real engineering'. That the process of wealth accumulation has been increasingly de-coupled from the productive economy was finally being accepted at the top of government, albeit a little late in the day.

By now something of a verbal war was being unleashed on the disproportionate power of finance capitalism. In March 2010, Richard Lambert, the director general of the CBI, told a business audience in London that hostile takeovers and what he called 'Jack Welch capitalism'—a relentless drive to improve returns to shareholders at the expense of other stakeholders—had created a big problem for industry. Businesses could never be 'a positive force for good', creating wealth and jobs, he declared, while short-term shareholder value is the main boardroom aim.

A week later, Paul Polman, boss of Unilever, said that the company had already stopped offering guidance to the stock market on potential profits. 'It is very easy for me to get tremendous results very short term, get that translated into compensation and be off sailing in the Bahamas ' he declared. 'But the goal for this company—and it's very difficult to do—the goal is to follow a four- or five-year process. We need to change the strategy and the structure as well as the culture.'

The research evidence is that the chase for shareholder value has left a trail of failures. In the US, the collapse of Enron can be traced to a corporate culture based on a single performance goal. The failure of Lehman Brothers had much to do with excessive executive rewards. In the UK, the obsession with fast returns also contributed to under-investment and the nation's poor record on competitiveness. Both dividend payments and executive rewards came to assume a greater priority over capital investment in the UK compared with competitors, even though this is rarely in the medium or longer term interest of shareholders or companies.

Such skewed priorities forced executives to concentrate less on the future than on satisfying the demands of their financial masters, bringing a corrosive impact on Britain's long-term industrial performance. In a detailed study of the impact of different investment strategies on advanced manufacturing in the UK, US, France, Germany and Japan, a Sheffield University study found that UK financiers tended to shun close long-term engagement with individual businesses to a much greater extent than elsewhere. In the UK, and to a lesser extent the US, the investment process was much more dominated by impersonal institutions obsessed with short-term returns and with little interest in the individual companies in which they invest.[328]

In continental Europe, in contrast, companies have been under less pressure for short-term performance from their shareholders and the banks that have supported them. A large chunk of Germany's banking system consists of a network of regional banks aimed at supporting the *Mittelstand*, local small and medium-sized businesses. In the UK, small firms have suffered from the increasing concentration of financial power in the large London-based boardrooms.

An empirical study of the United States found, for the period from 1973 to 2003, a negative relationship between the growth of 'financialisation'—the growing importance of financial markets—and the real economy, leading to a decline in real investment at the firm level. 'First, increased financial investment and increased financial profit opportunities may have crowded out real investment by changing the incentives of firm managers and directing funds away from real investment. Second, increased payments to the financial markets may have impeded real investment by decreasing available internal funds, shortening the planning horizons of management, and increasing uncertainty.'[329]

Driven by the desire to build big personal fortunes, the 'long term' is a phrase rarely to be heard on Wall Street and City trading floors. In the UK, domestic industry has found it difficult to get adequate funding for new start ups, innovation and expansion. When credit has been advanced to small and medium-sized business it has mostly involved excessive rates and complex terms. While the banks do continue to lend on a medium to long-term basis to some industries—such as defence and pharma-ceuticals where the fruits of investment take years to deliver a return—this is the exception. Investing in the companies of the future has become an increasingly fringe activity of finance. Britain's comparative advantage used to lie in manufacturing—now it lies in what one commentator has described as 'reckless gambling'.[330]

Short-termism is endemic to the role played by the City. Money caroms around the world at infinite speed in search of the fastest buck. Company chief executives, lured by 'golden hellos' and protected by generous pay-offs, rarely stay in their jobs long enough to see a coherent business strategy through to fruition. Business is increas-ingly geared to speed. Investment banks depend on a fast turnover of business activity and encourage change at the top. As a result, the UK (London and the South-East in particular) has too many jobs associated with financial engineering and its spin-offs—the law, accountancy and property—and too few in productive, entrepreneurial, hi-tech sectors of the economy from design and software to green technology and engineering.

Britain still has a number of world beating companies, built over decades. Rolls Royce is a high quality global player, employing 39,000 skilled workers worldwide. While James Dyson outsourced production from Wiltshire to Malaysia he has recently doubled his army of inventors, scientists and engineers to 700 in his quest for new products. Some industries—from health and the creative industries to high tech manufacturing and business services—have flourished.

The scale of the collapse in Britain's industrial base can sometimes be exaggerated. Half of the nation's exports are manufactured goods. But although the UK is still the seventh largest manufacturing nation in the world and has many successful small firms with a strong track record on innovation, its position is precarious in many key industries of the future. Because of an increasingly endemic myopia guiding investment decisions—with excessive value given to short-term over long-term returns, the nation is weak in a range of high-technology sectors especially electronics, computer software, chemicals and telecommunications. The main exceptions to this pattern—pharmaceuticals and aerospace—are both special cases, protected by a mix of regulation and patent protection while having governmental and quasi-governmental bodies as customers. Yet these sectors make up less than a tenth of FTSE 100 companies, compared with a quarter from banking and finance.

Germany, Japan and France and, to a lesser extent, the US, have a much heavier bias towards high value-added chemical and physics-based companies. This is a key reason why the UK has been sliding towards a low-wage, low value-added, lowish knowledge-based economy.

The destabilising role played by the City is well illustrated by the case of Vodafone, the telecoms conglomerate that runs the largest mobile network in the world and on most counts, a highly successful company. It was City pressure that persuaded Vodafone to embark on an aggressive expansionist policy at the end of the 1990s. Despite spending close to £200 billion on a worldwide acquisitions policy—including the buying of Mannesman—its market value had plunged to around £85 billion by 2010. While its share price hit 440 pence in the days after the deal, it had slumped to 80 pence by 2006 and had only recovered to 170 pence by early 2011. The City's relentless demands for over-performance ended up delivering disastrous returns for shareholders.

By 2010, the City, faced with a company worth a fraction of its former value, made new demands on the chief executive, Vittorio Colao, to embark on a reverse strategy of divestment—to sell its businesses in America, France and Poland, all aimed at boosting immediate returns. Although the company's previous management team had greatly overpaid for its acquisitions, breaking up a world-beating industrial giant made little long term business sense. The German, Swiss and Japanese stock-markets don't set out to dismantle their nations' biggest companies.

Short-termism is evident too in the falling length of time shares are now held, the increasing use of selling short and the increasing volatility in share price movements. Twenty years ago institutional investors such as pension funds and insurance companies were much more focused on the long term and shares were typically held for several years. According to the Bank of England, shares were held for an average of five years in the 1960s. By 2007, this had fallen to an average of seven months. Most fund managers turn over their entire portfolio in one or two years. Rapid turnover means that companies are being constantly forced to dance to the stop-go whims of transient investors, a problem compounded by the role played by hedge funds and investment banks.

The proportion of UK plc owned by hedge funds has grown from less than one per cent in the early 1990s to around 15 per cent today. Up to 70 per cent of US and 50 per cent of traded shares in London are accounted for by hedge funds and other 'high frequency traders'. They account for around 60 per cent of trading volume in high risk derivative products.[331] Hedge funds—which draw their capital mainly from wealthy individuals—grew rapidly from the millennium. Their control of global cash rose six-fold from some $450 billion in 2000 to $2600 billion in 2007, before falling back to $1850 billion in 2009.[332]

Hedge funds grew to such heights because of the 1982 repeal of the US ruling, introduced in the 1930s, that required all traded funds to be regulated by the Securities and Exchange Commission, the American equivalent of the Britain's Financial Services Authority. The repeal allowed hedge funds to escape such scrutiny.

Today there are still several thousand funds globally. In the United States, which accounts for around two-fifths of this total, hedge-funds are concentrated in upmarket New York suburbs like Greenwich, Connecticut. London is home to 450 funds—about 80 per cent of the European total—managing a combined £250 billion. Although a number of funds collapsed in the fall-out from the recession, they are still bunched in Mayfair which has become the third axis of financial power in the UK after the Square Mile and Canary Wharf. Most are highly discreet operations, based in small modern office suites, usually hidden behind little more than an inconspicuous nameplate, and rarely employing more than 30-40 people. The funds are one of the most obscure parts of the finance industry, lacking in transparency and accountability and very weakly regulated. They may be run from London and New York, but nearly all funds are registered offshore, at least a third in the Cayman Islands and a tenth in the British Virgin Islands.[333]

The richest of the London-based operators is the American born Louis Bacon who joined the ranks of the world's sterling billionaires in 2010 after increasing his fortune by 40 per cent in a single year. Bacon owns a Belgravia mansion, a 171,000 acre ranch in Colorado, a Long Island estate, a mansion in the Bahamas, a grouse moorland in Scotland and three private polo grounds. This has enabled him to move in Britain's most aristocratic circles. He is sometimes known as 'the godfather', largely because his company, Moore Capital, with investments of close to £12 billion, has achieved returns averaging close to 30 per cent since it was founded in the early 1990s.

Moore makes money for his clients, mostly individuals, and himself, by what he likes to call 'risk management', betting on the future direction of markets—equities, bond prices, currencies, commodities, debt. Sometimes he bets that prices will rise, sometimes that they will fall. Many of the more successful funds operate in a similar way, engaging in little more than speculation, though on a giant scale. Most are backed by highly sophisticated mathematically-based formulae which attempt to predict financial movements or spot a market in bonds or commodities that appear to be out of kilter. Those that get these calls right can make big money, whatever the economic conditions.

Even at the peak of the meltdown, a handful of investors chalked up some of the biggest individual payouts in the industry's history.[334] In 2009, David Tepper of Appaloosa Management, a hedge-fund based in suburban New Jersey, pocketed an estimated $4 billion for eight months work. A former Goldman Sachs trader, the 52-year old Tepper—who keeps a sculpture of a pair of testicles in his office—had taken advantage of the economic panic spreading across America to take a giant bet. When the beleaguered Wall Street banks, from Citigroup to the Bank of America, came to be bailed out by the government, Tepper's fund banked a massive profit.

Hedge funds have a highly controversial history. The industry itself defends its role on the grounds that it spots over-valued companies and currencies before others and thereby prevents bubbles occurring. While this may be true on some occasions, for the most part, the hedge fund industry has been a factor in the rise of instability both for individual companies and national economies. Funds greatly distort the reward structure in finance while enjoying a good deal of inside market knowledge which brings them huge trading advantages, advantages that have been used not for the benefit of the economy but to enrich a few thousand managers and clients.[335]

Hedge funds have been associated with a number of financial and banking shocks. In Japan in the late 1990s they were called *hagetako fando* ('vulture funds'). In 2005, Franz Müntefering, the head of Germany's SDP party, dubbed them 'a swarm of locusts'. In the US they have been likened to 'rabid dogs'. In the summer of 1997, hedge funds mounted a series of speculative raids against a number of South-East Asian currencies which the funds believed were greatly over-valued. While the funds made big money, they helped deepen the economic turbulence facing the countries concerned, from South Korea to Indonesia. Mahathir Mohamad, the Malaysian Prime Minister, called them 'rogue speculators' for helping to precipitate the crisis. What had been created was a financial system in which emerging countries could suffer great floods of 'hot money' followed by great droughts, hardly a sound basis for stability or growth.

A year later, the largest of America's hedge funds—the Greenwich-based Long Term Capital Management—had to be bailed out by a consortium of Wall Street banks to the tune of $3.6 billion to save the fund. It had been brought to its knees by a mix of poor investments and massive over-leverage. Leveraging offers potentially higher profits but only by greatly increasing the risk. As traders describe the risk, funds can 'eat like chickens but shit like elephants'. Leveraged one hundred times, LTCM had been turned into an elephant. It was a high profile warning that was, apparently, quickly ignored. Levels of leverage across the financial system continued to mount adding to the risk that eventually brought the global economy to its knees.

Hedge funds are specialists at targeting companies in short-term difficulties, enabling them to make a quick profit by betting that their share price will fall. They do this by 'shorting'. This involves borrowing shares and then selling them in the hope that they will fall in value and can be bought back at a cheaper price when the time comes to return them. Companies which issue profit warnings greater than City expectations can get hammered out of all proportion to the scale of the warning and a company's actual prospects. When the 'low cost' British airline Easyjet announced a gloomy forecast in the Spring of 2004, 110 million shares changed hands in a matter of hours, plunging its share price by 30 per cent. A week before, Nokia had been give the same treatment. 'It shows how distortion, manipulation and the use of overwhelming force have become endemic in the market', wrote the *Evening Standard*'s Anthony Hilton: 'Hedge funds and the prime brokerage activities of investment banks are turning the place into a casino where genuine long-term investors and companies are overwhelmed by their superior financial resources. If this continues, the stock market is stripped of its usefulness and becomes as much value to society as a high-stakes poker game.'[336]

Hedge funds have also played a controversial role in a number of takeover bids. A US hedge fund provided a key part of the financing for the US businessman, Malcolm Glazer's bid for Manchester United. Cadbury's fell to Kraft in 2010 largely because its shareholders—

THE COST OF INEQUALITY

many of which were hedge funds—smelt a quick profit. Indeed, hedge-funds upped their stake in the company from 5 to 30 per cent during the takeover battle. As Lord Mandelson, the then Secretary of State for Business, Innovation and Skills and hardly an enemy of business, complained: 'In the case of Cadbury and Kraft it is hard to ignore the fact that the fate of a company with a long history and many tens of thousands of employees was decided by people who had not owned the company a few weeks earlier, and probably had no intention of owning it a few weeks later.'[337]

Funds often take a punt on the outcome of such deals, and then have a vested interest one way or the other. In some cases, it is claimed that funds buy shares in order to swing the vote on a merger or takeover proposal, not to further the interests of the company, but to manipulate the share price in the direction of an earlier bet.[338]

Investment banks, awash with profits, also started to set up internal hedge funds, essentially a way of gambling with their own money. From the middle to the end of the 1990s, a number of banks—from Salomon Brothers and Goldman Sachs to Merrill Lynch and Drexel Burnham, Lambert—started to operate their own proprietary trading arms using the firm's own rather than their customers' money and investing mostly at the high risk end of the market. In this way profits were siphoned off to finance takeovers, invest in hedge funds or bet on commodities and currency movements. Such activity undoubtedly added considerable risk to the system as a whole. Nick Leeson, for example, was a key member of Barings proprietary trading team and at least some of the money he was investing came from the proprietary trading budget. As the investment banks were very lightly regulated, the authorities mostly had little idea about the scale or character of such activity.

Such trading has become highly attractive to the banks. While they get paid a commission from managing money from clients, they pocket all the gains from managing their own money. For a while, with market conditions especially favourable to such activity, these accounts generated substantial profits, while those running these highly secretive and opaque accounts would end up at the top end of banking salaries. Mark McGoldrick, nicknamed 'Goldfinger', who ran a 'special-situations' fund for Goldman Sachs—invested in a variety of obscure and illiquid investments, from Japanese golf courses to Thai auto loans—earned $70 million in 2006, but left a year later to set up his own hedge fund.

The investment banks have always been highly guarded about the role of such trading. Although they have also claimed that the desks played a minor role, they accounted for a significant proportion of revenue at the height of the financial boom. In the case of Goldman Sachs, a study by the University of Massachusetts found that such trading accounted for some 64 per cent of the bank's net revenue in 2006 and 2007.[339]

Another key way in which the increasing power of the City has been bad news for other sectors of the economy has been through the growing and to most, disproportionate, rewards available in finance. Just as London became a magnet for the money of the world's new super-rich, the City became a magnet for the country's best graduates. A job at one of the new glitzy investment banks offered money along with status and fast-living, especially as the City pay premium started to rise after Big Bang. Industry seemed dull, tame and very poorly paid by comparison with manipulating and growing other people's money. In the 1970s students from the country's leading business schools wanted to go into big industry. In the early 1980s their preference was for consultancy. By the end of the decade, it was finance. Michael Lewis, the trader who wrote of his experiences at the American bank, Salomon Brothers, in the best-selling *Liar's Poker*, tells the story of a talk he gave to students at the London School of Economics in 1986. Lewis had obtained an MSc in economics at the school and had joined Salomon's two years earlier.

When he arrived at the lecture hall to talk about the obscure workings of the bond market, he expected a tiny group of earnest students. Instead it was full. 'When one seedy-looking fellow who was guzzling a beer in the back shouted that I was a parasite, he was booed down. After the talk I was besieged not with abuse, and not with questions about the bond market, but with questions about how to get a job at Salomon Brothers.'[340]

The pull of the City speeded up from the 1990s as finance started to develop ever more esoteric financial products like derivatives. These products were mostly built around the predictions of the fiendishly complex mathematical formula developed by very highly paid mathematicians, economists and physicists. These models, it was claimed, could predict with great accuracy the future path of a whole range of financial variables from equity and commodity prices to interest rates and house prices. According to their architects, by anticipating and controlling the level of risk, finance could increase the level of liquidity in the markets and improve the level of efficiency with which resources were allocated, thus enabling a higher level of national and world economic activity.

This claim seemed to be vindicated when two hedge fund partners, Myron Scholes and Robert Merton, won the Nobel Prize for economics in 1997. Their Greenwich-based firm, Long Term Capital Management had been founded by John Meriwether, a former highly successful bond trader at Salomon, Lewis's boss and widely believed to be the inspiration for the *Bonfire of the Vanities*, Tom Wolf's 1980s novel of Wall Street excess. For a while the heavily-leveraged operation grew to be one of the most lucrative of the American hedge funds.

Even when their award-winning formula failed and LTCM collapsed in 1998, nearly bringing Wall Street down with it, the modelling and recruitment continued. The best American and British PhD econometricians, mathematicians and physicists continued to pour into Wall Street and the City, where they could earn huge multiples of the salaries on offer in industry or academia. Their highly paid role—to find financial, currency and pricing anomalies that could be exploited. Although there has always been a sniffy attitude in the UK towards 'trade and industry' amongst the British educational elites, the lack of graduates for the productive sector of the economy gradually started to ring alarm bells. A report by the economic forecasting group, the ITEM Club, in 2004, pinned some of the blame for the poor performance of the manufacturing sector in the UK on the success of finance in sucking in the pick of Britain's graduates. 'The City is like the cuckoo in the nest, growing ever larger and crowding out sectors that might otherwise be viable.'

That an overreaching financial sector has been to the detriment of other parts of the economy including small businesses, advanced manufacturing and parts of the regions came to be a view increasingly widely held. According to another account of Wall Street, 'The finance sector attracts a big chunk of the smartest, most hard-working and most talented individuals. That represents a huge human capital opportunity cost to society and the economy at large.'[341]

In March 2007, just before the walls of the global financial dyke finally burst, Sir John Gieve, Deputy Governor of the Bank of England, warned that while the growth of financial markets has had many positive aspects, 'we have seen renewed worries that London's prominence and the wealth it attracts and generates may be distorting the broader economy—that it may be more a cuckoo in the nest than a golden goose.'[342]

10

WALKING AWAY WITH GIANT JACKPOTS

Debenhams is Britain's third largest department store. First opened as a draper's shop in Central London's Wigmore Street in 1813, it progressed to department store status when it acquired its prime Oxford Street site in 1919. Over the next 80 years it expanded to 150 outlets. Although the chain has never risen to blue-chip ranks, it has been a successful, growing and profitable company for close to 100 years.

In 2003, it joined the growing list of public companies to be snapped up by private buyers. Britain's private equity houses, or leveraged buyout firms as they are known in the US, are essentially asset supermarkets and have become increasingly powerful players in the last decade. Nearly always registered offshore, these houses target vulnerable or poor-performing public companies, take them off the stock market into private ownership and away from public scrutiny.

With its strong asset base, Debenhams was a sufficiently lucrative catch that it became the target of a bidding war between a number of private equity houses in the summer of 2003. The war was won by a consortium comprising the British firm, CVC Capital, and the American companies Merrill Lynch Global Private Equity and David Bonderman's Texas Pacific Group. The consortium—Baroness Retail Ltd—outbid the rivals, eventually paying £1.72 billion for the chain.

Private equity has become one of the principal routes to personal wealth. As well as Debenhams, Bhs and Arcadia, former UK public companies taken private since 2000 include the AA, HMV, Harvey Nichols, Hamley's, Homebase, Tommy Hilfinger, Little Chef, Somerfield and Halfords. To date, the biggest to have succumbed are the former FTSE 1000 companies, Alliance Boots and EMI. In the early 1990s, private equity employed a twentieth of the private sector workforce. Today it accounts for a fifth, an expansion made possible by the burgeoning financial surpluses of the past two decades.

The biggest British names behind the private equity boom of the last decade have been Permira, Apax and CVC. Private equity companies obtain their capital mainly from pension funds, insurance companies, banks, endowments, foundations and increasingly, the privately wealthy. The partners running the firms, who mostly prefer to remain out of the limelight, not always successfully, include Damon Buffini of Permira, Sir Ronald Cohen of Apax and Mike Smith of CVC. These partners are so well paid—at a 'gravity-defying' rate, according to the *Economist* magazine—they have made colossal fortunes in just a few years.[343]

They make their money largely by charging much higher fees to investors than those of other fund managers. In the UK, private equity firms operate what is known as a 'two plus twenty' fee policy. This involves an annual management fee of 2 per cent on the funds invested and an additional—typically 20 per cent—share of profits on the fund.

This profit—or 'carry' as it is known—is generated in a number of ways, particularly from the sale of existing company assets, squeezing costs and suppliers, re-ordering finances to extract as much cash as possible and the re-selling of the company at a later date. Until 2008, private equity firms were able to exploit special tax privileges which meant that partners—who take their profits in the form of capital gains rather than income—would pay tax on these gains at a much lower rate than that paid by others. The industry gossip was that private equity partners often paid no more than 4-5 per cent in tax on their multi-million pound annual incomes.[344]

While such tax advantages passed mostly unnoticed during the economic boom years, they eventually became the subject of a public outcry. As Nicholas Ferguson, chairman of SVG Partners and one of the early founders of private equity, put it in June 2007: 'Any commonsense person would say that a highly paid private equity executive paying less tax than a cleaning lady or other low paid workers can't be right.'

Labour liked to boast that it had created the most lenient tax system in the world for new businesses. But the revelations about the way the tax rules were being exploited forced the Chancellor, Alistair Darling, to bring private equity partners broadly into line with other taxpayers. This was achieved only by reducing the overall tax rate on capital gains from 40 to 18 per cent, a figure later increased to 28 per cent by the new Conservative Chancellor, George Osborne, in his first budget. Although this brought all capital gains tax payers into line, it still left a major discrepancy in the tax system. Those who earn money from capital, which includes groups like buy-to-let landlords, are still being charged at a lower rate than salaried staff who have to pay tax at 40 per cent if they earn above the higher rate threshold.

Private equity is even more significant in the US, and the source of some of America's biggest fortunes. In 2006 private-equity buyouts—with $156 billion of new capital to invest—accounted for a quarter of all acquisitions. Such was its firepower, the global buyout industry secured $400 billion to be invested in 2007. With leverage, that represented up to $1500 billion in potential buying power—enough to buy McDonalds 35 times over.

Companies that are privately owned in the US include the $88 billion agri-business Cargill, the $74 billion United States Postal Service and the largest of them all, the $98 billion diversified manufacturer, Koch Industries. Koch is owned by two brothers, both multi-billionaires, who between them have poured $100 million into think tanks and foundations campaigning against climate change legislation—Koch has been named as one of the top ten air polluters in the US—and against a number of Obama Administration policies, from health-care reform to the economic-stimulus programme.

One of the oldest and biggest US private equity players is KKR, the firm behind the buying and break-up of RJR Nabisco. It owns a great diversity of companies—from Beijing and Johannesburg to Caracas and Bangkok. It acquired Alliance Boots in 2007 in a deal worth $12 billion. Heavily funded by a range of bank loans, from JP Morgan to the Royal Bank of Scotland, Alliance Boots was the first FTSE 100 company to be taken private, and then based not in the UK, but in Gibraltar. In the US, as in the UK, the biggest private equity titans have been able to extract huge fees from deals, entirely by restructuring existing companies, enough to take them close to the top of the American rich lists.

What the private equity barons have done is to use the global abundance of cheap money to find a way of scooping a giant jackpot, 'life-changing amounts of money' according to corporate analysts.[345]

The process of profit taking usually takes little more than 2-4 years of financial and managerial restructuring. The companies acquired are treated essentially like a cash machine, first to pay off the debt, and then to reward those who financed the deal, irrespective of the consequences for the future of business, staff or the local workforce.

Debenhams is a classic example of the way this works. The acquiring consortium put up around a third of the cost of purchase in equity and borrowed the rest to finance the deal. Although this was a fairly aggressive level of leverage, it was far from unusual. The deal was struck well before the credit bubble at a time when the banks were so flush with cash they would compete with each other to lend on such schemes. Not only does such leveraging enable private equity firms' cash reserves to go much further, it brings big tax savings. As the interest on the debt can be offset against profits for tax purposes the high levels of borrowing in private equity have often reduced corporation tax payments to zero. Debenhams—which paid corporation tax of £40 million the year before it was taken over—stopped paying corporation tax altogether in the time it was under private ownership. Other purchased companies—from the AA to Boots—have enjoyed sharp reductions in their corporate tax bills.

Having acquired the chain, the consortium installed a new top management team and operated it as a private company for nearly three years. The consortium paid off the purchase loan within two years by the sale of the stores' property portfolio. This was then leased back greatly increasing the stores' rental costs. It also extracted a number of cash sums through several refinancing deals.

The effect of this financial restructuring was to saddle the group with some £2 billion worth of debt. It had mortgaged itself heavily while losing its principal asset—its property base. Such 'asset-stripping'—selling assets to generate a short-term cash flow—is the usual route by which the acquisition debt is paid off. Because of this newly acquired debt burden, the board was forced to cut back sharply on capital spending on improving the quality of stores. Cutbacks in capital spending is a relatively common feature of the 'private equity effect'.

Debenhams was sold back to the stock market in 2006 for a share price of 195 pence. At the beginning of 2011, the price had sunk to 60 pence, a massive loss in shareholder value. One detailed academic study of the company has concluded that Debenhams became a 'much more fragile company than it was before the public to private transaction'.[346] The fall in the share price was mainly the result of its greatly weakened financial situation arising from the restructuring and added debt burden during private ownership. It was a pretty epic hangover which accounted for the company's underperformance after it was refloated.

While Debenhams has floundered and its shareholders suffered heavy losses, the group that bought it more than tripled the value of its original investment over 30 months ('abnormal returns' according to one academic account) through a mix of refinancing, cost cutting, reduced capital spending, property sales and the proceeds from the sale of nearly two-thirds of the company in 2006.[347]

The industry claims that its principal aim is to add value by improving the performance of companies. There is no evidence of this in the case of Debenhams. The history of the deal suggests that the consortium was only ever interested in a quick profit. 'The holding period was extremely short [thirty months] and reminds of the "buy-it, strip it, flip it" description often cited by private equity detractors', is how the academic study described the deal. 'There are strong hints to suggest that the private equity backers were only interested in short term returns and tried to extract as much value as possible, to the detriment of the longer term financial health of the company.'[348]

The return made on the re-engineering of Debenhams was high, but by no means exceptional in the world of structural refinancing. The industry delivered some racy returns for both investors and partners before the onset of the credit crunch. Texas, for example, boasted an annual average rate of return of 37 per cent between 2001 and 2004, compared with an annual return of only 3.4 per cent on mid-market funds.

Whether the private equity boom has been in the longer term interest of the companies—and the wider economy—has been the subject of bitter debate. While the industry claims to have a good record on managing the companies it acquires, on investment, jobs and efficiency, the evidence is that this process of short-term industrial and financial restructuring has had a very mixed effect on both the American and British economies, much of it negative.

Some poorly performing companies—such as the restaurant chain Pizza Express and the *moules-et-frites* chain, Belgo—have been made leaner and fitter, adding value through better financial discipline and improved management. In some cases, companies have been saved by a judicious takeover. Others have been well run.

But many takeovers have had damaging consequences. Moreover, the process of restructuring always takes place behind a veil of secrecy. Privately owned companies have few of the disclosure obligations of public companies. It doesn't have to be like this. Melrose, for example, is a public company specialising in turning round poorly performing engineering companies and has a good track record in improving the value of companies it has acquired, without the secrecy or leverage typical of private equity.

Few private equity companies have been held for longer than a handful of years, inviting the criticism that the takeovers are not there for the long term and mostly have little commitment to a company's staff and community, while exacerbating the short-termism that has long dogged the British economy. The evidence is that in most cases, the exceptional returns have been generated more by the extraction of *existing* than by the creation of *new* value with the inevitable result that the takeover targets have ended up financially weaker.

Indeed, the lion's share of these high returns have come not from improved efficiency and management but from the multiplier effect on returns enabled by financial 'leverage'. Take, for example, a private equity firm that bought a company for £1 billion and borrowed 70 per cent of the cost, a typical level of debt on many early deals. If it sells the company three years later for say £1.3 billion (a typical rise during the early 2000s), it would have made £300,000 merely by investing the same amount, a 100 per cent return. In the case of the fourteen most successful deals between 2005 and 2007, ones which yielded exceptionally high returns, as much as a half of these yields came from financial engineering, almost a third from the stock market boom, and less than a fifth from improved management.[349]

Once debt leveraging is stripped out, the returns achieved suggest 'mixed and in some cases, even mediocre results'. According to a study by Manchester Business School, the main impact of private equity has been the use of financial engineering to 'rearrange claims for the benefit of those who own equity, and ensure value capture by a managerial elite of general partners who run funds and senior managers who run the operating businesses invested in.'[350]

While the architects of public-to-private deals have walked away with giant jackpots, companies have mostly been stripped of their key assets, especially property portfolios, and landed with heavy debt burdens. In others high returns have been achieved by squeezing suppliers and big lay-offs of staff. Some deals have failed completely. Just how risky to staff and customers private ownership can be is starkly illustrated by the collapse of Britain's fourth largest retail chain, the department store, Allders. The chain was founded in 1862 and grew to 45 outlets in areas as diverse as Croydon, Coventry and Oxford. In 2003, the chain was taken private by Terry

Green, formerly chief executive of Bhs but who had fallen out badly with the store's owner, Sir Philip Green. He hoped that taking Allders private would enable him to emulate his former boss and enter the ranks of super-rich retailers. In the event, Green and most of the staff lost their jobs, and Allders' pension fund—with 3500 members—was left with a big £70 million black hole.[351]

The high returns enjoyed initially by the private equity business model were also heavily dependent on the exceptional economic conditions of the time—a mix of easy and cheap credit and rising asset prices. While these artificial conditions brought huge leverage-enhanced profits from the millennium, even notional returns have slumped sharply in more recent years. There were plenty of warnings. In 2006, the Financial Services Authority declared that private equity companies were 'increasingly being financed ... with a capital structure that is unsustainable in the long term.'[352]

Many of the companies taken over in the mid-2000s are now in danger of drowning in a sea of debt. In 2007, the year the credit crunch struck, the world's largest banks had committed some $300 to $400 billion in loans for deals that were in the process of being concluded.[353] Many of these were to come unstuck. In 2010, one of the UK's leading firms, Candover Investments, announced it was being forced to wind itself up following the heavy debt problems incurred in a number of its investments. Founded in 1980, Candover's investments had included Jarvis Hotels, Bourne Leisure, owners of Butlin Holiday camps and the luxury yacht maker, Ferretti. At the peak of its success it had even made a failed bid for the Telegraph Group. According to a study by Moody's of the top 10 largest US private equity buy-outs completed at the height of the boom between 2004 and 2007, six had already defaulted on at least some of their debts by the end of 2008. The report also found that private equity firms invest virtually no capital in the companies they buy.

The growth of financial surpluses, the demands for a quick buck and the growing divorce between finance and productive activity has had a powerful influence on the fate of many British, American and international companies. The prospect of lucrative fees and abnormal returns became one of the principal motivations for the surge in corporate restructuring of the last 20 years, enabling financiers, bankers and hedge fund operators to march to the top of the rich lists alongside industrial, technology and retail entrepreneurs often by cynically extracting existing value from the companies they restructured.

Forbes started its annual list of America's 400 wealthiest families in 1982. The list was and still is limited to 400 names because 'the Four Hundred' was a familiar shorthand term for high society during the 'Gilded Age' in 1870s America, the period when unprecedented fortunes were being accumulated in railways, oil and steel. Mrs William B. Astor, the wife of one of the richest of the group of multimillionaires, used to hold regular social events for those 'who matter' and only 400 people could fit into her personal ballroom on New York's Fifth Avenue.

The composition of the top 400 has changed sharply over time. The first 1982 list contained no hedge fund or private equity barons. These were industries about to be born. Gradually their founders have worked their way into and up the list. The premier division of American billionaires (the top 50) is still dominated by new technology tycoons—from Bill Gates and Paul Allen of Microsoft to Larry Ellison of Oracle and Larry Page and Sergey Brin who invented Google. The top 50 also includes retailers like the Walton family who own Wal-Mart and Jeff Bezos of Amazon along with manufacturers like the confectioners, Forest and John Mars.

The next group of 150, in contrast, is riddled with Wall Street financiers and hedge fund and private equity operators who have made their fortunes through the financial re-engineering of existing companies. They include Henry Kravis, one of the co-founders of KKR in 1976—worth $3.4 billion, one of his fellow co-founders, George Roberts—worth $3.2 billion, and David Rubenstein, co-founder of the Carlyle group.[354] These have acquired fortunes well beyond even the most generous remuneration packages offered by banks and public companies.

The trend in the UK has been very similar. Here, it was the *Sunday Telegraph* which first considered publishing a contemporary British list of the super-rich. In 1983, Ivan Fallon, the paper's then City editor, and a colleague, Dr Philip Beresford, were having lunch at Claridge's with Tiny Rowland, the controversial head of Lonrho, and once the owner of the *Observer* newspaper. When Rowland suggested a '*Forbes*' list for Britain, Fallon and Beresford set to work by phoning potential candidates. One of those contacted, the Duke of Devonshire and one of Britain's biggest landowners, summoned the paper's editor, John Thompson, to his club, White's, where he was suitably rebuked. The Duke of Atholl, also contacted by the paper, made it clear to the paper's then owner, Lord Hartwell, that he could forget shooting grouse across the duke's 147,000 Scottish acres if his name appeared in the list. The idea was quickly dropped.

Some years later, Fallon and Beresford both moved to the *Sunday Times*. The paper's owner, Rupert Murdoch, and the then editor, Andrew Neil, were less fearful of establishment threats. Nevertheless, the lesson had been learned and the work began in total secrecy. The list was compiled through secondary sources rather than direct contact and other staff were kept in the dark. The first the entrants knew of it was when the *Sunday Times* duly published its first list of the 200 richest Britons in 1989. It contained a few blunders, such as including a bankrupt and someone who had died eight months earlier, but proved a great boost to circulation.

Initially the annual ritual of being ranked and evaluated by a bunch of newspaper journalists did not go down well with many of those listed. On publication of the first 1989 list, the *Sunday Times* received all sorts of threats over inclusion and accuracy. Many came from the landowning aristocracy who appeared to prefer their finances to remain hidden from the public gaze.

Others have been less reticent. The porn king David Sullivan wrote to the *Sunday Times* enclosing his accounts and declaring himself grossly undervalued in the 1990 list at £60 million. In 1991, he was upgraded to £100 million. Peter de Savary, the property developer, has made the occasional appearance and likes to make phone calls beginning, 'Hi, number 65, this is number 44.'

The *Sunday Times* list is highly revealing about the changing character of British top society. The first reliable list (of 400) published in 1990 contained a number who had made money in the post-war decades including property developer Harry Hyams, the food retailer, Garfield Weston and the advertising supremos, the Saatchi brothers. Nevertheless, it was dominated by landowning aristocrats and the heirs of nineteenth century industrialists like the glass-making Pilkington family, Lord Levehulme of Lever Brothers and the Earl of Iveagh, scion of the founders of the Guinness empire.

Over the next 20 years, as in the United States, the composition of the richest was to change. The proportion of landowners and industrialists with inherited wealth slipped.[355] Although there were some financiers in the 1990 list—from the break-up king, James Goldsmith to the legendary financier Tiny Rowland—the number of City bankers and financial deal-makers has been rising sharply. In 2010, nearly a fifth of the richest 1000—including 51 hedge fund owners—made their money through banking and finance whereas only 11 per cent made it in industry or engineering. Thirteen partners at the American investment bank, Goldman Sachs—famously described by *Rolling Stone* magazine as a "vampire squid wrapped around the face of humanity"—made it into the top 1000.[356]

A certain level of finance-led industrial restructuring that forges more competitive and sustainable companies is inevitable and necessary. Mergers sometimes make sound business sense, while some companies need stronger management. Economies have to evolve and adjust as some companies fail, new ones emerge and the success stories of the past are overtaken by new techno-logical developments and the industries of the future.

Innovation is the lifeblood of economic dynamism and inevitably involves some pain or 'creative destruction' as the Austrian economist, Joseph Schumpeter, described it in *Capitalism, Socialism and Democracy* published in 1942.

It is a process of change that inevitably brings winners and losers. If the industrial restructuring of the last thirty years had been driven by business innovation aimed at improving productivity and long-run performance, creating new jobs and wealth along the way, the dislocation involved would have been defensible. But the evidence is that the business restructuring of recent times has been poorly associated with creating greater dynamism and building the productive strength of the economy. Rather it has been heavily driven by the goal of higher share prices and short-term financial gains for the few, aims which are often the enemy of successful innovation. While some deals have improved long-term company performance, the overall impact of the boom in deal-making has been very mixed, with a significant proportion having an overall negative impact on the fortunes of the companies involved.

Finance has played a central role in the increasing con-centration of income and wealth largely because of the re-distributive impact of much City-powered industrial activity. Britain's financial and business elite have found ways of scooping up both a larger chunk of existing wealth and of the proceeds of growth in the economy. Some of this growth is down to efficiency gains stemming from some financial and industrial restructur-ing. Yet while such activity has delivered towering rewards, the evidence is that much of the explosion of deal-making—from private equity business to wider acquisitions—has a poor record when it comes to improving efficiency and adding economic value. As Bank of England Executive Director, Andy Haldane, has shown, the gross value added of the financial sector in recent decades has been massively exaggerated.[357]

Instead, a good deal of financial business has had an important side-effect, that of transferring *existing* wealth, the stock of industrial and business assets that has been carefully built over long periods of time. This process of transfer is at the heart of much financial activity of recent times.

The chase for personal enrichment—a central driver of all private enterprise economies—was once more closely related to wider economic progress. In the last thirty years, that link has been largely broken. Whether today's super-rich have been able to acquire such giant fortunes because of a new age of super-skill or because they have been able to rig the system in their interests has been much debated. Certainly, some of the personal wealth boom of the last two decades is down to exceptional wealth and job-creating entrepreneurial activity which has added to productive capacity. The founders of Facebook, Google and Yahoo have presided over a profound and entirely positive business and social revolution. Some venture capitalist companies have a strong record in encouraging the formation of new products and services. There are thousands of successful modern entrepreneurs who have become rich by founding new companies, inventing new products or improving business processes. They include the British inventor and engineer, James Dyson, the owner of the Swedish global Ikea chain, Ingvar Kamprad, and Tim

Waterstone who modernised bookselling in the UK by setting up his national book chain using a £1000 redundancy cheque from WH Smiths.

Each of these has become rich by creating new wealth, business and jobs. They are a group that have rightly been defined as 'the deserving rich', a group 'who deserve their hard-earned places, those who, through a mix of exceptional skill, effort and risk-taking, have contributed to increasing the size of the cake by creating new wealth and in ways which benefit others as well as themselves. Most opinion would regard them as "deserving" of exceptional rewards.' Yet the evidence is that an increasing proportion of today's super-rich fall into the category of the 'undeserving rich', a group 'who rig the system to enrich themselves by unfairly grabbing a larger size of the cake at the expense of someone else.'[358]

The World Bank economist, Branko Milanovic, has used a similar distinction between what he calls 'good' and 'bad inequality'.[359] Personal fortunes that arise from exceptional personal risk-taking, innovation and merit are examples of good inequality. Today, most of the wealth gap is arguably the product of bad inequality.

Although there are plenty of individual examples of the modern tycoon taking big personal financial risks to help improve productive potential and spread opportunities, a growing proportion of trading activities, big business deals and accountancy practices of recent times have involved less a process of value creation that would have increased economic strength, and more a diversion and change of ownership of existing value and wealth. Many of today's business and financial oligarchy have used their growing economic muscle to seize a larger share of the national and global cake for themselves. Far from being legitimate rewards for unprecedented success, runaway executive pay, soaring Wall Street and City fees and record bonuses have often been the product of this process of diversion.

All mergers and acquisitions involve a transfer of ownership, a rearrangement of existing wealth and sometimes value creation as well. But the winners from industrial and financial restructuring and most forms of speculative activity have been almost entirely confined to the small business and financial elite controlling the processes. This is a group that can be seen in many ways as modern day *rentiers*—people who let their fortunes grow not by getting their hands dirty, or through the sweat and risk of creating new products or growing existing firms but by skimming off existing wealth—a group Keynes once dismissed as 'functionless investors'. The losers from this skimming process have mostly been weaker nations, staff, small shareholders and suppliers and taxpayers.

This process of wealth transfer has occurred in a variety of ways. The world's dictators from Africa to the Middle East have used their power to grow rich off the back of their country's natural stores of mineral wealth. Other extreme examples include the myriad business scandals—from Robert Maxwell's raid on the Mirror staff's pension fund to jailed financier Peter Clowes fraudulent savings scheme—with tycoons lining their own pockets by fleecing staff and customers. When Barings was brought to its knees by the rogue derivatives trader, Nick Leeson, in 1994, the funds to finance his dealing had been provided by small savers who had subscribed to a bond issue issued by the bank. The bondholders lost everything.

While there is nothing new about rogue businessmen, the deregulation of finance became something of a charter for abuse. The last twenty years of 'self-regulation' have been riddled with examples of the high level mis-selling of financial products, ones that have caught a majority of the population at some stage. These include the mis-selling of personal pensions, endowment mortgages and precipice bonds. Most savings schemes have come with excessive and often hidden costs. A report by David Pitt-Watson, chair of Hermes Focus Asset Management, showed that up to 40 per cent of the accumulated value of a private pension in Britain is lost in fees, one of the highest charging rates in the developed world.[360]

No other industry is allowed to operate the commission structures that characterise the finance profession. Although there has been nothing explicitly illegal about much of this activity, and no executives have been prosecuted, the pension and savings scandals of the last twenty years have enriched financial and insurance company executives at the expense of millions of smaller investors in a transfer of wealth from customers to executives.

In the United States, the fund management industry has been revealed time and again to be 'skimming off' value from investors. In 1999, stock analysts employed by investment banks were found to be deliberately plugging technology stocks knowing them to be over-valued. In its issue of May 14, 2001, *Fortune* magazine carried a picture of Mary Meeker—a superstar analyst with Morgan

Stanley—on its cover with the headline 'Can we ever trust Wall Street again?' Henry Blodget, an internet stock analyst at Merrill Lynch and one of the most enthusiastic promoters of dotcom shares, continued to make wild predictions of future share values of companies like Amazon to clients in 1999 and 2000 even when the bubble was at its most overblown. He was later revealed to have described the very stocks he was promoting as 'junk' and 'crap' in internal e-mails.[361]

What had been exposed was that much of the equities research establishment was essentially corrupt, talking up companies as long as they put juicy investment banking contracts their way. Wall Street firms were in effect touting tech stocks without revealing that they were collecting investment banking fees for selling them. Few of the Wall Street giants appeared to be giving objective advice. Ten major financial houses, from Goldman Sachs to Lehman Brothers, later paid a collective fine of $1.4 billion imposed by the US regulators for feeding misleading stock market research to investors to drum up business and fees.[362]

'The world's largest skimming operation' is how one republican senator from Illinois described the American mutual fund industry at a 2003 Senate hearing into abusive trading practices. He went on to describe the $7000 billion business as a 'trough from which fund managers, brokers and other insiders are steadily siphoning off an excessive slice of the nation's household, college and retirement savings.'

Many of the big American business scandals of the early 2000s involved a mix of wealth transfer and destruction largely caused by their executives' obsession with becoming super-rich. When the string of giant companies—from Enron to WorldCom—collapsed, it was because their bosses had been taking massive risks with their companies in order to build their own personal fortunes. Enron, WorldCom and Tyco were brought to their knees by a series of accountancy tricks used to siphon off corporate wealth to a handful of executives, leaving tens of thousands of employees losing their jobs, health care plans and pensions.

As these bankrupt companies were heading for the rocks, the top executives often continued to try and further enrich themselves—quietly exercising their stock options in the weeks before their companies collapsed. Gary Winnick, chairman of the communications company Global Crossing, the international fibre optic network operator, sold shares worth a staggering $734 million just before his company went under. These once publicly feted men were lining their pockets in full awareness that their employees and small investors were about to be stuffed.[363] One critic described the cashing in of share options at the time as a 'titanic redistribution of wealth achieved by corporate leaders'.[364]

The abuse of the market in poorly regulated products was spectacularly revealed by the case of the American hedge fund boss John Paulson. In 2007, Paulson clocked a profit of $3.7 billion in one year through a highly controversial deal that correctly predicted the collapse of derivatives linked to sub-prime mortgages. Paulson was betting that the mortgages would fail.

It later emerged that Goldman Sachs, the investment bank handling the deal, had sold the mortgage-backed security—largely a pool of sub-prime mortgages called

Abacus—onto unsuspecting clients in full knowledge that if Paulson was right these customers would make huge losses. The losses helped bankrupt the German Bank IKB and cost the Royal Bank of Scotland, and the British taxpayer, close to £600 million. Paulson, with Goldman Sachs, was deliberately creating toxic assets in order to profit from their failure, effectively a massive institutional transfer of wealth. Goldman Sachs was later fined $550 million—the largest such fine in history, $250 million to be returned to investors and $300 million paid to the U.S. Treasury.

In a good deal of the finance-driven deal-making of recent times, companies, their staff and shareholders have been treated as lottery tickets, to be manipulated by executives or to be bought and sold at will to the highest bidder. Take the case of the finance-led acquisition boom of the last fifteen years. Its supporters say this has been a sign of a healthy economy, providing necessary restructuring while keeping management on their toes through the threat of takeover. The reality is rather different. Once the takeover game played a largely productive role in the efficient allocation of capital resources, but those days are largely gone. While some mergers have led to more dynamic companies and added value, most deals have involved a process of upward wealth transfer, often as a direct result of extensive disruption to workforces from changed working conditions to loss of jobs.

Indeed, shedding jobs has been a central objective of such deals, necessary to pay for the costs incurred and to drive the promised productivity gains. When the insurance giant Aviva paid £1.1 billion for RAC in 2005, it led to the shedding of 1700 jobs at the car rescue firm.

A year later, the merger of Boots and Alliance UniChem involved the loss of at least 2250 jobs at Boots. When a coalition of private equity investors, including KKR, took over German telecom company Tenovis in 2000, they reportedly laid off 2500 of the 8000 workers and forced some of the remaining workers to accept a 12.5 percent paycut in exchange for the right to keep working. KKR bought the company for $400 million, and sold it for $635 million a few years later.

When the American firm Kraft bought Cadbury in 2010, it immediately reneged on a commitment, made before the takeover was signed, to keep open Cadbury's plant at Somerdale in Bristol and save 400 jobs. The merger led to the loss of 150 jobs at Cadbury's head office in Uxbridge. While workers on the factory floor faced new uncertainties over their futures, Todd Stitzer, the Cadbury chief executive, received about £20 million in cash and shares, and Henry Udow, the chief legal officer, close to £8 million. Shortly after the takeover, Irene Rosenfeld, the chief executive of Kraft Foods, was voted the second most important woman in the world—after US first lady, Michelle Obama—by *Forbes*.

Kraft is no stranger to the 'zap labour' rule. After it bought another British chocolate company, Terry's, in 1993, it rationalised its European confectionery operations, with the loss of over 2500 jobs, nearly a tenth of the company's European workforce. In 2005, despite earlier promises, it closed Terry's factory at York—where it made the chocolate orange—with the loss of 316 jobs. Production was moved to cheaper facilities in Sweden, Belgium, Poland and Slovakia.

Many deals have failed spectacularly, leading to both

wealth transfer and destruction. The merger of AOL and Time Warner in 2001 led to some of the largest losses in corporate history. The Royal Bank of Scotland's takeover of ABM Amro in 2007 was to have disastrous consequences for the bank, its staff, shareholders and customers and the British taxpayer.

One study of the impact of recent mergers in the UK, US and continental Europe concluded that 'shareholders of acquirers experience wealth losses on average or at best break even... The odds of positive and significant value creation for acquirer shareholders may even be less than 50 per cent, which is what you would get with the toss of a fair coin.' Another study found that two-thirds of deals destroy shareholder value.[365] In an analysis of 200 major European deals in the post-millennium years, management consultants the Hay Group found that just 9 per cent of deals meet all their objectives. This figure plummeted to 'an alarming 3 per cent of mergers and acquisitions by British companies' according to the report.

In the most extreme cases, such deals have led to the collapse of whole companies. The destruction of Marconi, one of Britain's industrial success stories, is a classic example of the dangers of reward-led restructuring. The company was sunk in the late 1990s by a City and acquisition-led strategy which brought colossal fees for those driving the deal, but which ultimately brought the company down.

In 1996, a new chief executive, George Simpson, inherited GEC from the old-school industrialist, Arnold Weinstock, who had built the electronics giant over a lifetime. Urged on by his investment bank advisers,

Simpson broke up the company by selling off the arms factories to British Aerospace, renaming the company Marconi and reinvesting in American telecommunications companies. It was a fatal error. When the telecom boom collapsed in 2000, the new investments proved to be worthless. The former giant company was destroyed, there were mass lay-offs and Simpson—who was one of the first batch of businessmen to be made a peer by Tony Blair—quickly did a bunk with the usual controversial pay-off.

The Marconi executives inherited a successful company and a cash pile of over £2 billion, embarked on a failed gamble to cash in on the telecommunications fad and left the company bankrupt. 'It rests with the boosterish analysts who failed to question the perpetual high growth Marconi (and its rivals) saw in telecoms; the corporate financiers who facilitated its absurdly expensive cash acquisitions; the bankers who extended loan facilities without asking the right questions' wrote Martin Dickson, City Editor of the *Financial Times*.[366] Twenty years ago GEC was Britain's third largest company. In 2005, Marconi was sold to Ericsson of Sweden for £1.2 billion. The company had been destroyed from within. While the staff faced mass redundancy and the shareholders lost most of their investment, those responsible for the company's fate were left with handsome severance payments.

ICI, another of Britain's leading manufacturing companies at the beginning of the 1990s, has been wrecked by another failed acquisition-led strategy. The chemical company restructured its operations and detached its successful pharmaceutical division into a separate business, Zeneca, in the middle of that decade. The remaining business was re-launched with great fanfare and a new goal—maximising shareholder value.

The new ICI embarked on an extensive programme of acquisitions and disposals that failed in almost every respect. The share price peaked in 1997 and then went into a decade long decline. In 2007, ICI ceased to exist as an independent company. Both Marconi and ICI are illustrations of the effect of the dominance of the City, of the new 'deal-driven culture', of the risks of being in hock to financiers interested in little more than the fast buck.

Most of these deals have been more or less one-way bets for those executing them. Whatever the medium term outcome of the deals, their architects hang onto the inflated fees and bonuses paid for organizing them. There have rarely been penalties—except for staff and investors—if the deals go wrong. Post-mortems don't happen. 'Every year in the City is year zero' as one insider put it. 'Nobody takes responsibility if a merger fails. As soon as one is executed and the fees are banked, it's onto the next.'

11

THE BIGGER PICTURE

In November 2008, a few weeks after the UK was officially declared to be in recession, the Queen and the Duke of Edinburgh were invited to the London School of Economics to open a £71 million academic extension to the 200 year old university. After the official opening, the royal couple were given a briefing on the roots of the international crisis by Professor Luis Garicano, director of research at the School's management department.

While the Queen is renowned for studiously avoiding controversy, she pointedly asked, at the end of the briefing, 'Why did nobody see it coming?' It was the very question that was on the public's lips. No doubt the Queen—who had lost up to a fifth of her own personal fortune at this stage of the downturn—thought that the LSE was as good a place as anywhere to get an answer. Put slightly off his mark, Professor Garicano told the Queen: 'At every stage, someone was relying on somebody else and everyone thought they were doing the right thing.'

Nearly eight months later, on June 17, 2009, a group of leading economists and historians gathered at the British Academy in Carlton Terrace, a few hundred yards away from Buckingham Palace, to discuss the question posed by the Queen. Those attending included Treasury permanent secretary Nick MacPherson, Professor Tim Besley, a member of the Bank of England's monetary policy committee, and the eminent historian of government, Professor Peter Hennessy of Queen Mary College.

Following the meeting, a three-page letter summarising the outcome of the forum was sent to the Palace. The letter, signed by Professors Besley and Hennessy, blamed the crisis on the 'psychology of denial' that gripped the financial and political world in the run-up to the crisis. 'Some of the best mathematical minds' were involved in risk management but 'they frequently lost sight of the bigger picture.' Many believed that risks had been safely dispersed and 'virtually removed' through 'an array of novel financial instruments ... It is difficult to recall a greater example of wishful thinking combined with hubris.'

Wishful thinking was widespread but not universal. Indeed there is a long list of economists who did see the crisis coming. One of the first was J K Galbraith. Invited to speak at the London School of Economics in 1999, just after his 90th birthday, the Harvard scholar poured a damp shower on the optimism of the late 1990s. 'In the U.S., we are having another exercise in speculative optimism.... When you hear it being said that we've entered a new era of permanent prosperity ... you should take cover. . . . Let us not assume that the age of slump, recession, depression is past.'

A few years later, in 2004, Stephen Roach, the chief economist at investment banking giant Morgan Stanley wrote that America has no better than a 10 per cent chance of avoiding economic Armageddon. Paul

Krugman had argued for years that a housing bubble was replacing the internet bubble that burst at the turn of the millennium. In 2005, at the annual gathering of central bankers at Jackson Hole, Wyoming, Raghuram Rajan, then chief economist at the IMF, warned of impending disaster arguing that financial innovation had made the system much more prone to collapse, not less.

Such views were treated as heresy at a time when freer markets were being feted for dispersing risk and creating sustained growth. 'I exaggerate only a bit when I say I felt like an early Christian who had wandered into a convention of half-starved lions ', is how Professor Rajan later described the reaction to his paper.[367]

These warnings were brushed aside by those with the power to take the action that might have mitigated the impending crisis. In April 2006, Anne Krueger, deputy managing director of the IMF announced that 'the world economy has rarely been in better shape.' International finance had created systems that had 'helped to make the banking and overall financial system more resilient', was the conclusion of the IMF in its annual report for that year. A few weeks before it was clear that the economic game was up, Frederick Mishkin, a governor of the Federal Reserve said that the Fed's forecasting model predicted that banking problems stemming from the slump in the housing market would be a minor blip.

In the UK, the man with responsibility for steering the economy away from the rocks continued to pour praise on the nation's economic performance. In his final budget speech in March 2007, Gordon Brown told the House of Commons, to great cheers from the Labour benches, that after years of sustained growth, 'Britain's growth will continue into its 59th quarter... and then into its 60th and 61st quarter and beyond. And we will never return to boom and bust.'

Such triumphalism was echoed in the corridors of the Square Mile and Wall Street. Leading financiers continued to make big claims for the global system they had constructed. Through their efforts, levels of risk in world finances were being lowered, the availability of money in financial markets raised and higher levels of national and world economic activity enabled. The banking industry had long argued that it was their innovations that underpinned the post-millennium boom. Financial invention, it was claimed, smoothed the way to the efficient allocation of resources and the higher liquidity that would enable faster growth.

The market convulsions that began in the summer of 2007 exposed the reality behind these claims. Of course, any finance system needs the freedom to take risks to innovate and invest. Without this economies would stagnate. The question is the level of risk. Far from managing risk more effectively, what was finally revealed was a pattern of reckless and self-serving lending that made the international finance system much more prone to instability and collapse than was necessary to ensure dynamism.

This heightened level of risk was in part a product of the hiked levels of cash surpluses generated by flush personal bank accounts and growing corporate profits. Most of this giant pool of cash was recycled through the financial system, adding to the volume of footloose capital rushing through the global economy and con-tributing to a glut of liquidity and mounting credit-fuelled consumption from the middle of the 1990s.

But the loading of unnecessary risk also stemmed from another source—the apparently compulsive obsession with building ever larger personal fortunes. Decisions on trading and innovation at most levels of banking and finance came to be dictated by the personal rewards they would generate. It was in this way that a series of perverse incentives became endemic to the new finance system. Funding went to areas that delivered the highest immediate returns irrespective of their wider economic merits.

In investment banks, for example, the move to compensation ratios of 50 per cent meant that rewards depended on turnover. As a result, the volume of deal-making rather than its quality became paramount. As Manchester University academics have put it: 'The comp ratio created (and presently still creates) a turnover related bonus pool which provides a direct incentive for the firm's senior employees to increase turnover from which they will take a predetermined cut.'[368]

Credit levels ballooned out of control because it was in the interest of bankers for them to do so. Indeed, the interests of financiers and bankers came to be increasingly at odds with the needs of the wider economy. As the finance sector grew bigger and more powerful, it became a money making rather than a wealth-creating machine, a mechanism for enriching the few, while making the world economy less robust. This ballooning risk stems from three overlapping factors.

First, the world's rising cash surpluses ended up in riskier and riskier forms of investment. This was in part because the super-rich demanded racier and racier returns. In the US and the UK, wealth management teams operating inside investment and specialist banks enjoyed booming business. Many of these companies started to handle only clients offering substantial sums. In the UK, for example, the wealth management firms Fleming Family and Partners, JO Hambro and Sarasin only handle a group known in the industry as 'ultra high net worth': those with assets to spare of at least £10 million.

Some of the money supported proprietary trading desks in investment banks. Yet using the banks' own capital in this way loaded additional risk and potential conflict. 'Not only do they risk putting their own interests before those of their clients', as the *Economist* magazine argued in 2007, 'they are also increasingly exposing themselves to the dangers of an abrupt turn in the credit cycle. They are arranging ever bigger debt issues for private-equity firms and hedge funds and so are encouraging a borrowing binge that could breed financial instability.'[369] While such trading was initially hugely profitable, they exposed the larger banks to the vagaries of the market, and accounted for a good deal of the losses incurred in the meltdown of 2008. They were, according to a study by the University of Massachusetts, 'one of the main components of what most mean by the "financial crisis".'[370]

One of the main beneficiaries of the international wealth boom was the hedge fund industry. Without the greater concentration of wealth at the top, the industry would not have grown to the size it did. Rich individuals hold around 40 per cent of all hedge fund assets and have demanded above-average performance in return for premium fees. As a result, such funds became what one analyst has described as 'betting syndicates for the very rich'.[371]

The $2600 billion held by funds in 2007 was higher than the foreign exchange surpluses created by major Asian exporting nations, but was applied in a much more capricious way. They accounted too for a very high proportion of trading activity on the New York and London stock exchanges.[372] The hedge fund industry had been 'pushing the limits of financial regulation for decades.'[373] When the US Congress pushed for tougher regulation of hedge funds in 2008, the industry's lobbying organisation, the Managed Funds Association, spent $17 billion on donations to politicians with influence.[374] An increasing number of companies and countries came to know only too well what it was like to be on the receiving end of hedge fund speculation. Because of this 'active' management—a strategy of moving huge sums of mobile money in and out countries, markets, commodities and companies often at great speed—they have the firepower to do serious economic damage.

Moreover, while hedge funds rely heavily on wealthy individuals, an increasing share of their funding has been coming from once risk-averse endowments and institutional investors. In 2010, Yale University had 28 per cent of its endowment fund invested in hedge funds and 27 per cent in private equity.[375] In the same year, despite the lack of transparency, the high charges and the greater risk involved, UK pension funds invested an average of 8.1 per cent of their portfolios in hedge funds. This was a fourfold increase over 2003.[376] Indeed, pension funds had steadily reduced their exposure to equities in the decade to 2009—from 74 to 55 per cent—and moved more money into riskier asset classes from property and commodities to private equity.[377]

Neither proprietary trading nor hedge fund activity serve much wider economic purpose than to make big money for the world's wealthiest individuals. They were developed to boost profits, bonuses and personal wealth for partners and clients, thereby reinforcing the concentration of wealth at the top and adding to the casino nature of global finance. What also became clear in 2007 and 2008 was that the mighty funds, for all their Harvard, MIT and Oxbridge trained staff, were not nearly as prescient as they once liked to claim. While some made big money out of the crisis, most failed to foresee the imminent collapse of financial markets.

The second factor driving risk was the growth of much higher levels of leveraging. To capitalise on new money-spinning opportunities, banks and hedge funds increased their borrowing to huge multiples of their capital reserves. In this way they unshackled billions of dollars held as a cushion against potential losses, upping their level of investment in a range of financial instruments, and their profit. This greatly magnified their profit, but only by escalating the level of debt in the financial system.

While leveraging is one of the oldest tricks in the banker's book, what emerged after 2000 was a form of 'super-leverage' with loan to deposit ratios driven to historic highs. Many US, UK, Icelandic and Irish banks all adopted business strategies supported by smaller and smaller capital bases. To drive their growth and profit strategies, the banks had to rely increasingly heavily on short-term borrowing from the international money markets, a strategy that simply exposed them to even higher levels of risk. It was a classic banking error of borrowing short and lending long.

Moreover, the banking system grew larger even during the crisis itself. At the end of 2009, fifteen European banks—including the Royal Bank of Scotland, Barclays and the Paris-based BNP Paribas—each still had assets larger than their home economies. The figure stood at ten in 2006. In the three years to the end of 2009, European bank assets grew by a quarter while US banks grew by a fifth. In the UK, the five largest banks—HSBC, Barclays, RBS, Lloyds and Standard Chartered—had, between them, assets close to four times the size of the economy. This is more than five times the levels held a decade earlier. The banks had been taking advantage of the period of cheap money to borrow in the wholesale markets to boost trading and increase lending, thus expanding their balance sheets through the credit bubble.[378]

One of the key consequences of this rise in leveraging was that in the UK, financial sector debt grew sharply from some 46 per cent of GDP in 1987 to 245 per cent in 2009. The level of debt in the UK financial sector stood at £3400 billion in 2009. This was double that of the non-financial sector and four times public sector debt. This sharp rise in the liabilities held by finance is a clear sign of the extra risk arising from the business strategy of the last 15 years.[379]

The third source of the escalation of risk was through what the *Economist* has described as 'the alchemist's trick of turning debt (mostly leaden) into derivatives (mostly liquid).'[380] Derivatives have little to do with the underlying

259

purpose of banking. They have come to be used as a new form of money while their growth turned the global financial system into a 'giant money press'.[381] It was this boom in the derivatives market—creating money out of thin air—that drove the explosion of credit and liquidity in the global economy.

'Derivatives' is a generic term for a great variety of different financial instruments of varying risk and complexity. In the past they have played a useful economic function to control for the level of uncertainty. One of their main early functions, for example, had been to help farmers guarantee the future price of commodities which can be subject to large fluctuations. As other financial variables—from exchange rates to oil prices—became more volatile in the 1980s and 1990s, they became much more widely used as a form of protection against such price swings.

But what happened from the middle of the 1990s was an explosion in their use for largely speculative purposes. Between 1994 and 2007, the value of the global market in derivatives exploded from $12,000 billion to $591,000 billion (see figure 4.1). It had risen in a decade from twice to ten times the size of global output, adding another twist to the upward spiral of risk.[382]

With investors demanding higher and higher yields, financiers looked for more innovative ways of making money. The greater the risks, the more the rewards mentality prevailed. A rising proportion of the new products—created by an elite club of credit derivative experts, all firm believers in the superiority of free markets—became little more than devices to gamble on the movement of exchange rates, commodity and share prices, interest rates and most dangerous of all, house prices. 'Banks devised a host of new tricks for offering investors better returns', according to the *Financial Times's* Gillian Tett, and a leading expert on derivatives, 'which invariably revolved around creating products that employed more leverage, as well as more complexity and risk.'[383]

For a while, the derivatives market was highly lucrative for the investment banks issuing them and the institutions buying them. In the heady days of the 'great moderation', when economies and markets were booming, derivatives provided apparently easy money for bankers, financiers and wealthy investors. The products were marketed by banks to clients as a way of boosting their wealth. Again, incentives were being distorted by the prospect of enrichment.

The whole business became deliberately clouded in complexity and opacity, eluding even those charged with controlling the process. 'I think, generally speaking, they are very valuable' is how Ben Bernanke, by then Chairman of the Federal Reserve, replied to a quizzing by the US Senate banking committee about the risks associated with derivatives in November 2005. 'With respect to their safety, derivatives, for the most part, are traded among very sophisticated financial institutions and individuals who have considerable incentive to understand them and to use them properly.' Even top bank bosses often had little understanding of the new devices—variously called 'inverse floaters', 'time trade' and 'LIBOR squared'—and being created by the highly paid alchemists who the letter to the Queen called 'financial wizards'. As the market grew at lightning speed, so the instruments on offer became more and more exotic, more and more lucrative and more and more dangerous.

They also became a key mechanism for upping leverage. Although the banks were required by global banking rules to hold capital reserves of at least 8 per cent of the loans on their books, they found a number of clever ruses for by-passing these requirements. Indeed, the world's largest banks were perhaps not so unaware of the risks they were taking with the lending boom. Just in case, they found a new way of protecting themselves from the risk of default. This protection took the form of what is known as securitisation where loans—a mix of credit card debt, conventional and sub-prime mortgages and financial loans, from the highest to the lowest risk—were split, diced and mixed up into financial packages and then sold onto other investors. Most of these packages—known as collateralised loan obligations—offered enticing rates of return, especially those containing a higher proportion of risky debt.

Mostly constructed and marketed by investment banks from Lehman Brothers and Bear Sterns in the US to Deutsche Bank and UBS in Europe, with even the highest risk packages endorsed by the credit ratings agencies, they were bought by a mix of financial institutions thus ending up as assets on their balance sheets. Such were the juicy returns on offer, they were snapped up by the discerning and undiscerning alike.

What was being created was a 'shadow banking system', largely hidden and little understood by regulators. Many of the instruments were removed from balance sheets enabling the issuing banks to bypass international rules on capital requirements, while the credit risks were cleverly passed on to others. While risks were escalating, they were being taken with other people's money with the knowledge that if the bets went wrong someone else would pick up the bill. Nevertheless, the hope was that because high and low risk loans were mixed up and spread around through these packages, the whole system would prove fail-safe.

This might have been the case in the early days of the expansion of credit derivatives, but as the trade exploded, so did the risks. Again there were plenty of warnings. In 2003, the billionaire investor and long one of the richest in the world, Warren Buffett, dismissed derivatives as 'financial weapons of mass destruction'. Felix Rohatyn, a legendary Wall Street figure who worked at the Wall Street corporate financiers, Lazard Freres, called them 'financial hydrogen bombs'.

Such was the growing supremacy of finance, there was mostly only minimal oversight of the new activity—from proprietary trading to derivative activity. In 2006, only a quarter of all lending occurred in regulated sectors a fall from 80 per cent in the 1980s.[384] This was deliberate. The authorities on both sides of the Atlantic had been happy to endorse a regime of self-regulation—effectively trusting the banks to manage their own risks. Yet instead of self-discipline this license brought a mass free-for-all. On those few occasions when the regulators started to get nervous about what was being created, the Wall Street lobbying machine went into overdrive. In 1994, no less than four anti-derivatives bills in Congress were shelved.[385]

Just as derivatives have been at the heart of many

historic bubbles, their misuse was central to a number of recent corporate scandals from Enron to the Italian dairy giant, Parmalet.[386]

Dozens of companies were brought to their knees in this way via a business strategy heavily geared to enriching company and investment bank executives. If the business incentives had been linked more closely to medium term success, and de-linked from immediate personal enrichment, the outcomes are likely to have been very different.

For a while the electric growth in this market seemed to serve the global economy well. But what was being played was a dangerous game of pass the parcel. Those left holding the massive bundle of 'toxic debt' when the music finally stopped in the late summer of 2007 were a mix of American and European banks, pension funds, insurance companies, individual investors and taxpayers. What had finally been exposed in the subsequent meltdown was a complete failure of the much lauded finance industry. One of the biggest losers was the British insurance giant, the Prudential, which lost half a billion dollars on credit related derivatives.

It has been argued by some that executive rewards at the large banks had little to do with the crash. Because bonuses have been increasingly paid in the form of shares, it is argued, the executives had every reason to run a steady ship and remuneration packages did not distort incentives by encouraging recklessness. The academic evidence, however, suggests otherwise. A study of 14 Wall Street Chief Executive Officers by two American economists has found that in the eight years to 2008, these banking heads bought $36 million worth of shares and sold $3.54 billion. The executives sold 100 times more than they bought, suggesting that, despite their persistent denials, they were far from unaware of the direction in which the economy was being steered. If they were confident of their strategies, they would have held onto this stock.

The same study suggests that the way bank chiefs were rewarded encouraged reckless business strategies and excessive risk-taking. 'Managerial incentives matter—incentives generated by executive compensation programs led to excessive risk-taking by banks leading to the current financial crisis.'[387] The IMF has come to a similar conclusion. 'The search for yield and acceptance of higher risk was in part driven by banks' compensation packages for their staff that in effect rewarded undue risk taking.'[388] Simon Johnson, former chief economist at the IMF and now at MIT, put it a little more bluntly. The chiefs were more 'knaves than fools'.[389]

Two decades earlier, long before the tsunami of new financial instruments, the American economist, Hyman Minsky—who died in 1996—had warned that deregulated financial markets would intensify the tendency of market economies to speculation and instability. Minsky was a post-Keynesian economist and critic of the free-market school who developed what he called the 'financial instability hypothesis' that integrated the role of finance into the Keynesian framework. In *Stabilizing an Unstable Economy*, published in 1986, he argued that Wall Street and other financial centres would generate destabilizing forces, making the behaviour of the economy incoherent and subjecting economies to serious threats of financial and economic instability.

Because success would breed excess, financiers—sitting on the prospect of ever higher profits—would find ways of gearing their performance to generate even higher returns, irrespective of the risks being played with the economy. Such excess would generate credit boom and bubbles and simply make the economy ever more vulnerable to even the slightest shock. Minsky's analysis was remarkably prescient. He was one of few economists to have so early predicted the 'credit crunch' and the resulting near-collapse of the global financial system.[390]

The mass liquidity pumped into the global economy merely accentuated the course of the economic cycle, raising the height of the boom and lowering the base of the slump. Little of this explosive injection of cash produced anything of lasting economic benefit. Some of it fed unsustainable and destabilizing 'grey markets' at the height of the credit bubble as the richest and most impatient of the newly enriched offered huge cash sums to jump the queue for the rarest of the new trophy assets.

With order books for private jets full for years to come, desperate buyers were paying premiums of up to £5 million to jump the queue for the top-of-the-range £22 million Gulfstream G550. With a similar wait of three years for the Aston Martin AMV8, places on the waiting list were changing hands for tens of thousands of pounds.

Much of it fuelled the boom in industrial restructuring. Some went to high profile businessman—from Russia's Oleg Deripaska to India's Lakshmi Mittal—to expand their global empires. But private investment (as a proportion of output) remained roughly stagnant in the UK in the decade to 2007 and in most developed economies. While business investment rose in the United States in the 1990s—especially in computer technology—it slumped from 2000.[391]

Instead of paying for an expansion in the global and national infrastructure, the over-supply of credit led to a series of destructive asset price bubbles—in commodities, company valuations and property: '....the search for high-return investment by those who benefited from the increase in inequalities led to the emergence of bubbles. Net wealth became overvalued, and high asset prices gave the false impression that high levels of debt were sustainable.'[392]

With huge leveraged sums available for buy-outs, the price of companies rose to exceed their real value. By the mid-2000s, buy-out specialists were often paying hugely inflated sums for private takeovers. When Guy Hands of Terra Firma paid £4.2 billion for the record producer EMI in 2007, it was greatly in excess of what the music company was really worth. Three years later it was sold for little more than half this value.

Oil prices rose fivefold between 2002 and 2008, peaking at $145 per barrel. Land values soared. The Dow Jones Index doubled between February 1997 and October 2007, a rise not matched by a growth in the real value of companies, and way ahead of corporate productivity growth. By the middle of 2008, prices for raw materials like copper, silver and raw sugar reached all time highs, many doubling in less than a year. While mainstream economists initially argued that these hikes were the product of 'economic fundamentals'—soaring demand from fast expanding economies like China—the crash made it clear that the commodity bubbles were heavily driven by short-term speculative activity. Goldman Sachs was estimated to have made $1 billion from commodities trading in 2009 alone.[393]

'To give a sense of the scale of this big investor speculative rush, the money invested into commodities indexes grew by a staggering 2500 per cent, from around $10 billion in 2002 to $250 billion by March 2008', wrote the BBC's *Newsnight* editor, Paul Mason, in his book *Meltdown*. After the crash, commodity prices collapsed, by much more than could be accounted for by output falls, largely because investors withdrew their money as fast as they had injected it. Thus the Dow Jones food index halved in the four months from July 2008, wheat and crude oil lost two-thirds of their market price and the Dow Jones AIG Commodity Index plummeted to 122 from a peak of 238 in July. As Mason put it: 'Had "powerful" fundamental economic forces really changed so much in such a short space of time? Certainly, by the autumn of 2008 the futures market for commodities was reflecting the expected onset of recession. But it is also clear that billions of dollars were pulled out of the commodities markets as the meltdown of September-October forced both hedge funds and large institutions to deleverage—that is, to call in and pay back the loans that had been fuelling one speculative bubble after another.'[394]

The most damaging bubble of all occurred in property. With the re-birth of property mania, commercial property developers found a near bottomless pit of finance for shopping malls, hotels and luxury housing developments from Dubai and Ireland to the Spanish Riviera and the banks of the Thames. In parts of the UK—from Manchester and Leeds to Sheffield and

Newcastle—the property boom left a positive legacy of improved city centres, offering new publicly funded art galleries, concert halls and open space alongside gleaming new shopping malls. Developments in these areas would not have been built but for the post-millennium property boom. Nevertheless, most of this global property boom ended in failure.

In some countries such as Spain and Ireland, there was a massive boom in the construction of new homes. When the money ran out, swathes of new holiday homes along the Spanish coastline from Malaga to Alicante ended up empty or half-finished, a skeletal symbol of the consequences of unrestrained markets. Dubai's attempt to turn the Gulf state into a billionaire's playground was brought to an abrupt halt when its decade-long building boom ended in a massive $25 billion default. Ireland's economy imploded largely as a result of reckless lending by the banks to property speculators. In the United States, most of the legacy of new house building now stands boarded up.

The huge property bubbles being created by the great surge in mortgage lending from 2000, in both the US and the UK, especially in the sub-prime market, was made possible by securitisation. Although mortgage loans had traditionally been held on the issuers' own books, they were now parcelled up into packages, sometimes mixed with other debt, and sold on as bonds to outside investors with generous yields. In this way the banks would still collect hefty fees for providing the mortgages, could greatly expand their lending without having to increase their capital base and could shift risky assets off their own balance sheets.

The mortgage-based derivative, or collateralised mortgage obligations as they were called, had been developed in the 1980s and was initially used with largely beneficial effects, improving access to conventional mortgages and lowering their cost. But what started as a success story turned, after 2000, into a competitive scramble unleashing more and more complicated products and a greatly excess supply of mortgage credit. The demand for these products—and their yields—exploded. Lenders would have been more cautious if they had held onto the loans as in the past, but now such leveraged lending was passed, often within days, on to others.

Most of these re-packaged mortgage bonds were initiated by American and British (led by Northern Rock) banks. The lion's share was then sold by London brokers, spreading around the world's financial institutions. Those buying them included other banks, hedge funds, proprietary trading accounts and even pension funds. This is how the financial contagion eventually spread.

Although this hike in lending led to a series of national construction booms, most of the expansion in lending was felt in rising prices. In the 7 years to 2007, house prices in the UK rose by almost 90 per cent in real terms. Although the rise was, at 50 per cent, more muted in the United States, this was still the greatest house price boom in American history. In the US the boom launched a frenzy of new construction and was a key source of growth in the US economy from 2000.

This heavily leveraged lending became increasingly concentrated amongst households with the highest risk of default—especially in the United States—largely on the assumption that the property boom would continue indefinitely. For a while these rises in paper wealth were used to justify further injections of credit. That a destructive cycle was being created with only one possible outcome was largely missed or ignored by those who count.

When the housing boom faltered in the United States, triggering the credit crunch, the losses incurred by the banks were mostly associated with rising levels of defaults on loans made to sub-prime borrowers in the US. The losses incurred by British and European banks, for example, arose initially largely from reckless investment in securities backed by US subprime mortgages.

Despite the bubbles that were building across a number of markets, the regulatory authorities took no action. Yet there had been plenty of earlier examples of their destructive power. In the 1920s, it was the property followed by the stock market bubble that led to the 1929 Crash. In the early 1970s, Heath's freeing up of the banks had provided a classic warning sign of the impact on property markets as house prices surged out of control. The bursting of the Japanese property bubble in 1989— which sent the nation into a decade-long spiral of deflation—was another.

In the US, Alan Greenspan had long argued that the role of the Federal Reserve was to prevent consumer price inflation, and had no role when it came to inflation in the price of assets. Yet, the excessive rises in asset prices are as much, if not a greater, cause of economic fragility.

City alchemists paid to devise models to assess risk said the chances of a crash were infinitesimal. The compliance, control and risk departments of banks—there to ensure the rules are followed and to prevent excessive risk-taking—were mostly removed from the decision-making process. In 2003, Ron den Braber, a risk controller at the London office of the Royal Bank of Scotland, warned his bosses that the bank's models were underestimating the risk of credit products. But when the Dutch statistical expert raised the alarm, he faced so much hostility he was forced to leave. Two years earlier, Sherron Watkins, vice-president of corporate development at Enron sent an email to her boss, the chief executive Kenneth Lay warning that 'funny accounting' would 'implode in a wave of financial scandals'. In return she was made to feel like an 'outcast'.

In July 2007, a few weeks before the crisis broke, Chuck Prince, then head of Citigroup, was being interviewed by the *Financial Times* in Japan. One of the highest paid executives in the US, Prince told the paper that he was not worried by the turmoil brewing in the US sub-prime market as there was still plenty of liquidity in the financial markets: 'When the music stops, in terms of liquidity, things will be complicated. But as long as the music is playing, you've got to get up and dance.'

Prince was hardly alone. Perverse incentives—Minsky's 'incoherence'—continued to work to keep the money-making machine at full throttle even as the system became ever more over-bloated. It may have made short-term business sense for Citigroup—and the other banks—to carry on making money while the going was good, but it was to add to the scale of the disaster that was to ensue.

'If you are running a newish hedge-fund which has

persuaded £50 million or so out of a few gullible investors and you want a chance of getting rich quick, buying all this stuff makes sense', according to one hedge-fund manager, speaking in 2006, on whether to buy any of the various packages associated with US sub-prime mortgages. 'Sure everyone knows the sector is going to blow up, but no-one knows when, and in the meantime you can make excellent returns from fiddling around with mortgage-backed securities and their many derivative products. You can charge whopping performance fees until the crash comes, then when it comes you just shut up shop and go home. Your clients will have lost money but as long as you get a couple of years at the trough, or even just one good one, you'll be set up for life'.[395]

Such were the distorted incentives at work, many added to their fortunes by ruthlessly gambling that a crash would happen. In the early months of 2007, a young trader at Goldman Sachs, Fabrice Tourre, was sending emails to his girlfriend that boasted of how he had sold toxic mortgage bonds to 'widows and orphans'—Wall Street's term for gullible investors. To this trader, the end was imminent. As he put it in an email on January 23 2007: 'More and more leverage in the system, the system is about to crumble at any moment,"[396]

Andrew Lahde, a 37-year old head of Lahde Capital, a smallish real-estate hedge-fund based in Santa Monica, California, made an 870 per cent profit in 2007 by shorting the sub-prime mortgage market through derivatives. Six months later he quit. 'I was in this game for money,' Lahde wrote to his clients in a two-page 'goodbye' letter explaining how he had come to hate the hedge-fund business and those who had risen to the top of finance. 'The low-hanging fruit ... was there for the taking.'

12

THE SCALE OF THE TASK AHEAD

Despite the evidence of the economic limit to inequality, little or no domestic or global action is being taken to cap and reverse the rises in the concentration of income and wealth of the last two decades. The world's political leaders did move to take decisive measures to prevent a more damaging fall-out from the inequality-induced credit crunch of 2007. That the crash proved to be less destructive than that of the 1930s was largely down to the speed and scale of action by the authorities. The regulators may have been asleep on the watch in the build up to the crash, but at least one of the lessons of the 1930s had been learnt.

To avert a deeper catastrophe, huge sums were poured into a largely insolvent banking sector across the globe with individual banks given state guarantees for their debts. In an attempt to keep credit flowing in the aftermath of the Lehman Brothers collapse, the United States Federal Reserve lent massive sums to banks, hedge funds and even rich individuals. Goldman Sachs received loans of $600 billion and Morgan Stanley close to $2000 billion. In the UK, the Royal Bank of Scotland, HBOS and Northern Rock were taken into full or part-public ownership to prevent them from failing. Without this taxpayer support, the banking system would have collapsed. As a result, banking debt—which still exists—was transferred to the state with public sector debts increasing sharply across the globe.

While one of the lessons of the Great Depression has been learnt, most have not. The 1930s slump led to the complete recasting of economic thinking. The hands-off policies of the early inter-war years and the belief in balanced budgets were replaced by the imposition of much stronger constraints on banking and the birth of state intervention to manage the level of demand. The soaring income gap of the time was capped and then set on a new path of decline. The imbalance between wages and profits was corrected. This was a reversal of thinking that while slow in coming, contributed to economic stability and prosperity across most of the world, while bringing a halt to the mounting bank failures of the 1920s.

Following the growing instability that culminated in the crash of 2008, a rethink on a similar scale might have been expected. As Alan Greenspan, one of the architects of the pro-market model, admitted in 2008: 'The whole intellectual edifice (has) collapsed'. Yet, despite the scale of the meltdown and the massive rescue of the banking system the economic orthodoxy of the last thirty years remains largely intact. Business Schools and economic departments across the United States and the United Kingdom are still pumping out the virtues of unfettered markets. The British Treasury still recoils from policies that might 'distort the market'. There has been a good deal of hand-wringing about the role of the banks and of the regulators, but as yet, no substantive challenge to the dominant belief in the virtues of self-correcting markets, powerful finance and high levels of inequality.

Having feted the finance sector for years, senior politicians, on both sides of the Atlantic, initially talked tough about the need for root and branch reform. 'Bring back the guillotine … for bankers' cried Vince Cable, then Liberal-Democrat Treasury spokesman in the *Daily Mail* on February 9, 2009. 'The bonus-hunting bankers … stand charged with destroying wealth on a massive scale.' George Osborne was equally critical in opposition. 'It is totally unacceptable for bank bonuses to be paid on the back of taxpayer guarantees,' he told the *Guardian* in August 2009. 'It must stop.' Yet, despite near universal public anger and the huge global rescue operation, the measures taken to date fall far short of the steps that are needed to rebalance the economy and tackle the level of inequality.

In the United States, the Dodd-Frank Wall Street Reform Act passed in July 2010 tightened some of the rules governing the US financial system. While hailed, by its architects, as the most sweeping overhaul of US financial regulation since the 1930s, its numerous critics have attacked it for being a shadow of what is needed and failing to remove the personal incentives to pursue short-term profits. Indeed, a number of amendments to toughen up the Act—on capital ratios, leveraging and breaking up the biggest banks—were killed off in Congress under pressure from the White House. Moreover, subsequent negotiations to finalise the details of the new rules have led to further watering down. 'Taken overall, the reform effort amounts to tinkering with the existing system rather than fundamentally reforming it' wrote John Cassidy in the *New York Review of Books*. 'Any comparison with FDR's regulatory response to the Great Depression is specious.'[397]

New rules—called Basel III—were drawn up by the group of 27 central bankers across the world imposing tighter restrictions on banks' capital requirements. Yet these are less stringent than thought necessary by analysts to prevent another bout of irresponsible lending and will not be fully implemented until 2019.

In the UK, before they left office, Labour imposed a £3.5 billion 'supertax' on bank bonuses. The incoming coalition chancellor, George Osborne, introduced a permanent levy on banks' balance sheets to replace this one-off measure. This financial activities tax is to operate from 2011 at a rate adjusted to ensure it raises a maximum of £2.5 billion a year. Analysts calculate that the net revenue from the levy will be much lower because it will be offset by the planned cut in corporation tax from 28 to 24 per cent. Some banks could actually stand to make a net gain from the tax changes. Just how easy it is for banks to avoid tax was revealed in February 2011 when Barclays was forced by persistent lobbying by the newly elected Labour MP, Chuka Umunna, to declare that it paid just £113 million in corporation tax in 2009 on record profits of £11.6 billion. That was a mere one per cent compared with the official corporation tax rate of 28 per cent.

Instead of the radical shake-up being promised in 2008, the financial system at the beginning of 2011 still looked very much as it was in 2007. One by one a variety of proposals for tighter control of banking were dropped or weakened. Successive meetings of the world's leading finance ministers failed to agree on reform. An early promise by President Obama to cap Wall Street bonuses at $500,000 was quietly dropped. Proposals for a global tax on financial transactions were sidelined.

In the UK, the banks were eventually pressured into agreeing to a limited disclosure of earnings, though one that fell far short of the requirement that applies in the public sector where the pay of all officials earning over a relatively modest £55,000 is now made public. Yet fuller disclosure is essential to encouraging more responsible remuneration packages. Interviewed by the Treasury Select Committee in December 2010, two of Britain's most powerful bankers, the chief executives of Lloyds and RBS, admitted they did not know how much their top staff were paid. 'I would not venture a guess' as Eric Daniels, the head of Lloyds, put it.

To date, the myopic compensation packages that have fuelled economic instability and held back productive investment remain largely in place while there have been no substantive proposals for the tighter control of those activities which largely play the market—from hedge funds to derivative trading. Under Dodd-Frank the big US banks still don't face any hard limits on the amount of debt they can take on; neither do their international competitors, such as Barclays, Deutsche Bank, and UBS. A significant but undetermined amount of derivatives trading is exempt from the new regulations. The banks have agreed to raise their capital ratios, to limit their own internal trading accounts and allow more consumer protection, but that's about it.

'It is hard to see how any of the fundamental problems in the (financial) system have been addressed to date' said Neil Barofsky, the independent inspector general for the US bank bailout, in his official report to Congress in February 2010.[398] Barofsky claimed that the financial system had become more dangerous because the banks still have an incentive to take excessive risks, knowing that the government would step in again when their speculative bets go wrong rather than bring down global finance. Even if the bailout 'saved our financial system from driving off a cliff back in 2008, absent meaningful reform, we are still driving on the same winding mountain road, but this time in a faster car.' In his quarterly report issued a year later, he warned that the 'too big to fail issue' had not been resolved. The big financial institutions 'and their leaders are incentivised to engage in precisely the sort of behaviour that could trigger the next financial crisis, thus perpetuating a doomsday cycle of booms, busts and bailouts.'[399]

Much of this failure to impose tougher regulation is down to the continuing power of finance to block reform. In the US, the Obama administration—whose senior economic advisers have nearly all come from Wall Street—is little more than a prisoner of the corporations and the super-rich's lobbyists. With American elections becoming more and more expensive, Obama's 2008 Presidential campaign and that of the Republican's were financed heavily by Wall Street and American business. Without their money, Obama would have lost. In return finance has been able to ensure that he, as with earlier Presidents, serve their interests.[400]

According to Simon Johnson, a dominant 'financial oligarchy' not only played a central role in creating the crisis. 'More alarming, they are now using their influence to prevent precisely the sorts of reforms that are needed, and fast... The government seems helpless, or unwilling, to act against them.'[401] While Johnson was talking mainly

280

about the power of Wall Street, the City has also gained a firm hand over the political process. Just as the banks convinced successive governments that an unconstrained financial sector would be in the wider interests of the economy, intense lobbying ensured that the kind of tough proposals being talked about at the height of the crisis were dropped or weakened.

As a result, it has been largely business as usual in the way economies are run. The division of output is still too heavily geared in favour of profits, while the wage-productivity gap is set to continue to widen. UBS's 'golden age of profitability' has continued through and beyond the crisis.[402] Wall Street banks enjoyed $55 billion in profits in 2009, their highest level in history, and paid over $20 billion in bonuses, pay-outs that were only possible because of lavish state support. Far from exercising restraint in return for taxpayer help, pay rose even more quickly than revenue, so that during the slump, the share of revenue handed out in compensation rose by nearly a fifth.

These soaring profits were down to low interest rates, taxpayer bailouts and the lessening of competition. The banks could make big money merely by borrowing from one arm of government—the Federal Reserve—at close to zero interest rates and then lending back to another arm by purchasing US bonds at an interest rate of 3 to 4 per cent and pocketing the difference. Others clocked up sizeable profits by speculating with near-free money. 'Any moderately competent Wall Street trader could generate large returns for his desk and a big bonus for himself' argued John Cassidy, 'without actually doing what banks are supposed to do: furnishing money to firms and funding capital investments.'[403] The banks have also been able to operate with even less competition. During the crisis, more than 300 banks failed in the United States, most notably Lehman Brothers, while others such as Merrill Lynch, were taken over by others.

It is a similar picture across corporate America. At the end of 2010, the 500 largest American companies held $2400 billion in cash or short-term investments. This is nearly three times the level held in 2008, and is the equivalent of a sixth of the size of the output of the American economy.[404]

The UK's largest corporations have also been storing up large piles of cash. By the middle of 2010, while wider living standards were falling, Vodafone had built a cash surplus of $14.3 billion, BP $12.8 billion and AstraZeneca $10 billion. UK-based non- financial companies held a total cash surplus of some £650 billion with UK banks, the product of slashed costs, worker lay-offs and dividend cut-backs. The largest firms on the continent also held large cash piles.[405] Far from investing this huge pool of cash in a way which could have helped boost recovery, the UK and the continent's largest firms were simply hanging onto it.[406]

This has been especially true of the banks. The UK's top five banks made profits of £15 billion in the first half of 2010. Yet, despite government pressure, and three banks remaining in part public ownership, lending to UK businesses fell steadily from 2007 while net lending—new lending less repayments—was negative in the first half of 2010.[407] Since the crash, the UK financial sector has been on a lending strike to the real economy.

This lack of lending to smaller companies, in both the

US and the UK, has nothing to do with a lack of cash. Indeed the banks have found the income to finance a number of high level business deals. Lucrative merger and acquisition activity—sluggish in 2009—has been rising sharply. In the first six months of 2010, Goldman Sachs earned close to $1 billion for advice on such deals. In the UK, banks also started funding the next wave of speculative investment. Witness the loans secured for the £11 billion Kraft takeover of Cadbury and another loan of $2.8 billion in September 2010 provided by Barclays and JP Morgan Chase to the private equity firm 3G Capital to buy out Burger King.

By the end of 2010, hedge funds and private equity firms that had not fallen by the wayside had mostly rebuilt their cash positions and were sitting on capital in excess of $3.500 billion, with a third of this held by private equity. 'The only way as an industry we can invest these enormous sums will be to go back to doing lots of pre-packaged deals provided to private equity firms by investment banks and doing even more pass-the-parcel deals—just to get this money out the door' is how Guy Hands, founder of the British private equity company, Terra Firma put it in November of that year as the money started flowing again. Hands, who lost $2 billion buying EMI for an inflated price, had learned the hard way. 'And in my 30 years of investing, whenever I have seen deals done just to get the money out of the door, it does not end well.'[408]

Despite widespread calls for the shrinking of the finance sector, the banks not only remain 'too big to fail'. As shown earlier, they grew even larger through the downturn. 'We are sowing the seeds for the next crisis," said David Lascelles, senior fellow at the London-based research group, the Centre for the Study of Financial Innovation. 'What we have been doing in the last two years is making banks much bigger. It really goes against the currents of the time.'[409]

While little of substance has been achieved to tighten banking regulations, the scale of income concentration looks set to intensify. Initially, many members of the global financial and business elite were themselves casualties of the credit crunch. One of the world's largest hedge funds, Citadel, lost $9 billion of investors' money at the height of the crisis. Some top bankers lost their jobs, though not their pensions or pay-offs. Initially, the world's super-rich saw their collective wealth plunge.

In the event, the slump in the fortunes of the very rich was very short-lived. In the United States in 2010, eight hedge fund managers earned more than $1 billion. In that year, the wealth of the world's richest 50 rose by a fifth. In the UK, the collective wealth of the top 1000 climbed 30 per cent. According to the *Forbes* 2011 list, the number of global billionaires rose to a record 1210, with their collective wealth of $4500 billion a third larger than the size of the German economy. The collective wealth of the global super-rich is now back above the record levels recorded in the year of the crash.[410] This sudden revival is in stark contrast to the 1930s when the rich as a group took a pounding from which they took decades to recover.

The rebirth of big fortunes has been led by financiers and business executives, as pay and bonuses in the largest companies has continued to soar. 'It seems that the days of earnings restraint by FTSE-350 directors were short-lived', said Steve Tatton of Income Data Services in October 2010. 'It is as though the recession never happened.'[411] The lack of reform has provided license for the persistence of disproportionate executive rewards. Close to 3000 City staff took home more than one million pounds in 2009—including more than 300 at the Royal Bank of Scotland—while bonuses in that year were about the same as annual lending to small businesses. These bonuses had their own role to play in the build up to the crisis. If financiers had taken less from 2000, the banks could have accumulated substantially more in capital to cushion the crisis.

Goldman Sachs set aside $16 billion for bonuses and salaries for 2010, just a little below the level of 2009 despite a 13 per cent fall in revenues. The scale of such bonuses is a classic example of market failure caused by accumulated economic power. Such rewards are simply not available in other parts of the economy. Yet none of the proposals to regulate banks more effectively deal fully with the issue of market failure and excess profit. The same perverse incentives that have starved the real economy remain intact. Trading decisions are still more heavily influenced by the pattern of available rewards than the wider needs of the economy.

The front-line engineers of the market system—the financiers, bankers and corporate executives—have built a system that has largely fire-walled their own wealth against economic failure. It is a system designed to ensure that the winners are able to hang onto the gains they have extracted from the model of shareholder capitalism that they so carefully constructed in their own interests.

The reversal in the fortunes of the very rich in the

early days of recovery is in stark contrast to those of the wider population. In both the US and the UK, living standards for the majority have been hit by a combination of rising unemployment and frozen or falling real wages. In the United States, the burden of the recession has been borne almost entirely by the workforce.

While employment levels fell by over 6 per cent during the downturn, output fell by less than half this rate. 'They threw out far more workers and hours than they lost output' according to Professor Andrew Sum of North Eastern University, Boston.[412] This is one of the key explanations for soaring profits and cash reserves. Business took advantage of the slump to freeze pay, cut hours and shed labour. Gross corporate profits rose by 57 per cent in the 18 months to the beginning of 2010, reaching close to $1600 billion. In July 2010, cash at the nation's nonfinancial corporations stood at $1840 billion, a 27 percent increase over early 2007 and a level not seen in the past half-century.[413] 'Having taken everything for themselves, the corporations are so awash in cash they don't know what to do with it all', commented the *New York Times*.[414]

While profits boomed, wage and salary payments fell by $122 billion over the same period. The effect of these trends was that while productivity increased sharply—by over 6 per cent between the end of 2007 and the beginning of 2010—the gains from this rise all went to corporate profits. 'There can be no robust recovery as long as corporations are intent on keeping idle workers sidelined and squeezing the pay of those on the job' added the *New York Times*.[415]

Since the downturn there have been concerted efforts

across the United States, mostly by big business, to further weaken the bargaining power of labour. In Wisconsin, the state's Republican governor, Scott Walker, even tried in February 2011 to introduce a bill designed to remove collective bargaining and other union rights. In an echo of Ronald Reagan's war on air traffic controllers in the 1980s, this was an attempt to dismantle what was left of union power, one which led to sustained protests across the country.

A similar divide has been emerging in the UK. After falling in every year from 2005-2010, real take-home pay is now predicted to continue to fall for the next year or two at least. This is the first time since the 1920s there have been six successive years of falling real living standards, a process that started well before the crash. In both the US and the UK, the likelihood is that wages will continue to lag productivity post-recovery, living standards will continue to stagnate while the wealth and income gap will remain at historic highs. Indeed, the new independent economic overseer set up by the Coalition, the Office for Budget Responsibility, has forecast that the United Kingdom's wage share will continue to fall until 2016.[416]

The risk now is that the fundamental economic factor that has driven rising instability and created the conditions for the crash—the two-decade long growing wage-productivity gap in both the UK and the US—is set to continue. The gains from growing productivity during the recession have been swept up almost entirely by profits, with wages slumping in real terms. Corporate cash balances are at near record highs while the world's super-rich are nudging up their share of global wealth.

It seems that, far from fostering a job-creating investment boom, the British and American economies are being steered towards another destructive wave of speculative activity that will feed the next round of asset bubbles, inching, in the process, closer and closer 'to the cliff'.

Building more robust and less turbulent economies, necessary conditions for avoiding a repetition of 2008-2009, requires a response on the scale of that of the 1930s. What is required is a set of interlocking measures that tackle the root causes of instability—the unequal distribution of the gains from economic progress and the higher concentrations of income, wealth and power. These measures would aim at modifying the extent of 'pre-distribution', the distribution of rewards *before* the application of state income support.

What is needed is a new 'contract with labour' that accepts that, because of the limits to the role of state transfers, inequality is best tackled at source via the guarantee of work and decent wages and the capping of excess rewards at the top. This would require putting inclusion at the heart of national economic policies by raising earnings floors, securing a better balance between wages and profits, closing productivity-wage gaps and breaking up the excessive concentrations of income and wealth at the top. Because excessive levels of inequality have such important consequences for the functioning of the economy—through the effect on demand, borrowing and state finance—the goal of keeping a limit on the degree of concentration should also be elevated to one of the key economic targets, alongside the pursuit of economic growth and the control of inflation.

The reduction of inequality needs to happen on an international scale with those countries like the United States and the United Kingdom, with some of the heaviest concentrations, leading the way. Such a strategy, aimed at making the world less vulnerable to instability would require the construction of a new political, economic and business model that raises the wage share, shrinks the role of finance and ends the way short-term profits and share prices are valued above all other objectives. It was the US and the UK that took the lead in introducing and promoting the new capitalism and should now play the same role in building a different, more economically inclusive model.

Capping and then reversing the declining wage share is inevitably a medium to long term goal that requires a major shake-up in the Anglo-Saxon labour market and finance-centred business model. The de-linking of living standards from productivity growth has been driven largely by a combination of a more ruthless business model and the weakening of labour's bargaining power. This strategy has led to more jobs, but of declining quality, and in both the UK and the US, the rise of low paid, low skill, low security jobs alongside enhanced profitability. Constructing a new economic and business model is, of course, a highly ambitious goal. It needs a set of deep-seated reforms, to be implemented over a ten year period, in the following areas.

First, the single business goal of shareholder value should be reformed. What is needed is a move away from 'Jack Welch capitalism'—an obsession with profits whatever the impact on others—to a model that brings a better balance between the public interest and market

289

freedom. This means a more equitable distribution of the national cake, a rewards system more closely linked to real performance and a more productive use of profits: more John Lewis, less Jack Welch; more wealth-creating enterprise, less wealth-diversion from existing companies. Corporations do not operate independently of wider society. They depend on public services—from transport to education—and the largest of them wield great power over staff, consumers, small shareholders and often governments. Yet that power is mostly wielded without regard for the consequences for these groups. This holds even more so in the case of finance where despite the wider economic importance of the sector, there is no sense of the social or public good.

Although shareholder value remains the dominant business model in both the US and the UK, there are plenty of other forms of profitable private enterprise, small and large, that operate a different value system that recognises the wider implications of corporate behaviour on employees and society. In the UK, some medium sized companies—such as the Emma Bridgewater Pottery in Stoke—make a healthy profit while maintaining domestic production even though they could increase profits by moving overseas. While most other bike companies have moved production to the Far East, Bromptons, the award-winning folding bike manufacturer, assembles its bikes individually in its west-London factory. In 2010, production increased to 28,000 bikes, 75 per cent of which were exported. The mutually owned building societies and the John Lewis partnership—which maintains a fixed maximum ratio between staff pay at the top and bottom—adopt a value system that aims to serve the interests of staff and customers as well as the company.

There is also a long history of successful intervention by government to restrict corporate freedoms when they impinge too heavily on ordinary citizens. President Roosevelt's New Deal measures greatly curbed the freedom of American big business, a model of intervention that brought economic success for close to half a century. In the UK, the post-war era also saw a string of policies designed to protect the workforce from the negative impact of the market.

As the economic commentator, Will Hutton, has argued for many years, the current business model should move towards a multiple stakeholder model of the corporation that enshrines in law the idea that corporations have responsibility to a wider group than just shareholders, including staff, the local community and the taxpayer.[417]

Such a move should include tighter controls over activities—such as takeovers which are currently not regulated at all—where the primary motive and effect is wealth-transfer. Governments should have the power to impose, on national interest grounds, minimum lengths of share ownership for voting rights to prevent speculative share purchases and where necessary, block a hostile takeover by transient institutional investors. Independent studies have shown that greater controls would have only a minimal impact on the economy, but would greatly reduce the probability of crises.[418]

Secondly, the UK and the US currently have the most de-regulated labour markets amongst the world's developed nations, offering only minimal levels of workplace protection.[419] The evidence is clear, that countries with a high coverage of collective bargaining tend to have lower earnings dispersion. There is nothing unusual about labour being given a stronger voice in the workplace. Compared with the rest of Europe, the UK has one of the lowest proportions of workers covered by collective bargaining arrangements.[420] In Germany and several other continental countries the unions are more integrated into workplace decision making in a way which brings a much more co-operative approach to the running of business and the economy.

As part of the new contract with labour, Britain should move more closely to the continental European practice, especially the 'flexicurity' model followed mainly in Scandinavia. These nations have both highly interventionist policies—which combine worker security with a flexible response to technological advance—and a strong record on employment generation, labour force participation and growth. They are characterised by strong collective bargaining and workforce protection along with generous welfare benefits buttressed by stringent job search requirements and time limits on the duration of benefits.

In contrast to the Anglo-Saxon experience of high earnings inequality and high levels of in-work poverty, the flexicurity countries have combined high employment with much lower levels of wage inequality. Moving to such a model would enable a gradual rise in minimum wage levels in relative terms, the extension of the living wage—which pays roughly 30 per cent more than the minimum—and a fairer distribution of workplace, pre-tax incomes. The academic evidence is that there is room for strengthening the current floor without threatening job creation.[421]

Thirdly, breaking up the big concentrations of income and wealth requires much tougher policies on personal taxation. In the US, high incomes and large wealth holdings are very lightly taxed, largely as a result of a decade long series of tax cuts on the wealthiest initiated by George W Bush and continued by Barack Obama. As Warren Buffett, the world's third-richest person, has put it: 'people at the high end, people like myself should be paying a lot more in taxes. We have it better than we've ever had it.'[422]

Despite the introduction of a new top 50 per cent tax rate on high earners, the UK's tax system continues to be regressive, taking more proportionately from the poor than the rich. Several changes are needed. Most important, the tax system should be recast until this pattern is reversed. Indeed the British tax system was progressive until the mid-1980s.[423] The progressive principle was advocated by the father of economics, Adam Smith in his book, *The Wealth of Nations*, published in 1776. It is a fundamental principle of fairness long enshrined in most national tax systems, and has been endorsed time and again by tax commissions. As the 1993 Ontario Fair Tax Commission put it, 'After sifting through the arguments we have concluded that a fair tax system is one based primarily on the ability-to-pay principle, and that in turn, requires the overall tax system to be progressive. Progressivity is a fundamental component of tax-fairness.'[424]

Other changes are needed too. Limits should be imposed on the extent to which leveraged loans can be used to offset profits in the case of acquired companies. To prevent high levels of earnings being disguised as a capital gain, such gains should be taxed at the same rate as income with an adjustment to tax windfall gains more heavily than entrepreneurial success. Wealth should be taxed more heavily, with, for example, capital transfers being more highly taxed.[425]

The American academic, Robert Shiller—an economist with a strong track record in predicting financial bubbles—has called for a much more radical proposal on the tax system, that it should be indexed to the level of income inequality. Under what he calls 'The Rising Tide Tax System', taxes would automatically become more progressive if inequality became more acute. Shiller has found that if such a reform had been instituted 30 years ago in the United States, even in a partial form, economic inequality would have been lessened.[426] More progressive systems of income tax can help to dampen turbulence as they act as 'automatic stabilisers', reducing the tax take and encouraging consumption during downturns and imposing a break when the economy becomes overheated.

A much more concerted attack is also needed on tax avoidance. One possibility for the UK is the imposition of a minimum tax rate for earnings over £100,000, while still allowing the use of reliefs and allowances. Richard Murphy of Tax Research UK has estimated that a proposal to set a minimum average rate of 32 per cent on incomes over £100,000 rising to 37 per cent at £150,000 and 40 per cent on £200,000 and above would raise additional revenue of some £6 billion a year, equivalent to raising personal allowances by more than 10 per cent.[427]

Globally there also needs to be a much tougher line on tax havens. There is no reason why the UK Government should not lift the veil of secrecy by insisting on the same standards of disclosure and accountability as apply in the UK with its own Crown Dependencies and Protectorates such as Jersey and the Cayman Islands.

Fourthly, a number of finance-specific measures are needed which remove current perverse incentives to risk and ensure finance carries out its primary function—of providing the level of credit and liquidity needed to finance world trade and productive investment. As has been widely recognised by a number of commentators, including Meryyn King, the new global rules on capital ratios do not go nearly far enough to solve the 'too big to fail' problem. One radical proposal would be to impose a statutory limit on the size of bank assets in relation to GDP.[428] Another would be to internalise the risk either by holding top executives legally responsible for bank failures with heavy penalties, or by making directors hold a minimum proportion of the banks' capital. At the moment, bankers are playing with other people's money. If directors knew that their own money was on the line, this would reform the current perverse incentive structure that encourages excessive risk-taking and risk-inflated remuneration levels.

An alternative would be to split the banks into separate institutions—retail and investment. This would overcome current conflicts of interest and has an impressive array of backers from a number of progressive economists to Mervyn King. If this 'narrow banking' option was introduced, the retail banks would be protected from collapse, while the riskier investment banks would not.

Removing this protection from 'casino banking' would itself reduce the incentive to risk as the bankers—rather than taxpayers—would end up with responsibility for their actions. Nevertheless, it is an idea that has been given a largely lukewarm reception by the Commission on Banking established by the coalition government and chaired by Sir John Vickers.[429]

The most effective way of tackling excessive levels of remuneration in finance is by action on bank profits. Finance has been generating 'supernormal' profits for years. These excess profits have been driven by rates of return that are much greater than can be achieved in most other forms of business activity. It is this differential that has led to the expansion of finance and the maldistribution of resources between finance and other sectors. These higher returns arise from a mix of cheap money, state guarantees and the lack of a competitive market in finance and should be brought into line with those available in other sectors. It is these artificially boosted profits that are the source of the heavily skewed pay and bonuses in finance.

Attempts to moderate pay and bonuses by government regulation are unlikely to work in a world where finance remains so powerful. New European regulations applied from January 2011 were designed to tighten rules on bonuses—with a maximum of 30 per cent paid in cash and the rest deferred for three to five years and only paid on proven performance. Yet this attempt to encourage a more long term view was thwarted by the banks which had already taken steps to sideline the move by large increases in basic salaries. HSBC, for example, doubled salaries for hundreds of its top staff. The most effective way of capping pay and bonuses is by tackling the mostly exorbitant banking fees and charges caused by a lack of proper competition in the industry.

In the last two decades, fees—for advice on business strategy and underwriting new share issues to handling government bond issues—have risen sharply. Although individual firms compete strongly for business, there is almost no variation in fee levels, which should long ago have been the subject of a proper Competition Commission Enquiry. Paul Myners, former Financial Services Secretary from 2008-2010, has called Britain's banking system 'oligopolistic'.[430]

Banks also stand accused of charging excessive rates of interest and imposing excessively stringent conditions on business lending. Indeed, small businesses claim these charges almost doubled in the two years to 2010, despite the Bank of England's base rate being at an historic low. This has also acted as a disincentive to smaller firms starting out or trying to expand from borrowing.

Sustained supernormal profits—a sign of a badly distorted economy—could also be tackled by a much tougher tax regime than the £2.5 billion financial activities tax on banks to operate in the UK from 2011. The need for stronger action has been recognised by the number of proposals discussed at international summits. One idea originally touted by the American administration is for a financial stability tax. This would pay for an insurance fund that could bail out the financial system, but it didn't feature in the Dodd-Frank reform bill and has faded from view, partly because it would risk exacerbating the 'too big to fail' problem.

Most effective in reining in the banks would be a global transactions tax levied on every financial deal. The idea was first mooted by John Maynard Keynes in the 1930s as a way of discouraging speculation. It was then resuscitated by the American Nobel laureate, James Tobin, in 1972, as a way of curbing the kind of currency fluctuations which followed the break-up of the Bretton Woods system of monetary management in 1971.

If the 'Tobin' or 'Robin Hood tax' had been in place in recent times, it would have limited the build up of surpluses while clawing back some of the excess profits from speculation. Even a moderate rate of tax would raise between one and 2.5 per cent of global GDP, a substantial sum that could be used to rebuild national economies. In the UK, the yield would be up to £25 billion—ten times the revenue to be generated by George Osborne's financial activity tax.[431] In the event, a possible transactions tax was kicked into the long grass by the G20 at their summit in Toronto in April 2010, largely because of resolute opposition from the United States.

There is no reason in principle why more than one of these taxes should not operate as they have different purposes, though there would clearly need to be a limit on the total revenue generated and any new tax regime would have to gel with progress on reducing fees and profits through tighter competition. The more effective such action, the less need for additional taxation, especially as there is always a risk that banks will simply maintain profits by passing the extra tax onto customers and shareholders.

Such measures would help restore the link between finance and productive activity. But to help fill the funding gap left by the private banking system and provide more support for the real economy, they should be buttressed by the creation of a state National Investment Bank, as called for by the Engineering Employers Federation and the Institute of Civil Engineers.[432] Its role would be to provide affordable loans and grants for infrastructure projects, social entrepreneurship and sound small and medium sized businesses. Potential targets would include low-carbon technology, alternative energy and the knowledge economy. This could be modelled on the German KfW banking group, founded in 1948 to help rebuild Germany's economy. It could be financed through a mix of revenue from new taxes on banks, market funding and the profits made when the government sells state-owned shares in the bailed-out private banks. This move would also help overcome the issue of the lack of competition amongst lenders. Indeed, 85 per cent of lending for small business loans comes from the four largest banks.

Tougher reform is a pressing economic issue. The strategy laid out above is far from utopian. The case for unfettered markets has been discredited. There is a growing public clamour for change. With the world's largest companies sitting on record cash reserves, there is no better opportunity for boosting wage shares. The last two all-embracing crises—in the 1930s and 1970s—led to massive upheavals in the way individual economies and the global financial system were run. A ten year timescale for change is longer than the time taken to dismantle much of the post-war apparatus in the 1980s.

Some of these measures—such as those designed to close the wage-productivity gap and build a more progressive tax system—could be implemented at a national level. Others—such as those on the taxation, bonus policies and size of banks—would ideally require global action.

There is now a growing body of opinion that accepts the failings of the economic strategy of the last thirty years. As Gordon Brown admitted in his own account of the crisis, *Beyond the Crash*, 'The crises of economic policy in the past century teach us that the conventional wisdom of the day can easily become the misjudgement of history.'[433] An increasing number of leading political and economic figures have called for a fairer distribution of national wealth.

In 2006, before the onset of the credit crunch, the Nobel-prize winning economist Robert Solow claimed that an economy that doesn't distribute its gain more widely is 'poorly performing'. In the same year Ben Bernanke said that corporations should 'use some of those (higher) profit margins to meet demands for higher wages from workers.[434] In 2007 Germany's finance minister called on European companies to 'give workers a fairer share of their soaring profits.'[435] In 2007, Robert Shiller warned that: 'The most essential long-term economic problem of this century is the risk that income inequality will get substantially worse... The mere prospect of a winner-takes-all world ought to strike fear into our hearts.'[436]

It was a theme echoed at the 2011 World Economic Forum at Davos. One senior business leader admitted to the meeting that during the crisis, companies across the world had 'sacrificed the workers to please the sharehold-ers' and called for a more 'humanistic' approach. At one plenary session, Bob Diamond, the chief executive of Barclays thanked the authorities for bailing out the financial system. Christine Lagarde, the (then) French finance minister, responded. 'Thanks were not enough. What the banks needed to do was lend more, improve their capital ratios and reform their compensation structures'.[437] Juan Somavia, Director-General of the International Labour Organisation, has said: 'Minimum wage setting and collective bargaining systems should aim to ensure that wage increases do not lag behind productivity.'[438]

The case for a higher wage share has also made in the study by Michael Kumhof and Romain Rancière for the IMF. They showed that the fall in the bargaining power of labour had been a key factor in both the 1929 and 2008 crashes. Upping the share of wages in GDP through 'the restoration of the lower income group's bargaining power', according to their findings, is the most effective way of preventing another major economic crisis. 'Without the prospect of a recovery in the incomes of poor and middle income households over a reasonable time horizon, the inevitable result is that loans keep growing, and therefore so does leverage and the probability of a major crisis.'[439]

In the UK, a number of influential figures—from the former director general of the CBI, Sir Richard Lambert, to the chairman of the FSA, Lord Turner—have heavily criticised the current finance business model, its lack of moral compass and its structure of perverse incentives. In a letter to the *Financial Times* on 28 September 2010, sixteen leading City financiers and lawyers launched an attack on finance's sole obsession 'with law and profit'.

The City, they argued, should also 'be motivated by, and subject to, a larger social and moral purpose which governs and limits how they behave.'

That reform has failed to go far enough was admitted by the Governor of the Bank of England, Mervyn King, in a remarkably frank speech in New York on October 25 2010.[440] The Governor accused the bailed-out investment banks of 'financial alchemy', criticised the proposed bank levy as a 'foolish' way to rein in the banks and called the new Basel III accord on capital ratios inadequate to 'prevent another crisis'. He summed up his views as follows: 'Of all the many ways of organizing banking, the worst is the one we have today.'

Whether these calls to action have much effect remains to be seen. There are many obstacles to reform. The banking and billionaire lobby continues to exercise a powerful grip on the US and UK governments and global finance forums. The Obama administration is weakened by both the mid-term election of a Republican dominated Congress at the end of 2010 and the continuing pressure to maintain the status quo from Wall Street. Although many of the changes proposed above—on size, tax and pay—should ideally be implemented on the global stage, summits have failed to achieve consensus around more radical proposals.

The danger is that the real lessons of 2008-2009 are being quietly buried. Yet, if the fundamental gap between rich and poor is not tackled, the limit to inequality will continue to be breached, bringing a persistence of the crises that have marred the global economy over the last twenty-five years, and a heightened risk of permanent recession.

ACKNOWLEDGMENTS

In the mid-1970s, the Wilson government appointed a Royal Commission on the Distribution of Income and Wealth. It seems remarkable now but the Commission was born out of a political climate that favoured the narrowing of the income and wealth gap in Britain, even though it had fallen sharply compared with the pre-war era. In the event, the 1970s was to prove the high point of equality across most of the developed world. From that decade, the level of inequality headed relentlessly in one direction, back towards the much wider gaps of the 1930s.

In the decades up to the 2007 crash, the question of growing inequality became increasingly marginalised as an economic and political issue. Before 2008, the overwhelming consensus across most of the political spectrum in the UK, and amongst most economists, was that inequality and big rewards at the top were good for the economy. Despite the efforts of a small group of academic researchers, think tanks and pressure groups, and their warnings of the dangers of more polarised societies, it was very difficult to rouse much interest in the counter view. That has now changed. Today, books attacking inequality not only tend to get noticed, some of them even sell well. There is a growing public appetite for radical measures to reduce the concentration of wealth and income at the top, not just in the UK, but across many other countries.

Despite the changing public and intellectual mood, the political response has been at best, muted. Far from reducing inequality, the turbulence of the last few years has, if anything, allowed the yawning income gulf to widen further. Moreover, although much has been written about the growing divide, and its consequences, these accounts have been confined mostly to issues of fairness. Perhaps the most important consequence, the impact on the economy, has been much less closely investigated. This book provides one attempt to fill that gap. It concentrates entirely on the economic impact of the surging levels of inequality—in the UK, the United States and elsewhere—of the last three decades.

There are a large number of debts I owe along the way. I am grateful

303

to *The Author's Foundation* for a grant towards the research costs. I would also like to thank staff at the British Library and especially at the Office for National Statistics for their patience and skill in responding to endless requests for help with locating and interpreting data. Both are invaluable resources that we rarely value highly enough. I have benefitted too from contributions from anonymous referees and from helpful feedback at seminars I gave on the subject of inequality and instability, including to the New Political Economy Network and to the Royal Society of Arts, 2009.

I would also like to thank members of the Economic and Social Affairs Unit at the TUC for many discussions around these issues and especially to Adam Lent, the former head of the Unit, for commissioning research on the economic impact of the super-rich, on the impact of wider economic trends on low and middle income households in Britain and on a largely forgotten group in Britain—'the squeezed middle'. I have drawn on this work, published in a series of TUC economic pamphlets in 2008 and 2009, and on other articles I had published in those years. The latter suggested, tentatively, that the fundamental cause of the 2008 crash lay, not in mainstream explanations, but in a growing level of economic fragility and turbulence that had their roots in the way the fruits of economic growth had become so unevenly shared.

Most important have been the ongoing discussions I have had with friends and colleagues, sometimes perhaps *ad nauseam*! I am especially grateful for invaluable comments on earlier drafts from Chris Garsten, Steve Schifferes and David Webster, even if we have not always been fully in agreement. A special thanks to Anne Rannie for her insights, encouragement and support and for keeping me almost sane through the whole process, never complaining about the weekends lost to the computer screen.

I must also thank my agent, Andrew Lownie, for keeping faith with the project despite scepticism from publishers, who mostly seemed to view this as yet another book on the crash, despite attempts to convince them it offered a wholly differentiated argument. A big thank you therefore to Martin Rynja of Gibson Square for swimming against the tide. I also need to thank Martin for insisting that a book aimed at a popular as well as a specialist market needed to be decontaminated from economic jargon. I doubt if I have fully succeeded.

NOTES

1   Robert J Shiller, *Inequality-Indexing of the Tax System*, The Tobin Project, 2007.

2   See, for example, W Hutton, *Them and Us*, Little Brown, 2010; D Dorling, *Injustice*, Policy Press, 2010; G Irvin, *Super Rich*, Polity Press, 2008; P Toynbee & D Walker, *Unjust Rewards*, Granta, 2008; S Lansley, *Rich Britain*, Politico's, 2006.

3   R Wilkinson and K Pickett, *The Spirit Level*, Penguin, 2009.

4   In 2008, the UK was ranked the seventh most unequal of the world's thirty richest nations. Amongst the European nations on this list, the UK was the third most unequal, behind Italy and Poland. National Equality Panel, *An Anatomy of Economic Inequality in the UK*, 2010, p 53.

5   C Goldin and RA Margo, 'The Great Compression', *Quarterly Journal of Economics*, vol 107, 1992; Kevin Phillips, *Wealth and Democracy*, New York, 2003, p 432.

6   *Ibid*. p 78.

7   WD Rubinstein, *Men of Property*, The Social Affairs Unit, 2006, ch 8.

8   *Ibid*. p 288.

9   Throughout the book we are concerned with economic inequality, and especially the increased concentration at the top of the distribution. There are a number of different ways of measuring inequality (income or wealth, pre- or post-tax income etc) and no single index or summary measure can encapsulate the character of the whole distribution. While these measurement issues are beyond the scope of this book it is important to note that all indices and measures of inequality have moved in the same direction over time. See also, AB Atkinson and S Morelli, *Inequality and Banking Crises: A First Look*, Mimeo, Oxford University, 2011.

10 AB Atkinson and T Piketty, *Top Incomes over the Twentieth Century: A contrast between European and English speaking countries*,

11 Oxford University Press, 2007, table 4.2. Wealth levels for individuals—a stock of assets rather than a flow of income—reflect the accumulation of assets over many years and will for most people exceed income levels in any one year. The total national level of wealth will be much higher than annual national income. In the UK, for example, while the annual output of the economy stood at some £1.5 trillion in 2009, the volume of wealth—a mix of cash, savings, shares, bonds, property and accrued pension rights—was around £6.7 trillion.

12 S Lansley, *Rich Britain*, Politico's, 2006, Appendix, p234-236, and Office for National Statistics, *Share of the Wealth*, December 2004. The definition of marketable wealth includes property (but not accrued pension rights) as well as liquid assets like cash, savings and shares and bonds. If property is excluded, the top 1 per cent enjoy an even higher share of the nation's wealth, while the distribution of liquid assets is even more unequal. According to Tulip Financial Research, the specialist wealth consultants, the top 45,000 people (0.1 per cent of the population) in 2002 enjoyed a third of all liquid assets (marketable wealth that includes cash, savings and shares), averaging more than £8 million each. See Tulip, *Britain's Millionaires: The Powerhouse of Private Investment*, Tulip Financial Research, 2002.

13 The raw figures, based on estate returns, will almost certainly understate the actual share of wealth enjoyed by the top one per cent because they are based on declared levels of wealth and most of the very wealthy have ways of disguising the true level of their worth.

14 HM Revenue and Customs.

15 Figures provided by Datamonitor, *The Global Wealth Report*. See, too, the figures

NOTES

provided by wealth consultants, Tulip Financial Research, *op. cit.*

16 S Lansley, *op. cit.* Appendix.

17 P Krugman, *The Great Unravelling*, Allen Lane, 2003, p 220.

18 P Krugman, 'The Rich, the Right and the Facts', *American Prospect*, 1 September, 1992.

19 P Grier, 'Rich-Poor Gap Gaining Attention', *Christian Science Monitor*, 14 June 2005.

20 B Bernanke, *The level and distribution of well-being*, Federal Reserve, 6 February, 2007.

21 T Piketty and E Saez, 'Income Inequality in the US, 1913-1998', *NBER Working Paper 8467*, 2001; http://elsa.berkeley.edu/~saez/TabFig2006.xls.

22 T Piketty and E Saez, *Top fractiles income share (including capital gains) in the US, 1913-2006*, March 2008, Table A3. Piketty and Saez have presented a number of different versions of the data. Some sets include the impact of capital gains and some exclude it. The set used here relates to table A3 and includes capital gains. All the sets follow a very similar pattern. See http://elsa.berkeley.edu/~saez/TabFig2006.xls.

23 Edward Wolff, 'Recent Trends in Wealth Ownership, 1983-1998', Levy Economic Institute, April 2000; E Wolff, 'Recent trends in Household wealth in the US', *Working Paper no 589*, Levy Institute, 2010: http://www.levyinstitute.org/publications/?docid=1235.

24 JB Davies et al, 'The World Distribution of Household Wealth', *Discussion Paper, 2008/03*, United Nations University, 2008 p 19.

25 Piketty and Saez *op. cit.*

26 K Phillips, 'The New Face of Another Gilded Age', *Washington Post*, 25 May 2002.

27 Phillips, *Wealth and Democracy, op. cit.* p 109.

28 *Guardian*, 6 August 2005.

29 M Whittaker, *Squeezed Britain*, Resolution Foundation, 2010, p 24. Income is 'final income' which is 'original income' (mostly earnings), *plus* cash benefits and income-in-kind and *less* taxes.

30 J Hills, T Sefton and K Stewart (eds), *Towards a More Equal Society?*, Policy Press,

2009, p 26-27.

31 B Bell and J Van Reenen, *Bankers' Pay and Extreme Wage Inequality in the UK*, CEP, LSE, 2010.

32 T Cowen, 'The Inequality That Matters', *The American Interest Magazine*, Jan-Feb 2011; SN Kaplin and J Rauh, 'Wall Street and Main Street: What contributes to the rise in the highest incomes?', *Review of Financial Studies*, March 2010.

33 http://sociology.ucsc.edu/whorules-america/power/wealth.html; T Judt, *Ill Fares the Land*, Allen Lane, 2010, p 14.

34 G Domhoff, 'Wealth, Income and Power' in *Who Rules America?*, 2005: http://sociology.ucsc.edu/whorules-america/power/wealth.html.

35 See eg P Krugman, 'For Richer', *New York Times Magazine*, 20 October 2002. The gap in after-tax incomes has followed a similar trend. See eg, R Greenstein and I Shapiro, *The New Definitive CBO Data on Income and Tax trends*, Centre on Budget and Policy Priorities, 23 September 2003.

36 J Hills, *Inequality and the State*, Oxford University Press, 2004 p 31; Hyunsab Kum, *Inequality and Structural Change*, UNRISD Research Programme on Poverty Reduction and Policy, UNRISD, Geneva, 2008; OECD, *Growing Unequal? Income Distribution and Poverty*, OECD, 2008.

37 OECD, *ibid.*

38 J Galbraith, 'Inequality, unemployment and growth', *Journal of Economic Inequality*, Volume 7, June 2009.

39 Forbes, *The World's Billionaires*, March 2007.

40 D Rothkopf, *Superclass*, Little Brown, 2008, p 54.

41 *Ibid.* p xv.

42 UN, *The Inequality Predicament, Report on the World Social Situation*, 2005. Inequality has also been rising within most regions of the world, from Asia to Latin America. See, for example, I Ortiz and M Cummins, *Global Inequality: Beyond the Bottom Billion*, UNICEF, 2011, table 12.

43 JB Davies, *op. cit.* p 9 and 19. There is some evidence about trends in global inequality as measured using individual incomes across countries. One such study has concluded that global inequality has

NOTES

been rising over the last twenty years. See eg, B Milanovic, *Global Inequality Recalculated*, World Bank, 2010.

44 M. Feldstein, 'Is Income Inequality Really a Problem?', in *Income Inequality Issues and Policy Options: A Symposium Sponsored by the Federal Reserve Bank of Kansas City*, Jackson Hole, Wyoming, August 27-29, 1998.

45 A O'Hear, 'Equality', *New Statesman*, 23 April 2001.

46 R North, *Rich Is Beautiful: A Very Personal Defence of Mass Affluence*, Social Affairs Unit, 2005.

47 http://www.imf.org/external/np/vc/-2011/010411.htm.

48 JM Keynes, *National Self-Sufficiency*, 1933, Section 3, republished in *Collected Writings*, Vol. 11, 1982.

49 KO Morgan, *The People's Peace*, Oxford University Press, 1992, p 354.

50 L von Mises, *Ideas on Liberty*,Irvington, New York, 1955.

51 M Friedman and R Friedman, *Capitalism and Freedom,* University of Chicago Press, 1982, p133.

52 J Krieger, *Reagan, Thatcher and the Politics of Decline*, Polity Press, 1986, p 155.

53 A Glyn, *Capitalism Unleashed*, Oxford University Press, 2006, p 5.

54 Interview With Adam Posen, *Challenge*, July-August, 2008.

55 D Harvey, *A Brief History of NeoLiberalism*, Oxford University Press, 2006, p 43-44.

56 B Western and J Rosenfeld, *Unions, Norms and the Rise in American Wage Inequality*, Harvard Univeristy, March 2011.

57 *The Times*, 5 August 1974.

58 Office for National Statistics: compensation of employees (series HAEA) as a proportion of GDP (YBHA); http://www.statistics.gov.uk/statbase/expo data/files/1507162651.csv.

59 D Ricardo, *The principles of taxation and political economy*, JM Dent, 1821.

60 This is in some ways less the case in countries with a significant dependency on exports and investment for demand and growth. It would also be less of a problem if any shortfall of demand could be replaced by higher exports or investment, but this has not occurred in the UK dur-

61 ing the wage squeeze from the early 1980s. A Glyn & B Sutcliffe, *British Capitalism, Workers and the Profits Squeeze*, Penguin, 1972 p 16.

62 R Skidelsky, *John Maynard Keynes, 1883-1946*, Pan Books, 2003, p 238.

63 Glyn & Sutcliffe *op. cit.* ch 2; AB Atkinson, *The Economics of Inequality*, 2nd edition, Oxford University Press, 1983, ch 9.

64 Glyn and Sutcliffe, *op. cit.* p 5.

65 R Brenner, *The Boom and the Bubble*, Verso, 2002, p 17.

66 Glyn & Sutcliffe, *op. cit.* p 46.

67 Clause Offe, *Disorganised Capitalism*, Polity Press, 1985.

68 See O Giovannoni, 'Functional Distribution of Income, Inequality and Incidence of Poverty', University of Texas Inequality Project, *Working Paper No 58*, January 2010. .

69 Steven Greenhouse and David Leonhardt, 'Real Wages Fail to Match a Rise in Productivity', *The New York Times*, August 28, 2006.

70 A Glyn, *G-24 Policy Brief, no 4*, 2006.

71 S Lansley, *Unfair to Middling*, TUC, 2009.

72 Lansley, *ibid.* p. 11. The figures have been derived from the Annual Survey of Hours and Earnings (for 1997-2008), and the New Earnings Survey (for 1978 to 1996). The earnings figures have been adjusted for changes in the retail price index. The NES covers GB and ASHE covers the UK. There has been a similar, though less extreme, rise in the dispersion of wages over the period amongst women.

73 Lansley *ibid.*

74 S Lansley, *Life in the Middle*, TUC, 2009, pp 14-16.

75 ILO, *World of Work Report 2008: Income Inequalities in the Age of Financial Globalization,* ILO, 2008, p 10; Giovannoni *op. cit.*

76 S Lansley, *Unfair to Middling, op. cit.* p 7.

77 R Z Lawrence, *Single World, Divided Nations?*, OECD, 1997.

78 The wage index in figure 2.4 relates to all workers, both men and women. The rise in real wages has been even slower for men. There was no rise in real male wages from 1980 to 2007, while real wages for

NOTES

women rose by 25 per cent.

[79] See, for example, G Irvin, *Super Rich*, Polity, 2008, p 137 and L Kenworthy, *Slow Income Growth for Middle America*, 2008. There has been much debate amongst American academics about the phenomenon of stagnant or near-stagnant living standards. Some have argued that estimates of the scale of stagnation have failed to allow for falls in the size of families and for the rising value of workplace benefits, such as the rising cost of health insurance. See, for example, RJ Samuelson, 'The Real Economy Scorecard', *The Washington Post*, 3 September 2008. Other evidence suggests that allowing for these changes would have had only a minimal effect on the rising productivity-wage gap. See, for example. L Kenworthy, *Middle America's Standard of Living*, Spring 2010 and FS Levy and P Temin, 'Inequality and Institutions in Twentieth Century America', *MIT Working Paper, 07-17*, 2007.

[80] Economic Policy Institute, 'Productivity and Median and Average Compensation', 1973 to 2007, *State of Working America*, 2010.

[81] See, for example, 'Interview with Dr Ravi Batra', *Truthout*, 16 March, 2009; R Batra, *The Great Depression of 1990*, Dell Publishing, 1988.

[82] Juan Somavia, *The Challenge of Growth, Employment and Social Cohesion*, ILO, October 2010.

[83] See eg 'The Globalisation of Labour', *World Economic Report*, IMF, 2007.

[84] See, for example, S Machin, 'The changing Nature of Labour Demand in the New Economy and Skill-Based Technological Change', *Oxford Bulletin of Economics and Statistics*, 2001, issue 63, pp 753-76; J. Hills, *Inequality and the State*, OUP, 2004, p 79-83.

[85] See, for example, W Hutton, *Them and Us*, Little Brown, 2010.

[86] J Krieger, *Reagan, Thatcher and the Politics of Decline*, Polity Press, 1986, p 176.

[87] The data from 1971-2009 is the ILO unemployment rate (series MGSX, second quarter), seasonally adjusted. The figures for 1950-1970 were provided by the ONS. Because of changes in definitions, the series before and after 1970 are not strictly comparable.

[88] For the 1950s to the 1980s, *Social Justice*, Report of the Social Justice Commission, Vintage, 1994; for the 1990s and 2000s, ONS; http://www.statistics.gov.uk/elmr-/03_10/downloads/Table2_09.xls.

[89] P Edwards, *Non-standard work and labour-market restructuring in the UK*, Warwick Business School, 2006.

[90] R Taylor, *Britain's World of Work*, ESRC, 2002.

[91] TUC, *Hardwork, Hidden Lives, Report on Commission on Vulnerable Employment*, 2008.

[92] *Ibid.* p 17.

[93] Interview in Adam Curtis, *The League of Gentlemen*, BBC2, 1992.

[94] See, eg, R E Rowthorn & JR Wells, *De-Industrialisation & Foreign Trade*, CUP, 1987, ch 10.

[95] Glyn, *Capitalism Unleashed, op. cit.* p 98.

[96] *The New York Times*, 11 November 1984.

[97] H Perkin, *The Third Revolution*, Routledge, 1996, p 37.

[98] Glyn *op. cit.* p 135.

[99] Tom Nairn, *The Break Up of Britain*, 1981, p 392.

[100] I Gilmour, *Dancing With Dogma*, Pocket Books, 1993, p 71.

[101] RW Johnson, *The Politics of Recession*, Palgrave Macmillan, 1985, p 29.

[102] Quoted in Gilmour, *op. cit.*, p 70.

[103] ONS Workforce Jobs, by industry: http://www.statistics.gov.uk/downloads/theme_labour/LMS_FR_HS/WebTable05_2.xls; there was also a rise in the size of the workforce over the period.

[104] If business services are included (legal, accountancy and business consultancy), the figures for 2007 and 2006 rise to 14.5 per cent and 13.8 per cent respectively.

[105] S Lansley, *Do The Super-Rich Matter?*, TUC Touchstone Pamphlet, 2008, p 15.

[106] ONS National Accounts Yearbook.

[107] S Lansley, *Life in the Middle, op. cit.*, Appendix 1.

[108] *The Times*, 14 October, 1996.

[109] *Daily Mail*, 18 April 1996.

[110] In the 12 years from 1997 to 2009 alone, the proportion of the working population employed in managerial and professional

NOTES

occupations—from doctors, accountants, lawyers and software engineers to teachers, personnel officers, public servants and retail managers—rose from 34.7 per cent of the employed population to 43.5 per cent. Over the same period, the proportion working as plant and machine operatives fell from 9.8 per cent to 6.6 per cent. ONS, *Labour Force Surveys*, first quarter 1997 and 2009.

111 M Goos & A Manning, 'Lousy and Lovely Jobs: The Rising Polarisation of Work in Britain', *Review of Economics and Statistics*, 89, 2007, pp 118-33, figure 1.

112 Since 1999, there has been a slight moderation in this trend with a shift in jobs from the lowest paid decile to the second and third deciles, and a continuing, if slowing shift in jobs from the middle to the very top. See, for example, 'How Have Employees Fared?' *DTI Employment Relations Research Series*, No 56, 2006. The shrinking of the middle is a largely common trend with the middle third losing share across nearly all European nations.

113 P Gould, *Unfinished Revolution*, 2nd edition, Abacus, 1999.

114 Goos & Manning, *op. cit.* pp 118-33.

115 S Lansley, *The Livelihood Crisis*, TUC Touchstone Pamphlet, 2011, table 2.

116 The figure for 1997 comes from A McKnight, Low Paid Work in J Hills et al, (eds), *Understanding Social Exclusion*, Oxford University Press, 2002. The figure for 2009 comes from ONS, *Annual Survey of Hours and Earnings*, 2009.

117 ONS, *Annual Survey of Hours and Earnings*, 2009. http://www.statistics.gov.uk/-downloads/theme_labour/ASHE-2009/tab1_5a.xls.

118 The number earning below the level of the minimum wage fell from 1.28 million (5.6 per cent of the workforce) in 1998 to 242,000 (0.9 per cent of the workforce) in 2009.

119 Irvin, *op. cit.* p 131-2.

120 D Autor, 'The Polarisation of Job Opportunities in the US Labour Market', Centre for American Progress and The Hamilton Project, 2010.

121 R Crisp et al, *Work and Worklessness in*

Deprived Neighbourhoods, Joseph Rowntree Foundation, 2009, p 34.

122 A Felstead et al, *Skills at Work 1986-2006*, SKOPE, 2007; D Gallie et al, *Employment Regimes and the Quality of Work*, Oxford University Press, 2007.

123 Lansley, *Life in the Middle*, *op. cit.* p 20.

124 H Perkin, *The Third Revolution*, Routledge, 1996, p 40.

125 Lansley, *The Livelihood Crisis*, *op. cit.*

126 These are roughly comparable points in the economic cycle.

127 Lansley, *The Livelihood Crisis*, *op. cit.* figure 9.

128 Series UK SEAS1 and UK SEAS-BAK2008 provided by ONS; SIC 2003, category J 65-67.

129 Moreover, the lion's share of the best jobs created by the increasing dependency on banking have gone to London and the South-East. These regions have swallowed up over 40 per cent of all finance jobs while the north-east and Wales have less than 6 per cent between them. See Buchanan et al, *Undisclosed and Unsustainable*, Centre for Research on Socio-Cultural Change, Manchester University, 2009.

130 Centre for Cities, *Cities Outlook*, 2009.

131 Centre for Cities, Public Sector Cities, *Trouble Ahead*, July 2009.

132 Buchanan et al, *op. cit.* p 22.

133 J Hills et all (eds), *Towards a More Equal Society*, Policy Press, 2009, p 2.

134 *Ibid.* p 28.

135 Lansley, *Life in the Middle*, *op. cit.* figure 8.

136 H Roberts and D Kynaston, *City State*, Penguin, 2001, p 48.

137 S Lansley and H Reed, *The Red Tape Delusion*, TUC Touchstone Pamphlet, 2010, pp20-21.

138 Lansley, *Life in the Middle*, *op. cit.* p 28.

139 WD Rubenstein, *Men of Property*, Croom Helm, London, 1981, tables 3.3-3.7, p 62-66.

140 J Bakan, *The Corporation*, Constable, 2004, ch 4.

141 Lansley, *Do the Super-Rich Matter?*, *op. cit.* p 12-13.

142 C Toulouse, 'Thatcherism, Class Politics and Urban Development in London', *Critical Sociology*, Volume 18, 1992, p 62.

NOTES

143 D Kynaston, *The City of London, Volume IV*, Pimlico, 2001, chapter 22.

144 Z./Yen, *The Global Financial Centre Index*, City of London Corporation, March 2007.

145 http://www.ifsl.org.uk/media/2333/-Eco_con_of_UK_fin_ser_2007.pdf.

146 Centre for Research on Socio-Cultural Change (CRESC), *An Alternative report on UK Banking Reform*, University of Manchester, 2009, p 41.

147 Robin Blackburn,' Finance and the Fourth Dimension', *New Left Review*, 39, May/June, 2006.

148 Boston Consulting Group, *Investment Banking and Capital Markets*, Annual Reports.

149 Glyn, *Capitalism Unleashed, op. cit.* p 52. Elsewhere, the rise of finance proceeded somewhat less smoothly. In the 1990s, the growth slowdown in Germany and the Japanese banking crisis both led to slumps in the valuation of finance companies in those countries.

150 Merrill Lynch and Capgemini, *World Wealth Report*, 2010, figure 8.

151 José Gabriel Palma, 'The revenge of the market on the rentiers. Why neo-liberal reports of the end of history turned out to be premature', *Cambridge Journal of economics*, vol 33, issue 4, 2009.

152 IMF, *Global Financial Stability Report*, April 2009, Appendix Tables 3 and 4.

153 CRESC, *op. cit.* p 42.

154 Anthony Sampson, *The Midas Touch*, Hodder & Stoughton, 1989, p 13.

155 Quoted in R Roberts and D Kynaston, *City State*, Profile, 2002, p 116.

156 Bank for International Settlements, *Triennial Central Bank Survey, Foreign Exchange and Derivatives Market Activity*, September, 2010.

157 Harvey, *Neoliberalism, op. cit.* p 161; P Dicken, *Global Shift*, Guilford Press, 2003, ch 13.

158 N Shaxson, *Treasure Islands*, Bodley Head, 2011, p 74.

159 *Ibid.* p 78.

160 *The Observer*, 24 December, 2006.

161 M Hollingsworth and S Lansley, *Londongrad*, Fourth Estate, 2009, ch 4.

162 *Ibid.*

163 Michael Freedman, 'Welcome to Londongrad', *Forbes Global*, 23 May 2005; R. Skidelsky, *St Petersburg Times*, 4 January 2003; David Satter, *Darkness at Dawn: The Rise of the Russian Criminal State*, Yale University Press, 2003, p. 55.

164 J. Christensen, *Tax Distortions, Fiscal Dumping and Tax Fraud*, Tax Justice Network, 2003.

165 A. Mitchell, P. Sikka, J. Christensen, P. Morris and S. Filling, *No Accounting for Tax Havens*, Association of Accountancy and Business Affairs, 2002, p. 11.

166 Tax Justice Network, The Price of Offshore, 2005: http://www.taxjustice.-net/cms/upload/pdf/Briefing_Paper_-_The_Price_of_Offshore_14_MAR_2005.pdf.

167 Source: John Christensen, Tax Justice Network.

168 Quoted in Guy Adams, *Independent on Sunday*, 17 December 2006.

169 Jonathan Dee, *New York Times*, 9 September 2007.

170 *Forbes*, 16 November 2006.

171 P Beresford and WD Rubinstein, *The Richest of the Rich*, Harriman House, 2007.

172 Paul Krugman, *New York Times*, 20 October, 2002; a similar emphasis on changing social norms to explain the rising income share of the top has been made by Thomas Piketty and Emmanuel Saez, *Income inequality in the Unites States, 1913-1998*, NBER, Working Paper 8467, September 2001.

173 Krugman, *op. cit.*

174 Roberts & Kynaston, *op. cit.* p 142.

175 *Ibid.* p 153.

176 J. Cassidy, 'The Greed Cycle', *New Yorker*, 23 September 2002.

177 D. Henwood, 'A New Economy', speech to the Friday Forum, University YMCA, University of Illinois at Urbana-Champaign, October 1999.

178 *The Guardian*, 1 September, 2010.

179 H. Williams, 'How the City of London came to power', *Financial Times*, 21 March 2006.

180 Mervyn King, *From Bagehot to Basel and*

NOTES

Back Again, Bank of England, 25 October, 2010.

[181] See eg J Froud, S Johal, A Leaver and K Williams, *Financialisation and Strategy*, Routledge, 2006; T Golding, *The City*, Prentice Hall, 2001.

[182] Froud, *op. cit.*

[183] The *Independent*, 31 March, 2000.

[184] D French, *Branch Network Reduction Report*, Campaign for Community Banking, 2009.

[185] J Coney J, 'Fury over Britain's vanishing banks', *Money Mail*, 3 February 2010; see http://www.thisismoney.co.uk/savings-and-banking/article.html?in_article_id=498645&in_page_id=7.

[186] J Micklethwait & A Wooldridge, *The Company*, Weidenfold & Nicholson, 2003, p 180.

[187] William Duncan, *Ten Important Lessons From the History of Mergers & Acquisitions*, Ezine Articles, 2010.

[188] http://www.statistics.gov.uk/StatBase/-tsdataset.asp?vlnk=993.

[189] http://www.statistics.gov.uk/pdfdir/-ma0610.pdf.

[190] Will Hutton, *The State We're In*, Random House, 1995 p 163.

[191] Patrick Hosking, 'Merger Mania and Short Memories', *New Statesman*, 23 August, 1999.

[192] Philip Augar, *The Greed Merchants*, Allen Lane, 2005, p 171.

[193] 'Going Places', *Newsweek*, 15 May, 2006.

[194] M Wolf, *Financial Times*, 9 November, 2010.

[195] Roberts and Kynaston, *op. cit.* p 47.

[196] CRESC, *An Alternative report on UK Banking Reform*, University of Manchester, 2009, p 46.

[197] M Brewer et al, 'Racing Away? Inequality and the Evolution of Top Incomes', *IFS Briefing Note No 76*, 2008.

[198] *Ibid.* p 25.

[199] A Hilton, 'Do the City's Top Men really deserve their bonuses?', *Evening Standard*, 13 September 2006.

[200] Augar, *op. cit.*

[201] See Lansley, *Rich Britain, op. cit.* ch 4.

[202] S Lansley and A Forrester, *Top Man*, Aurum, 2006, p 244 -246.

[203] Quoted in *Daily Telegraph*, 6 June 1998.

[204] Interview with author.

[205] interview with author.

[206] Kenneth Rogoff, 'No Grand Plans, but the Financial System Needs Fixing', *Financial Times*, 8 February 2007.

[207] IMF, *World Economic Outlook, Database*, April 2009.

[208] *Ibid.*

[209] T Morgan, 'No Way Out', *Tullett Prebon Strategy Note 23*, 2011.

[210] GDP adjusted for inflation.

[211] R Skidelsky, *Keynes: The Return of the Master*, Allen Lane, 2009, p 118-120.

[212] Annual change in GDP, chained volume measure, seasonally adjusted (Office for National Statistics, series ABMI); http://www.statistics.gov.uk/statbase/TSD download2.asp.

[213] *Ibid.*

[214] Glyn, *Capitalism Unleashed, op. cit.* p 131.

[215] *Ibid.*

[216] World Economic Forum, *The Global Competitiveness Report*, 2009-10, 2009.

[217] G L Bernstein, *The Myth of Decline*, Pimlico, 2004, p 572.

[218] ONS, output per job for whole economy (series LNNP). Comparable figures are not available pre-1961.

[219] ESRC, *The UK's Productivity Gap*, ESRC Seminar Series, 2004; see also Office for Fair Trading, *Productivity and Competition*, 2007.

[220] N Bloom & R Griffiths, 'The Internationalisation of UK R&D', *Fiscal Studies*, 2001, vol 22, no 3.

[221] *Ibid.*

[222] Bernstein *op. cit.* p 537, 575.

[223] See eg, R Griffiths, *How Important is Business R&D to Economic Growth?*, IFS, 2000.

[224] Don Young, www.havingtheircake.com.

[225] Quoted in Niall Ferguson, *The Ascent of Money*, Allen Lane, 2008, p 164.

[226] Skidelsky, *Keynes: The Return of the Master*, *op. cit.* p 119.

[227] GDP at market prices, chained volume index, percentage change per quarter (YBEZ).

[228] Office for National Statistics, GDP at market prices, chained volume index, percentage change, quarter on previous quarter,

NOTES

YBEZ. See also, Office for National Statistics, 'Output and Expenditure in the Last Three UK Recessions', *Economic and Labour Market Review*, August 2010.

229 M Weale, 'Commentary: International Recession and Recovery', *National Institute Economic Review*, No. 209, July 2009.

230 M Wolf, 'This time will never be different', *Financial Times*, 28 September, 2009.

231 D Moss, 'An Ounce of Prevention', *Harvard Magazine*, October 2009.

232 Gerald Holtham, 'Workers of the World Compete', *Prospect*, December, 2008.

233 Palma, *op. cit.*

234 IMF, *Global Financial Stability Report*, April 2009, Appendix Tables 3 and 4: The figures for the Asian Savings Glut are from Palma, *op. cit.*

235 http://c0182732.cdn1.cloudfiles.rackspacecloud.com/fcic_final_report_full.pdf.

236 Holtham, *op. cit.*

237 Lansley, *Unfair to Middling, op. cit.*, S Lansley, 'How Soaring Inequality Contributed to the Crash', *Soundings*, Issue 44, Spring 2010.

238 David Moss, *Comments on Bank Failure/Regulation/Inequality Chart*, Harvard Business School, August 2010.

240 *New York Times*, 21 August 2010.

241 Moss, *op. cit.*

242 J Stiglitz is quoted in E L Glaeser, 'Does Economic Inequality Cause Crises?, *New York Times*, 14 December, 2010; JP Fitoussi and F Saraceno, *Inequality and Macroeconomic Performance*, Centre de recherché en economie de sciences Po, 2010; R J Rajan, *Faultlines*, Princeton University Press, 2010, chapter 1; Holtham, *op. cit*, 'Interview with Dr Ravi Batra', *Truthout*, 16 March, 2009; R Batra, *The Great Depression of 1990*, Dell Publishing, 1988; M Kumhof and R Rancière, 'Inequality, Leverage and Crisis', *IMF Working Paper*, WP/10/268, November 2010, p 3.

243 Kumhof and Rancière, *op. cit.*

244 D Laibson, 'Did Rising Income Inequality Help to Generate the Recent Financial Crisis?', The *Economist*, 29 August, 2010.

245 Glaeser, *op. cit.*

246 Atkinson and Morelli, *op. cit.* p 57.

247 JP Fitoussi and F Saraceno, *op. cit.*

248 M Iacoviello, 'Household Debt and Income Inequality, 1963-2003', *Journal of Money, Credit and Banking*, August, 2008.

249 Kumhof and Rancière, *op. cit.* p 3.

250 T Cowen, 'The Inequality That Matters', *The American Interest Online*, Jan-Feb, 2011.

251 Moss, *Harvard Magazine, op. cit.*

252 Ajay Kapur et al, 'The Global Investigator: Plutonomy: Buying Luxury, Explaining Global Imbalances', *Citigroup Equity Research*, October 14, 2005.

253 RN Goodwin, 'The Selling of Government', *Los Angeles Times*, 30 January 1997.

254 J Stiglitz, *The Roaring Nineties*, Allen Lane, 2003.

255 K Phillips, 'Too much wealth, too little democracy.' *Challenge*, September, 2002.

256 *Guardian*, 19.11.03.

257 *Time*, 26 February, 2011.

258 H Williams, *Britain's Power Elites*, Constable, 2006, p 164.

259 N Matthiason & Y Bessaoud, *Growth in City Donations to the Conservative Party*, Bureau for Investigative Journalism, February 2011.

260 CRESC, 2009, *op. cit.* p 23.

261 G Soros, 'The Crisis and What to do About It', *New York Review of Books*, 4 December, 2008.

262 BBC, *Panorama*, 8 October 2007.

263 *Ibid.*

264 A Brummer, *The Crunch*, Random House, 2009, p 11.

265 British Bankers' Association.

266 ONS: Volume of Retail Sales Index.

267 This compares with a previous peak of £22.2 billion in the third quarter of 1988 before it fell back with the onset of the recession of the early 1990s.

268 Bank of England: http://www.statistics.gov.uk/downloads/theme_social/Social_Trends38/06_13.xls.

269 The Young Foundation, *Sinking and Swimming*, 2009, p 54-55.

270 http://www.statistics.gov.uk/downloads/theme_social/Social_Trends38/06_13.xls.

271 ONS, *Social trends*, 2007, p 88; see also S

NOTES

Bridges et al, 'Housing Wealth and Accumulation in Financing Debt', in G Bertola et al, (Eds), *The Economics of Consumer Credit*, MIT Press, 2005.

272 *Social Trends, op. cit.* p88.

273 Department for Business, Enterprise and Regulatory Reform, *Household Debt Monitoring Papers*.

274 Council of Mortgage Lenders; *Social Trends, op. cit.* p89.

275 D Ben-Galim & T Lanning, *Strength Against Shocks*, IPPR, 2009.

276 ONS, *Wealth and Assets Survey*, 2009. Wealth is defined as all household goods and possessions including cars and owner-occupied houses after deducting financial liabilities.

277 S Verick and I Islam, 'The Great Recession of 2008-9', *IZA DP*, No 4934, May 2010.

278 Federal Reserve, Flow of Funds Analysis.

279 Johanna Montgomerie, 'A Bailout for Working Families', *Renewal*, vol 17, no 3, 2009.

280 M Kumhof and R Rancière, 'Inequality, Leverage and Crises', *Vox*, February 4, 2011.

281 N Shaxson, *Treasure Islands*, Bodley Head, 2011, p 166-172.

282 Brummer, *op. cit.* p 23.

283 *Ibid.* p 24.

284 *Ibid.* p 22.

285 CR Morris, *The Trillion Dollar Meltdown*, Public Affairs, 2008, p 70-71.

286 G Tett, *Fool's Gold*, Little Brown 2009 p 146.

287 D Harvey, *The Enigma of Capital*, Profile, 2010, p 17.

288 D Ramsey, *Prawn Cocktail Party*, Vision, 1998, p 25.

289 *Ibid.* p 26.

290 On the M4 definition—currency, current accounts and deposit accounts.

291 Ramsey, *op. cit.* p 28.

292 C Brown, 'Does Income Distribution Matter for Effective Demand?', *Review of Political Economy*, July 2004.

293 C Crouch, 'Privatised Keynsianism: An Unacknowledged Policy Regime', *The British Journal of Politics and International Relations*, 2009.

294 R Rajan, *Faultlines*, Princeton University

Press, 2010, chapter 1.

295 G Turner, *The Credit Crunch*, Pluto, 2009, p 35-47. IN the US, debt was assumed to rise by a third of its actual level and in the UK by a quarter.

296 J A Hobson, *The Industrial System*, AM Kelly, 1909.

297 J A Hobson, *Imperialism*, J Nisbet, 1902 p 112.

298 Quoted in R Overy, *The Morbid Age*, Penguin, 2010, p 60.

299 TJ Hatton and M Thomas, 'Labour Markets in the Interwar Pweriod and Economic Recovery in the UK and the USA', *Oxford Review of Economic Policy*, 26, 2010, pp 463-485.

300 R Skidelsky, *Keynes, The Return of the Master, op. cit.* p 70.

301 *Ibid.* p 69.

302 A J Badger, *The New Deal*, Macmillan, 1989, p 23.

303 See also A B Atkinson, *The Economics of Inequality*, 2nd ed, Clarendon Press, pp. 173-4; W. Kopczek and E. Saez, *Top Wealth Shares in the US 1916-2000: Evidence from Estate Tax Returns*, NBER Working Paper 10399, National Bureau of Economic Research, 2003; Atkinson and Morelli *op. cit.*

304 T Phillippon and A Reshef, 'Wages and Human Capital in the US Financial Industry', NBER Working Paper, January 2009.

305 Kendrick, John W. *Productivity Trends in the United States.* Princeton University Press, 1961.

306 DM Kennedy, *Freedom from Fear: The American People in Depression and War, 1929-1945*, OUP, 1999.

307 Badger, *op. cit.* p 30.

308 JK Galbraith, *The Great Crash 1929*, Penguin, 1992, p 111.

309 J Maskow, 'Poor Representation Creates Voter Apathy', *Battalion*, 2 November, 1998.

310 Phillips, *Wealth and Democracy, op. cit.* p. xvi.

311 *Ibid.* p 356.

312 Niall Ferguson, *The Ascent of Money*, Allen Lane, 2008, p 162.

313 JK Galbraith, *op. cit.* p 40.

314 M Kumhof and R Rancière, 'Inequality,

NOTES

Leverage and Crisis', *IMF Working Paper*, WP/10/268, 2010, Figure 1.

315 P Fortune, 'Margin Requirements, Margin Loans and Margin Rates, Analysis of History of Margin Credit Regulations', *New England Economic Review*, 2000.

316 R Lambert, 'Crash, Bangs and Wallop', *Financial Times*, 19 July 2008.

317 John Maynard Keynes, *The General Theory of Employment, Interest and Money*, Harcourt, Brace and World, 1936, p. 159.

318 *Ibid.* chapter 21.

319 JK Galbraith, *op. cit.* p 194-5.

320 JK Galbraith, *op. cit.* p 32.

321 Roger Middleton, 'Britain's Economic Problems, Too Small A Public Sector?', University of Bristol, 1997, p 30.

322 Carlota Perez, *Bad Samaritans*, Random House, 2007; Ha-Joon Chang, *Industrial Policy: Can We Go Beyond an Unproductive Confrontation?* University of Cambridge, 2009.

323 T Palley, *Financialisation*, Levy Economics Institute, Working Paper 525, table 10, 2007.

324 IFSL, Banking Report 2008, chart 25.

325 http://www.statistics.gov.uk/StatBase/-tsdataset.asp?vlnk=993.

326 Don Young, 'FTSE 100—the largest companies', 2007.

327 D Young and P Scott, *Having Their Cake, How the City and Top Managers are consuming British Industry*, Kogan Page, London, 2004.

328 Andrew Tylecote and Paulina Ramirez, *UK Corporate Governance and Innovation*, Sheffield University Business School, Discussion Paper, 2004.

329 Ozgur Orhanguzi, 'Financialisation and capital accumulation in the non-financial sector', *Cambridge Journal of Economics*, 2008.

330 H Williams, *Britain's Power Elites*, Constable, 2006, p 169.

331 T Dolphin, *Financial Sector Taxes*, IPPR, 2010, p 14.

332 *Ibid.* p 15.

333 J G Palma, 'The Revenge of the Markets on the Rentiers', *Cambridge Journal of Economics*, vol 333 issue 4, 2009.

334 *Absolute Return*, April 2010.

335 J Chapman, *Phasing Out Hedge Funds*, Public Policy Research, March-May, 2010.

336 A Hilton, 'Hedge Funds' Market Spoiler, *Evening Standard*, 12 May 2004.

337 Mansion House Speech March 2010 Available at http://archive.bis.gov.uk/-newsarchive/nds/clientmicrosite/-content/Detail.aspx-ReleaseID=411720&-NewsAreaID=2&ClientID=431.html.

338 Henry Hu and Barnard Black, Hedge Funds, 'Insiders and Empty Voting', *Finance Working Paper*, No xx/2006, European Governance Institute, p 12.

339 J Crotty, G Epstein and I Levin, 'Proprietary Trading Is A Bigger Deal Than Many Bankers and Pundits Claim', *Policy Note No 15*, February, 2010, Political Economy Research Institute, University of Masschusetts.

340 M Lewis, *Liar's Poker*, Coronet, 1991, p 141.

341 Cowen, *op. cit.*

342 Sir John Gieve, *The City's Growth: The Crest of a Wave or Swimming with the Stream?* March 27 2007.

343 *The Economist*, 25 November, 2004.

344 Peter Smith, 'A Public Relations Offensive on the Buy-Out High-Wire', *Financial Times*, 26 January 2007.

345 Dan Roberts, 'Hyper-capitalism', *Financial Times*, 2 May 2006.

346 Jules Domenichini, *Public to Private Transactions, A Case of Debenhams*, mimeo, 2009.

347 *Ibid.*

348 *Ibid.*

349 Martin Arnold, 'Profits of Buy-out groups tied to debt', *Financial Times*, 14 January, 2009.

350 J Froud and K Williams, 'Private Equity and the Culture of Value Extraction', *Centre for Research on Socio-Economic Change Working Paper no 31*, 2007, p 8; see also S N Kaplan & A Schoar, 'Private Equity Performance, Returns, Persistence and Capital Flows', *Journal of Finance*, vol 60, no 4, 2005.

351 A Brummer, *The Great Pensions Robbery*, Random House, 2010, p 185.

352 FSA, *Private Equity: A Discussion of Risk and Regulatory Engagement*, November 2006, p 64.

NOTES

353 CR Morris, *The Trillion Dollar Meltdown*, Public Affairs, 2008, p 8.

354 Forbes, *The World's Billionaires*, 3 March 2010.

355 Lansley, *Rich Britain*, op. cit. p 135.

356 *Rolling Stone*, 9 July 2009.

357 *The Contribution of the Financial Sector: Miracle or Mirage?* Speech by Andy Haldane at the Future of Finance Conference, London, 14 July 2010.

358 Lansley, *Rich Britain*, op. cit pp 209-210.

359 B Milanovic, *The Haves and Have-Nots*, Basic Books, 2011.

360 D Pitt-Watson, *Tomorrow's Investor*, Royal Society of Arts, 2010.

361 *Economist*, 16 November, 2002; F Partnoy, *Infectious Greed*, Profile Books, 2004, p 288.

362 *New York Times*, 29 April, 2003; The *Guardian*, 6 Feb 2004.

363 *Financial Times*, 31 July 2002.

364 R. Brenner, 'Towards the Precipice', *London Review of Books*, 6 February 2003.

365 S Sudarsanam, *Creating Value from Mergers and Acquisitions*, Prentice Hall, 2003, p 1-2; Mark Sirower, *The Synergy Trap: How Companies Lose the Acquisition Game*, Simon and Schuster, 2000.

366 *Financial Times*, 8 Sept 2001.

367 R G Rajan, *Faultlines*, Princeton Univesity Press, 2010, p 3.

368 Centre for Research on Socio Cultural Change, *An Alternative report on UK Banking Reform*, University of Manchester, 2009, p 47.

369 'The alchemists of finance', *Economist*, May 17th 2007.

370 Crotty, *op. cit.*

371 *Ibid.*

372 J Chapman, 'Phasing Out Hedge Funds', *Public Policy Research*, March-May, 2010.

373 E J Weiner, *The Shadow Market*, Oneworld, 2010, p 44.

374 *Ibid.* p 49.

375 *Ibid.* p 130.

376 Survey by JP Morgan Asset Management, 27 September, 2010.

377 http://www.towerswatson.com/united-kingdom/press/3767.

378 'European Banks Growing Bigger "Sowing the Seeds" of the Next Crisis', *Bloomberg*, December 1, 2009.

379 PricewaterhouseCoopers, UK *Economic Outlook*, November 2010.

380 'The alchemists of finance', *op. cit.*

381 'The Disappearing Dollar', *Economist*, 2 December, 2004.

382 G Tett, *Fool's Gold*, Little Brown, 2009, p 14.

383 *Ibid.* p 109.

384 Morris, *op. cit.* p 54.

385 Tett, *op. cit.* p46.

386 P Augar, *The Greed Merchants*, Allen Lane, 2005, pp 80-83.

387 S Bhagat and B Bolton, *Bank Executive Compensation and Capital Requirements Reform*, Mimeo, University of Colorado and University of New Hampshire, 2011.

388 http://www.ieo-imf.org/eval/complete/-pdf/01102011/Crisis_BP5_UK_Bilateral_Surveillance.pdf.

389 http://thegreatrecessionconspiracy.-blogspot.com/2011/02/simon-johnson-explains-how-wall-street.html.

390 H Minsky, *Stabilising an Unstable Economy*, Yale University Press, 1986; see also S Keen, *Debunking Economics*, Zed Books, 2001.

391 C Lapavitsas, Financialisation and Capitalist Accumulation, School of Oriental and African Studies, 2010.

392 Fitoussi and Saraceno, *op. cit.*

393 http://www.theecologist.org/News/-news_round_up/542538/goldman_sachs_makes_1_billion_profit_on_food_price_speculation.html.

394 P Mason, *Meltdown, The End of the Age of Greed*, Verso, 2009.

395 Merryn Somerset-Webb, 'Don't Believe the Hype', *Spear's Wealth Management Survey*, Issue 6, January 2008.

396 S Foley, 'Detailed in emails', *Independent*, 26 April, 2010.

397 The *New York Review of Books*, Nov 10, 2010.

398 Neil Barofsky, *Quarterly Report to Congress*, January 2010.

399 Neil Barofsky, *Quarterly Report to Congress*, January 2011.

400 The US November 2010 mid-term elections became the most expensive in history. $5 billion poured into the campaign,

nearly of all of it from Wall Street and the big corporations, with the Republicans receiving six times as much as the Democrats.

401 S Johnson, 'The Quiet Coup', *The Atlantic*, May 2009.

402 Steven Greenhouse and David Leonhardt, 'Real Wages Fail to Match a Rise in Productivity', *The New York Times*, August 28, 2006.

403 John Cassidy, *New York Review of Books*, November 10, 2010.

404 *Bloomberg*, 16 February 2011.

405 http://www.guardian.co.uk/business/-2010/nov/30/europe-biggest-companies-cash-pile.

406 D Weldon, 'Unlock the Surplus', *Red Pepper*, January 2011.

407 Bank of England, *Trends in Lending*, October 2010.

408 Quoted in N Pratley, 'Why Does Apax Want to Buy ISS', *Guardian*, 8 December, 2010.

409 'European Banks Growing Bigger "Sowing the Seeds" of the Next Crisis', *Bloomberg*, December 1, 2009.

410 *Sunday Times Rich List*, 2010, April 2010; Forbes, *The World's Billionaires*, March 2011; Merrill Lynch and Capgemini, *World Wealth Report*, 2010 and 2011.

411 IDS, *Directors Pay Report*, 29 October, 2010.

412 A Sum, *How the US Output Recession of 2007-09 led to the Great Recession in Labour Markets*, Northeastern University, Boston, MA, July 2010.

413 *Ibid.*

414 B Herbert, 'A Sin and a Shame', *New York Times*, 30 July 2010.

415 *Ibid.*

416 Duncan Weldon, 'Government Policies will further Squeeze the Wages of Ordinary Workers', *False Economy*, 3 February, 2011.

417 W Hutton, *The State We're In*, Jonathan Cape, 1995; W Hutton, *Them and Us*, Little Brown, 2010.

418 S G Cecchetti, *Financial Reform*, Bank for International Settlements, October, 2010; http://www.niesr.ac.uk/event/wef.php.

419 S Lansley and H Reed, *The Red Tape Delusion*, TUC Touchstone Pamphlet, 2010,

p 20-23.

420 International Labour Office, *Global Wage Report, 2008/9*, 2008, table 3, p 38.

421 Lansley and Reed, *op. cit.*

422 Interview with ABC's 'This Week With Christiane Amanpour', November 28, 2010.

423 Lansley, *Do The Super-Rich Matter?, op. cit.* figure 6.3.

424 *Fair Taxation in a Changing World*, Report of the Ontario Fair Tax Commission, University of Toronto Press, 1993, p 45.

425 R Prabhakar et al, *How To Defend Inheritance Tax*, Fabian Society, April 2008.

426 L E Burman, R J Shiller, G Leiserson, J Rohaly, *The Rising Tide Tax System*, Mimeo, Urban Institute, 2007.

427 Richard Murphy, *The Missing Billions*, TUC Touchstone Pamphlet, 2008, p32.

428 See, eg, S Johnson & J Kwak, *13 Bankers*, Pantheon, 2010.

429 *Interim Report*, Independent Commission on Banking, April, 2011.

430 P Myners, 'Break Up Britain's Uncompetitive Big Banks', *Financial Times*, 12 December, 2010.

431 Dolphin, *op. cit.* p 17-18.

432 EEF, *Manufacturing Our Future*, 2009.

433 G Brown, *Beyond the Crash: Overcoming the first crisis of globalisation*, Simon and Schuster, 2010.

434 *New York Times*, 20 July 2006.

435 *Financial Times*, 28 February 2007.

436 Robert J Shiller, *Inequality-Indexing of the Tax System*, The Tobin Project, 2007.

437 Quoted in M Elliott, 'Global Business', *Time*, February 14, 2011.

438 J Somavia, *The Challenge of Growth, Employment and Social Cohesion*, ILO, October 2010.

439 M Kumhof and R Rancière, 'Inequality, Leverage and Crisis', *IMF Working Paper*, WP/10/268, November 2010, p 22.

440 Mervyn King, 'From Bagehot to Basel and Back Again', Bank of England, 25 October 2010.

INDEX

AA, 226, 229
ABM Ambro, 124, 208, 248
Abramovich, Roman, 26, 105
Allders, 233-4
Alliance Boots, 226, 228, 247
Amazon, 236, 244
Apax, 226
Asia's saving glut, 151-2
asset bubbles, 32, 91, 157, 160, 199, 217, 264, 266, 267, 269, 271, 288, 294
Atkinson, Tony, 156
Augar, Philip, 125

Bank of England, the, 39, 150, 171, 181, 215, 224, 240, 297, 302
Barclays Bank, 121, 129, 259, 278, 279, 283, 301
Barofsky, Neil, 279
Batra, Ravi, 156
Beresford, Philip, 236-7
Bernanke, Ben, 19, 139, 151, 261, 300
Besley, Tim, 252
Bhs, 113, 129, 226, 234
'Big Bang', 95, 131, 168, 222
Blair, Tony, 74, 87, 88, 96, 97, 249
Bonderman, David, 111-4, 225
bonuses, see City and Wall Street bonuses
Bromptons, 290
Brown, Gordon, 69, 87, 97, 136, 140, 253, 300
Budd, Sir Alan, 65
Buffett, Warren, 263, 293
Bush, George HW, 17, 18, 28, 162
Bush, George W, 14, 40, 41, 136
Business Week, 14, 40, 41, 136

Cable, Vince, 277
Cadbury, 116, 124, 208, 220, 247, 283
Canada, 26, 49, 55, 140
capitalism, see 'managed' and 'market capitalism'
cash surpluses held by corporations, 102, 126, 159, 254, 255
Cash, William, 108
Cassidy, John, 277, 281
Catchings, Waddill, 190
Cayman Islands, the, 106, 109, 216, 295

Centre for Policy Studies, the, 36
Centre for Research on Socio-Cultural Change, Manchester University, the, 83
Chalfont, Lord, 41
Chicago, the University of, 34, 138, 156
China, 27, 30, 108, 126, 151, 152, 267
Citigroup, 160, 208, 217, 272
City and Wall Street bonuses, 9, 24, 86-8, 127, 130-4, 167-8, 242, 250, 258, 264, 277-8, 281, 284-5, 296
City fees, 88, 127-34, 167, 226, 229, 235, 242-4, 248, 250, 256, 269, 273, 297-8
City pay, 24, 25, 87, 116, 132-5, 144, 222, 242, 279, 281, 284, 296
Clinton, Bill, 137, 161, 162
Competition and Credit Control, 180
Confederation of British Industry, the, 70, 89, 210, 301
Conservative Party, the, 33, 51, 68-9, 80, 83, 87-8, 162, 203, 227
Cowen, Tyler, 158, 159
'crowding out', 203-5, 224
CVC, 225, 256

Daily Telegraph, the, 23, 29, 234
Darling, Alistair, 227
Debenhams, 8, 225, 226, 229-31
'deindustrialisation', 66, 67, 69, 76, 77
deregulation, 34, 115, 122, 123, 137, 143, 144, 149-50, 155, 162, 167-8, 186, 243
derivatives, 101, 127, 222, 242, 245, 259-64, 273, 279
'deserving' versus 'undeserving rich', 241
Dodd-Frank Reform Act, 277, 279, 297
'downsizing', 117, 205
downward mobility, 77-8
Drexel Burnham Lambert, 130, 220
Dyson, James, 7, 146, 213, 240

economic equilibrium, 30, 47, 51, 57, 190, 202
economic imbalance, 31, 47, 48, 57, 138, 276
Economist, the, 226, 256, 259
Ellison, Larry, 236
EMI, 208, 226, 267
Emma Bridgewater Pottery, 290
Enron, 109, 137, 210, 245, 264, 272

INDEX

European Exchange Rate Mechanism (ERM), 68, 204

Evening Standard, the, 133, 219

exchange controls, 68, 93

exchange rate policy, 39, 67, 68, 93, 94, 204, 260

Facebook, 7, 240

'financial deal-making', 14, 32, 99, 123, 205-6, 239, 246

financial deregulation, see deregulation

'financialisation', 120, 211

Financial Services Authority, 165, 171, 209, 215, 234, 301

Financial Times, the, 10, 119, 127, 150, 199, 249, 161, 301

Fitoussi, Paul, 156, 157

Ford, Henry, 77, 184, 185, 188

France, 49, 70, 140, 142, 145, 211, 214

Frankfurt, 95, 101

free markets, 18, 19, 28-30, 33-36, 138, 160, 265

Friedman, Milton, 34, 36, 69, 121, 138

Forbes, 7, 9, 26, 27, 110, 113, 235-6, 247, 284

Galbraith, JK, 115, 194, 196, 200, 202, 252

Garicano, Luis, 251

Gates, Bill, 256

GEC, 66, 248, 249

General Electric (GE), 38, 116

Germany, 26, 39, 49, 58, 70, 121, 122, 122, 130, 140, 142, 211, 214, 218, 292, 299, 300

Gieve, Sir John, 224

Gilmour, Sir Ian, 69

Glaeser, Edward, 156

global financial assets, 101, 152

globalisation, 65, 67, 107

Glyn, Andrew, 50, 52, 62, 143

Goldman Sachs, 29, 95, 99, 128, 131, 183, 217, 220, 221, 244-6, 268, 273, 275, 283, 285

Goldsmith, James, 123, 238

Google, 7, 236, 240

Great Depression, 1930s, 32, 62, 93, 154, 190, 192, 200, 276, 278

Green, Sir Philip, 111-4, 129, 134

Greenspan, Alan Sir, 19, 151, 187, 271, 276

Griffiths, Brian, 29

Guardian, the, 151, 277

Haldane, Andy, 240

Hands, Guy, 208, 267, 283

Harvard University, 20, 28, 154, 156, 252

Hastings, Sir Max, 10, 23

HBOS, 129, 134, 183, 275

Heath, Sir Edward, 41, 123, 180-1, 271

hedge funds, 24, 31, 99, 100, 103-4, 122, 128, 133, 162, 208, 215-23, 235-6, 245, 256-8, 268, 270, 272, 274, 283-4

Hennessy, Peter, 252

Hilton, Anthony, 133, 219

Hobson, John A, 188, 189

Holtham, Gerry, 154, 156

Hong Kong, 101, 121

Hoover, Herbert, 197

Hutton, Will, 291

Iacoviello, Matteo, 158

Income Data Services, 285

industrial restructuring, 64, 67, 123, 139, 238-9, 266

industrial revolution, the, 44, 48, 97, 113, 185

Institute for Economic Affairs, the, 33

International Labour Organisation, the, 55, 58, 301

International Monetary Fund, the, 9, 29, 30, 58, 90, 92, 95, 109, 137, 147, 156, 253, 265, 301

Ireland, 169, 268, 269

Irvin, George, 76

Japan, 27, 49, 70, 108, 120-1, 142, 150, 211, 214, 218, 221, 271

Johnson, Simon, 265, 280

Jones, Jack, 42

Joseph, Sir Keith, 36

JP Morgan, 228, 283

Kapur, Ajay, 160

Kennedy, JF, 115, 161

Keynes, John Maynard, 34, 48, 92, 138, 148, 186, 189-192, 199, 200, 242, 298

King, Mervyn, 9, 295, 302

Kohlberg Kravis Roberts (KKR), 123

Kraft, 208, 219, 220, 247, 283

Krugman, Paul, 17, 18, 19, 115, 143, 253

Kumhof, Michael, 156, 301

Kynaston, David, 96

labour market, 38, 64, 67, 69, 73, 77, 88-9, 95, 115, 137-8, 289, 291

Labour Party, the, 80, 84, 88, 89, 97, 189, 191, 209,

Lambert, Richard, 210, 301

Lamont, Norman, 62

Lehman Brothers, 97, 183, 210, 244, 262, 275, 282

318

INDEX

Leveraging, 101, 127-9, 198-9, 206, 218-9, 223, 225, 229, 232-4, 258-62, 267, 270, 277, 293, 301
Lewis, John, 290
'limit to inequality', the, 6, 157, 200, 275, 302
Lloyds Bank, 116, 121, 183, 259, 279
London School of Economics, the, 24, 33, 222, 251-2
Long Term Capital Management, 218, 223
low pay, 64, 75, 77, 81, 83, 85, 174
Lucas, Robert, 138, 139

Major, Sir John, 87, 108
Malthus, Thomas, 188
'managed capitalism', 37, 63, 141, 142, 148
Mandelson, Peter, 89, 209, 220,
'market capitalism', 34, 37, 51, 63, 141-2, 151, 153
Mason, Paul, 268
Manchester, 164, 268
Manchester Business School, 120, 133
Manchester United, 128, 219
Manchester University, 83, 103, 163, 255
manufacturing industry, 49, 66-70, 80-1, 98, 140, 145-6, 181, 184, 193, 207, 211-3, 223, 224, 249
McDonald, Ramsey, 191
Mellon, Andrew, 40, 191, 194
Mergers, acquisitions and takeovers, 124-5, 135, 205, 208, 238, 242, 246, 248
Merrill Lynch, 95, 99, 128, 130, 132, 220, 225, 244, 282
Merrill Lynch Capgemini, 100
middle-class, the, 71, 72, 76
'middle England', 60
Milanovoc, Branko, 241
Miliband, Ed, 60, 78
minimum wage, 25, 41, 88, 184, 292, 301
Minsky, Hyman, 147, 265, 266, 272
Mittal, Lakshmi, 26, 131, 266
Mont Pelerin Society, the, 33, 34, 36
mortgages, sub-prime, 164, 165-168, 171, 177-8, 182, 245, 262, 269, 271, 273
Moss, David, 154, 155, 160
Murdoch, Rupert, 237
Myners, Paul, 297

Neil, Andrew, 237
Newman, Katherine, 76
New Statesman, the, 28
New York, 31, 36, 91-3, 95, 96, 105, 109, 160, 216, 235, 257, 302
New York Times, 17, 20, 155, 286

NIESR, 148
Nixon, Richard, 40, 60
Nokia, 206, 219
Northern Rock, 167-9, 182, 183, 270, 275

Obama, Barack, 103, 228, 278, 280, 293, 302
Office for Budget Responsibility, the, 287
Ontario Fair Tax Commission, the, 293
OPEC oil crisis, 39, 141, 163
Organisation for Economic Co-operation and Development (OECD), 25-6, 66, 88, 149
Osborne, George, 203, 227, 277, 278, 298

Page,Larry, 236
Paulson, John, 245, 246
Phillips, Kevin, 22, 161
Piketty, Thomas, 20, 155
Plutonomy, 160
Posen, Adam, 39
poverty, 26, 41, 48, 75, 76, 83, 85, 88, 193, 292
'pre-distribution', 83, 288
Prince, Chuck, 272
private equity, 100, 103, 111, 114, 122, 133, 134, 159, 205, 208, 225-39, 247, 256-7, 283
'privatised Keynesianism', 186
productivity, 39, 40, 49, 55-9, 66, 98, 118, 138, 142-7, 159, 187, 193-4, 239, 246, 267, 281, 286-9, 299, 301
profits, profit share, 30-32, 43-52, 64, 80, 87, 96-9, 104, 149-50, 168, 183, 185, 193, 195, 198, 206, 210, 220-1, 234, 254, 258, 266, 276, 278, 281-2, 286-90, 294-7, 300
'profits squeeze', the, 49-51
proprietary trading, 220, 256, 258, 263, 270

Rajan, Raghuram, 156, 187, 253
Ranciere, Romain, 156, 301
Reagan, Ronald, 18, 28, 35, 38, 40, 41, 52, 61, 67, 98, 141, 161, 287
research & development, 146-7, 208
recessions, 11, 13, 34, 46, 47, 57, 61-2, 65, 67, 78, 82, 118, 136-41, 147-9, 154, 172, 191, 202, 251, 268, 286-7, 302
Ricardo, David, 45, 189
'Robin Hood' tax, 298
Rockefeller, John D, 23, 47
Rogoff, Kenneth, 137
Rolls Royce, 213
Roosevelt, Franklyn D, 91, 92, 190, 199, 291
Rowland, Tiny, 123, 236, 238
Royal Bank of Scotland, 121, 124, 128, 130, 183, 228, 246, 248, 259, 272, 275, 279, 285
Russian oligarchs, 26, 100, 101, 105, 126, 128

INDEX

Saez, Emmanuel, 20, 155
Saraceno, Franceso, 156, 157
Scanlon, Hugh, 42
Scargill, Arthur, 42
Schumpeter, Joseph, 239
'securitization', 262, 269
service economy, the, 61, 65, 66, 69-72, 77, 78
Shanghai, 101
'shareholder value', 115, 116-123, 158, 210, 230, 248, 250, 289-90
Shaxson, Nicholas, 104-5
Shiller, Robert, 294, 300
Skidelsky, Robert, 48, 148
Smith, Adam, 393
Solow, Robert, 300
Somavia, Juan, 58
Sorrell, Martin, 30
Soros, George, 163
South Korea, 206, 218
Spain, 121, 269
Spirit Level, The, 5
squeeze on wages and living standards, the, 5, 9, 10, 24, 30-1, 44, 52-3, 58, 77, 98, 154, 159, 179, 183
'squeezed middle', the, 60, 305
stagflation, 38, 186
Stiglitz, Joseph, 156, 161
Strauss-Kahn, Dominique, 29
strikes, 39, 42, 48, 49
Sunday Telegraph, the 236
Sunday Times, The 17, 203, 237
surpluses, financial, 31, 47, 98-104, 114, 126, 159, 205-6, 226, 235, 254, 298
Sutcliffe, Bob, 50
Switzerland, 105, 109, 119

takeovers, see mergers & acquisitions
tax havens, 89, 106, 107, 160, 295
Tax Justice Network, 107
Tepper, David, 217
Tett, Gillian, 261
Texas Pacific Group, 111, 113, 225, 231
Thatcher, Margaret, 29, 33, 35, 36, 38, 40, 42, 52, 60, 62, 65, 67, 69, 70, 88, 95, 141, 181, 204
Tobin, James, 298
Tokyo, 101, 108
trade unions, 38, 40-3, 48, 51, 61-5, 69, 70, 94, 117, 118, 122, 162, 181, 287, 292
Tullett Prebon, 140
Turner, Adair, 209, 301
Turner, Graham, 188

UBS, 52, 126, 262
Umunna, Chuka, 278
'underconsumption', theory of, 188-90
'the undeserving rich', the, see 'deserving' versus 'undeserving rich'
Unemployment, 38-43, 57-8, 62-5, 77-8, 136, 141, 142, 150, 164, 175, 180, 189, 190, 192, 286

'vanishing-middle', the, 60-83
Vickers, John Sir, 296
Vodafone, 124, 130, 214, 182
Volker, Paul, 103
von Hayek, Friedrich, 33, 92
von Mises, Ludwig, 36

Wall Street Journal, 18, 184
'wage-productivity gap', the, 55-7, 98, 154, 281, 287, 299
'wage share', the, 10, 44, 46, 49-59, 63, 83, 85, 154, 160, 176, 186, 287, 299, 301
wages, the squeeze on, see squeeze on wages
Wall Street crash, 1929, 30, 32, 40, 91, 150, 191
Walmart, 25, 236
Walmart, 25, 236
wealth, the transfer of, 32, 45, 82, 102, 159, 240, 242-50, 291
Welch, Jack, 116, 117, 210, 289, 290
Wolf, Martin, 127, 150
'working class', the, 60, 65, 71, 72, 76-8, 188-9
World Economic Forum, 29, 144, 300

Yahoo, 7, 240
Young, Don, 208, 209

Zhu, Min, 30